ADVANCES IN BUSINESS AND MANAGEMENT FORECASTING

ADVANCES IN BUSINESS AND MANAGEMENT FORECASTING

Series Editors: Kenneth D. Lawrence and
Ronald K. Klimberg

Recent Volumes:

ADVANCES IN BUSINESS AND MANAGEMENT
FORECASTING   VOLUME 9

ADVANCES IN BUSINESS AND MANAGEMENT FORECASTING

EDITED BY

KENNETH D. LAWRENCE

*New Jersey Institute of Technology,
Newark, USA*

RONALD K. KLIMBERG

*Saint Joseph's University,
Philadelphia, USA*

United Kingdom – North America – Japan
India – Malaysia – China

Emerald Group Publishing Limited
Howard House, Wagon Lane, Bingley BD16 1WA, UK

First edition 2013

British Library Cataloguing in Publication Data
A catalogue record for this book is available from the British Library

ISBN: 978-1-78190-331-5
ISSN: 1477-4070 (Series)

ISOQAR certified
Management System,
awarded to Emerald
for adherence to
Environmental
standard
ISO 14001:2004.

Certificate Number 1985
ISO 14001

INVESTOR IN PEOPLE

CONTENTS

LIST OF CONTRIBUTORS

James Algeo	Philadelphia Insurance Companies, Bala Cynwyd, PA, USA
Timothy R. Anderson	Engineering and Technology Management Department, Portland State University, Portland, OR, USA
Dorothy Cimino Brown	School of Veterinary Medicine, University of Pennsylvania, Philadelphia, PA, USA
Evelyn Brown	Department of Engineering, East Carolina University, Greenville, NC, USA
Shaw K. Chen	College of Business Administration, University of Rhode Island, Kingston, RI, USA
Shao-Shing Chen	National Space Program Office, National Science Council, Hsinchu, Taiwan
Paul Heath	Vidant Rehabilitation Hospital, Greenville, NC, USA
Laura Helms	Vidant Medical Center, Greenville, NC, USA
Xuan Huang	Department of MISQ, School of Business, University of Alabama at Birmingham, Birmingham, AL, USA
Olga Isengildina-Massa	College of Business, University of Texas at Arlington, Arlington, TX, USA
Rhonda Joyner	Vidant Rehabilitation Hospital, Greenville, NC, USA
Kristin Kennedy	Mathematics Department, Bryant University, Smithfield, RI, USA

Gary Kleinman	School of Business, Montclair State University, Montclair, NJ, USA
Ronald K. Klimberg	Haub School of Business, Saint Joseph's University, Philadelphia, PA, USA
John F. Kros	Department of Marketing and Supply Chain Management, College of Business, East Carolina University, Greenville, NC, USA
Min-Hua Kuo	School of Management, Shih Hsin University, Taipei, Taiwan
Mark T. Leung	Department of Management Science, College of Business, University of Texas, San Antonio, TX, USA
Kenneth D. Lawrence	School of Management Science, New Jersey Institute of Technology, Newark, NJ, USA
Sheila M. Lawrence	School of Management and Labor Relations, Rutgers, The State University of New Jersey, Middlesex, NJ, USA
Dong-Joon Lim	Engineering and Technology Management Department, Portland State University, Portland, OR, USA
Matthew Lindsey	Nelson Rusche College of Business, Stephen F. Austin State University, Nacogdoches, TX, USA
Stephen MacDonald	Economic Research Service, United States Department of Agriculture, Washington, DC, USA
Saverio Manago	Department of Marketing & Decision Science, Salem State University, Salem, MA, USA
Virginia M. Miori	Department of Decision and System Sciences, St. Joseph's University, Philadelphia, PA, USA

Amitava Mitra	Auburn University, College of Business, Auburn, AL, USA
Alan Olinsky	Mathematics Department, Bryant University, Smithfield, RI, USA
Youqin Pan	Department of Marketing & Decision Science, Salem State University, Salem, MA, USA
Jayprakash G. Patankar	The University of Akron, Department of Management, Akron, OH, USA
Robert Pavur	University of North Texas, Denton, TX, USA
Terrance Pohlen	Department of Marketing & Logistics, University of North Texas, Denton, TX, USA
John Quinn	Mathematics Department, Bryant University, Smithfield, RI, USA
Neil Runde	Engineering and Technology Management Department, Portland State University, Portland, OR, USA
Michael Salzillo	Mathematics Department, Bryant University, Smithfield, RI, USA
Brian Segulin	RoviSys, Aurora, OH, USA
Joanne Utley	School of Business and Economics, NCA&T State University, Greensboro, NC, USA
Nuo Xu	Department of MISQ, School of Business, University of Alabama at Birmingham, Birmingham, AL, USA

xi

PART I
HEALTH CARE

CENSUS FORECASTING IN AN INPATIENT REHABILITATION FACILITY

John F. Kros, Evelyn Brown, Rhonda Joyner, Paul Heath and Laura Helms

ABSTRACT

The application of forecasting to health care is not new. A frequent issue in many Inpatient Rehabilitation Facilities (IRFs) is the fluctuating and unpredictable census. With scarce resources, particularly physical therapists and occupational therapists, this unpredictability makes appropriate scheduling of these resources challenging. This research addresses the issue of patient admissions in an inpatient rehabilitation facility attached to an 861 bed level-one trauma hospital. The goal is to develop a predictive model for the IRF's Census to assist in resource planning (e.g., labor, beds, and materials).

Keywords: Inpatient census prediction; health care forecasting; rehabilitation; predictive modeling

Advances in Business and Management Forecasting, Volume 9, 3–13
Copyright © 2013 by Emerald Group Publishing Limited
All rights of reproduction in any form reserved
ISSN: 1477-4070/doi:10.1108/S1477-4070(2013)0000009004

INTRODUCTION

The application of forecasting to health care is not new. A frequent issue in many Inpatient Rehabilitation Facilities (IRFs) is the fluctuating and unpredictable census. With scarce resources, particularly physical therapists and occupational therapists, this unpredictability makes appropriate scheduling of these resources challenging.

The issue of patient admissions in an inpatient rehabilitation facility for a level-one trauma hospital are investigated in this chapter. A predictive model for census forecasting is proposed.

FACILITY BACKGROUND

The Vidant Rehabilitation Hospital, with two locations at Vidant Medical Center and Vidant Edgecombe, is a 91-bed inpatient rehabilitation program servicing eastern North Carolina. In operation since 1977, the rehabilitation hospital offers an accredited, comprehensive rehabilitation program that is part of a statewide network. Through the association with both Vidant Medical Center and the Brody School of Medicine at East Carolina University (ECU), patients have access to a full range of state-of-the-art medical services. Additionally, Vidant Rehabilitation Hospital is the area's leading rehabilitation training program for medical, allied health, and nursing students (www.vidanthealth.com).

Vidant Rehabilitation employees a number of physical, occupational, and speech therapists. The task of scheduling these care providers is complicated by fluctuations in the patient census. For this research, operations personnel from the rehabilitation facility have partnered with academicians from ECU in an effort to develop a forecasting model for the patient census. It is anticipated that such a model will enable better scheduling of resources.

The 75-bed rehabilitation facility at Vidant Medical Center cares for patients with many kinds of injuries, including spinal cord, neurological, orthopedic, and brain injury. Several months worth of data, including but not limited to referral location, date of admit, reason for admit, reason for non-admit, day of week, and time between referral and admit, were collected and analyzed. Basic data analysis (e.g., average admits per month and day, cross-tabulation of referral unit vs. day of week and rehabilitation admit unit, and lag time associated with referral date and admit date) enabled the research team to better describe the inflows to the rehabilitation facility.

The rehabilitation facility being studied receives their patients via referrals and subsequent evaluation by the rehab consult team. Approximately 80% of its patients are admitted from the attached hospital facility while the other 20% are admitted from other facilities in the area. The rehabilitation facility collects data on many variables, including admission dates, times, along with the unit from which the patients were transferred, that is, the outside medical facility or specific hospital unit.

Of the 80% patients who are admitted from the attached hospital, 45% are from three specific hospital units (Surgical Intensive Unit, Neurosurgical Unit, and Orthopedics) while approximately 35% are evenly distributed from other hospital units (e.g., Cardiac Intensive Care Unit, Cardio Vascular Intensive Unit, Family Medicine, Surgical Intensive Care Unit, etc.). The remaining 20% are from "outside" the hospital system. These admit data are used to develop the predictive model. However, before the authors could develop the model, a literature review was completed. The results of the literature review are next, followed by a section on data analysis.

LITERATURE REVIEW

Overall, forecasting has two roles in a health care organization: cumulative need for services and census planning. Analysis of demand, either on the service side or census side, drives hospital-wide decisions. Examples of these decisions include staffing, ancillary services, elective admission scheduling, and support services including cleaning, food service, and linens. In a sense, demand forecasting in health care is akin to aggregate planning in the manufacturing environment.

Pierskalla and Brailer (1990) provide an excellent overview of operations research techniques used in health care delivery, including forecasting. More specifically, Harrington (1977) and Hogarth and Makridakis (1981) provide seminal reviews of the major forecasting techniques used in the health care industry.

Demand forecasting is important for many aspects of health care operations research and management. Forecasting can be accomplished using qualitative or quantitative techniques. The chief difference between the two techniques is the degree to which subjective judgment influences the model. Qualitative approaches such as historical analysis employ analysis of similar settings or an organization's own institutional history to determine future demand. This technique tends to be a bit short-sighted in that it ignores any major changes in market make-up or changes within the organization.

The Delphi technique is another technique in which future predictions are extracted from the experts. The process is repeated until a consensus emerges. The main issue with the Delphi technique is that it is susceptible to ideological biases that make it difficult to use in settings where predictions may not conform to standard views of organization or reward structure.

While qualitative techniques attempt to formalize explicit expert judgment, quantitative techniques have implicit judgments (e.g., specification of the model). This impact of judgment, whether explicit or implicit, on the results of demand forecasting, can be strong (Hogarth, & Makridakis, 1981). Quantitative forecasting techniques are the focus of this work and therefore the models developed are quantitative in nature. The next section gives an overview of quantitative forecasting.

QUANTITATIVE FORECASTING TECHNIQUES/MODELS

Quantitative techniques include time series analysis (e.g., moving averages or exponential smoothing) and regression models. Time series analysis uses historical data to predict future demand. Typical time series models use an average of past data to form a forecast or employ a weighted average of past data to create a forecast. All time series data contain systemic variation.

A major source of systemic variation comes from outside effects in many demand time series data sets. Seasonal variation or changes in market make up or even day of the week often play a role in census determination. For example, data show that the number of visits to Emergency Departments are much higher on Mondays than on weekends. Therefore, time or past historical data is not the only variable that has an impact on census patterns, multiple factors play a role. While the time series models are common and easy to develop, it can be said that each of these models may fail due to additional systemic variation that is not accounted for. In turn, accounting for the largest amount of systemic variation in time series is the main goal of a forecasting model.

MULTIPLE LINEAR REGRESSION MODELS

Multiple linear regression models are commonly used in forecasting when multiple independent variables impact a dependent variable. In this study, the rehabilitation census can be considered the dependent variable while time, certain seasonal factors, technological factors, or data lag factors can be considered as independent variables. The general form of a multiple regression model is represented as:

$$Y_t = b_0 + b_1 X_{1t} + b_2 X_{2t} + b_3 X_{3t} \ldots + b_n X_{nt} + e_t \tag{1}$$

The Xs denote the independent variables while Y denotes the dependent variable.

As an example, Kamentzky, Shuman, and Wolfe (1982) use least squares regression analysis to determine the demand for pre-hospital care for making ambulatory staffing decisions. Johansen, Bowles, and Haney (1988) demonstrate a model for forecasting intermediate skilled home nursing needs. They combine elements of simple observational models and complex statistical approaches. Kao and Poldadnik (1978) describe adaptive forecasting of hospital census, demonstrating how institutional and exogenous variables can be used in forecasting models to improve accuracy longitudinally. Kao and Tung (1980) employ an auto-regressive, integrated moving average (ARIMA) time series model to forecast demand for inpatient services.

DATA ANALYSIS AND INITIAL MODEL DEVELOPMENT

While all of these studies investigated the use of forecasting techniques in health care, there were few that really addressed the issue of linking forecasts to improved resource planning. In our study, data were collected on admissions and discharges. It became evident that census patterns fluctuated and behaved in an unpredictable manner. Admission and discharges varied by referring unit and day of the week. ANOVA tests revealed that these variations were significant at the 5% level. Tables 1 and 2 display admissions and discharges by referring unit and day of the week.

The unpredictability contributes to the difficulty of scheduling appropriate levels of resources such as physical and occupational therapists. The contribution of this research is the examination of approaches for census modeling, the development of a prediction model, and the eventual integration of that prediction model into resource scheduling.

The predictive model we developed relates the hospital census, the date of consult, the referring unit, the date of admit, and the offset between consult date and admit date. We seek to answer the question "How can we use this information to predict the census for the rehabilitation clinic a week or more

Table 1. Admits by Unit and Day of Week (Approx. 4-Month Period).

Day of Admit	SIU	NSU	ORTH	Other VMC	Outside VMC	Total
Monday	23	40	16	57	22	158
Tuesday	33	70	29	76	31	239
Wednesday	40	68	24	85	55	272
Thursday	39	48	19	85	46	237
Friday	49	32	15	92	53	241
Saturday	13	5	10	25	16	69
Sunday	5	0	1	9	4	19
Totals	202	263	114	429	227	1235

Table 2. Discharges by Unit and Day of Week (Approx. 4-Month Period).

Day of Admit	SIU	NSU	ORTH	Other VMC	Outside VMC	Total
Monday	12	20	6	36	9	83
Tuesday	50	52	29	86	55	272
Wednesday	34	58	25	101	56	274
Thursday	43	62	34	94	54	287
Friday	58	61	16	97	45	277
Saturday	4	8	2	11	5	30
Sunday	1	2	2	4	3	12
Totals	202	263	114	429	227	1235

in advance to enable us to schedule labor resources to better match that census?" A model will be developed using existing data to predict short-term census fluctuation (i.e., 7 days).

THE PREDICTION MODEL

In order to develop the model, historical data were analyzed. It was determined that approximately 80% of the facility's patients come directly from Vidant Medical Center (VMC) acute inpatient units. Furthermore, as previously indicated, the data revealed that on any given day, three units at VMC account for approximately 45% of the census for the Pitt County location of Vidant Rehabilitation Hospital (hereafter referred to as the Rehabilitation Facility).

Our initial solution approach involved analyzing census data from VMC as well as consult and admit data from the rehabilitation facility to determine the average lag in days between consult at VMC and admit to rehab. We determined the lag for each of the three main VMC units that feed the rehabilitation facility and used these values in our forecasting model. The current census at the rehabilitation facility itself was also identified as an important variable.

An input/output model was developed to approximate when and from which unit patients were populating the rehabilitation facility. This work assisted in identifying variables for the predictive multiple regression model. Specifically, it helped to identify the lag times for the model variables Rehabilitation Census and unit referrals such as Orthopedics. Rehabilitation Census was defined as the number of patients populating the Rehabilitation Facility on a particular day whereas unit referrals were defined as the number of patients referred to the Rehabilitation Facility from a particular medical unit from the adjacent hospital.

A multiple regression model was developed using various input variables. A lag model (i.e., autoregressive model) proved to have the strongest predictive power. Independent variables of Time, Day of the Week, Rehabilitation Census for various Lags, Orthopedics Census for various Lags, Surgical Intensive Census for various Lags, and Neurosurgical Census for various Lags were used to develop a model to predict Rehabilitation Census.

STEPWISE REGRESSION AND PREDICTIVE MODEL DEVELOPMENT

The variables given in Table 3 were initially included in the model. The lag lengths were selected on the basis of the observations in the rehabilitation

Table 3. Initial Predictive Model Independent Variables.

Day of Week (MTWThF)
Neurosurgical Unit Lag 18 Days
Orthopedics Lag 12 Days
Rehabilitation Census Lag 1 Day
Rehabilitation Census Lag 3 Days
Rehabilitation Census Lag 7 Days
Rehabilitation Census Lag 18 Days
Surgical Intensive Unit Lag 14 Days
Time (Nov. 8, 2010 = time 1)

data. For example, the lags for the different units (Surgical Intensive, Neurosurgical, and Orthopedics) were chosen on the basis of time between consult and admit to the Rehabilitation Facility associated with a patient that is transferred from said unit. In addition, the lags for Rehabilitation itself were chosen on the basis of certain time frames within the Rehabilitation Facility itself (e.g., the lag of 7 days is associated with the facility's weekly discharge meeting while 18 days is associated with the average length of stay for rehabilitation patients). A step-wise regression was employed to identify those variables that were significant in census prediction. Table 4 displays the final variables that were statistically significant.

A final model was created, which included the variables Rehab Census Lag 1, Rehab Census Lag 3, Rehab Census Lag 7, Rehab Census Lag 18, and Time (in days). Statistically, the model explains approximately 75% of the variability in the data with all independent variables being significant at the 0.05 level (refer to Table 5). The mean absolute percent error for the model is roughly 5.8% or about 2.5 patients per day. The regression equation is as follows:

$$\hat{Y}_t = 31.10 + 0.42x_1 + 0.20x_2 + (-0.18)x_3 + (-0.17)x_4 + 0.14x_5 \quad (2)$$

It must be noted that the coefficients for the 1-day and 3-day lags are positive. This is expected since, in an operational sense, the previous 1-day and 3-day periods correspond to admissions. On the other hand, the coefficients on the 7-day and 18-day lags are negative. These lags correspond to discharges, specifically the weekly "wellness" meeting where many discharges occur, and the 18-day average length of stay of a typical rehabilitation patient. The time coefficient is positive in that the Rehabilitation area has seen some increase in the number of overall patients over the time frame being studied.

A typical set of independent variables from the Rehabilitation data is the 35th day of data. For the 35th day of data, the previous day's Rehabilitation Census was 52, the Rehabilitation Census three days prior was 51, the

Table 4. Final Predictive Model Independent Variables.

Rehabilitation Census Lag 1 Day
Rehabilitation Census Lag 3 Days
Rehabilitation Census Lag 7 Days
Rehabilitation Census Lag 18 Days
Time (Nov. 8, 2010 = time 1)

Rehabilitation Census seven days ago was 52, the Rehabilitation Census 18-days prior was 46, and the Time variable is 35 since we are studying the 35th day of the data. Employing regression Eq. (2) with $x_1 = 52$, $x_2 = 51$, $x_3 = 52$, $x_4 = 46$, and $x_5 = 35$, the forecast for the census at the Rehabilitation Clinic is as follows:

$$\hat{Y}_t = 31.10 + 0.42^* (52) + 0.20^*(51)$$
$$+ (-0.18)^*52 + (-0.17)^*46 + 0.14^*35 \approx 50.70 \qquad (3)$$

From Eq. (3), it can be seen that the regression equation produces a census of 50.70. However, in the case of the rehabilitation clinic, a portion (i.e., 0.70) of a patient is not possible, so it can be said that the census is 51. This compares very well with the actual Rehabilitation Census on the thirty-fifth day of data, which was 53. The model error is 2.30 out of the actual of 53 or approximately 4.4% (Table 5).

Patient Flow and Link to Resource Planning

Along with model refinement, a process flow map was created depicting what happens to a patient from the time a rehabilitation consult is conducted at VMC to the time the patient is discharged from the rehabilitation facility (see Fig. 1). There are various admission criteria considered by all inpatient rehab hospitals, as patients must require 24/7 physician

Table 5. Regression Output for Rehabilitation Predictive Model.

Regression Output		
R^2	74.2%	
ANOVA		
F Stat.	55.3	
Significance of F	<0.000	
Regression Variable	Regression Coefficients	p-Value
Intercept	31.10	0.000
Rehabilitation Census Lag 1 Day $= x_1$	0.42	0.000
Rehabilitation Census Lag 3 Days $= x_2$	0.20	0.026
Rehabilitation Census Lag 7 Days $= x_3$	−0.18	0.032
Rehabilitation Census Lag 18 Days $= x_4$	−0.17	0.013
Time (Nov. 8, 2010 = time 1) $= x_5$	0.14	0.000

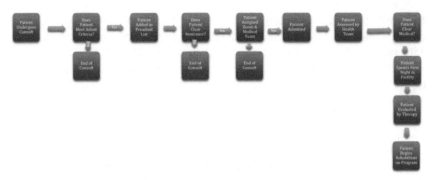

Fig. 1. Process Flow Rehabilitation Consult.

and nursing care, and be appropriate to participate in an intensive multi-disciplinary therapy program.

A patient is assigned a room, bed, medical team, nursing team, and therapy team prior to admittance. After admittance, a patient is assessed by physicians and nurses and then spends his/her first night. Patients are typically evaluated by a therapy team within 24 hours of arrival and are scheduled for their rehabilitation therapy program following this evaluation. The daily scheduling of nurses, occupational therapists, physical therapists, and speech therapists is impacted by the flow of the admissions process for each new patient.

CONCLUSION: FUTURE RESEARCH AND OTHER APPLICATIONS IN HEALTH CARE

Forecasting demand in a health care setting is not an easy task. Demand for rehabilitation services can be highly variable. The model developed here is able to explain 75% of the variability and is capable of forecasting the Rehabilitation Census within about three patients. Although that does make the model of value to the rehabilitation facility, additional refinements may be needed, as three patients does impact resource planning, such as number of therapists needed.

The ability to forecast patient census could be beneficial to many other types of health care facilities. The approach used here could be replicated and applied to other types of inpatient facilities including psychiatric facilities and drug addition treatment centers. Home health programs and hospice programs could also benefit from the ability to forecast demand for their health care-related services

The prediction of daily census along with aggregate demand forecasting is important for improving resource use and planning in health care organizations. It can be said that for any business, demand forecasting is an important component of capacity utilization and service quality. Likewise, demand forecasting, either inpatient, outpatient, or in the form of equipment (e.g., beds, x-ray machines, etc.), plays an important role in hospitals, nursing homes, outpatient practices, and in nearly every other organization within the health care system. Further research involves linking DRG codes to Rehabilitation Impairment Codes (RICs) to better establish the link between hospital patients and rehabilitation admits.

REFERENCES

Harrington, M. B. (1977). Forecasting area-wide demand for health care services: A critical review of major techniques and their application. *Inquiry*, *14*, 254–268.

Hogarth, R. M., & Makridakis, S. (1981). Forecasting and planning: An evaluation. *Management Science*, *27*(2), 115–138.

Johansen, S., Bowles, S., & Haney, G. (1988). A model for forecasting intermittent skilled nursing home needs. *Research in Nursing and Health*, *11*, 375–382.

Kamentzky, R. D., Shuman, L. J., & Wolfe, H. (1982). Estimating need and demand for pre-hospital care. *Operations Research*, *30*, 1148–1167.

Kao, E. P. C., & Poldadnik, F. M. (1978). Incorporating exogenous factors in adaptive forecasting of hospital census. *Management Science*, *24*, 1677–1686.

Kao, E. P. C., & Tung, G. G. (1980). Forecasting demands for inpatient services in a large public health care delivery system. *Socio-Economic Planning Sciences*, *14*, 97–106.

Pierskalla, W. P., & Brailer, D. B. (1990). Applications of operations research in health care delivery. In S. M. Pollock, M. H. Rothkopf & A. Barnett (Eds.), *Handbooks in operations research and management science* (Vol. 6). Amsterdam, The Netherlands: Elsevier Science.

FORECASTING ACTIVITY LEVELS AS A BASELINE FOR PREDICTING PAIN AND DISCOMFORT LEVELS IN CANINES

Virginia M. Miori, James Algeo, Brian Segulin and Dorothy Cimino Brown

ABSTRACT

Evaluating pain and discomfort in animals is difficult at best. Veterinarians believe however, that they can establish a proxy for estimating levels of pain and discomfort in canines by observing variations in their activity levels. Sufficient research has been conducted to justify this assertion, but little has been conducted to analyze the volumes of activity data collected. We present the first of a series of analyses aimed at ultimately presenting an effective predictive tool for canine pain and discomfort levels. In this chapter, we perform analyses on a dataset of normal (control) dogs, containing almost 3 million records. The forecasting analyses incorporated multiple polynomial regression models with transcendental transformations and ARIMA models to provide effective determination and prediction of baseline normal canine activity levels.

Keywords: ARIMA; canine activity levels; activity monitors

Advances in Business and Management Forecasting, Volume 9, 15–32
Copyright © 2013 by Emerald Group Publishing Limited
ISSN: 1477-4070/doi:10.1108/S1477-4070(2013)0000009005

INTRODUCTION

Assessment of pain and discomfort in animals is a difficult process at best. Observing animal behavior over time can provide an indication of the level of pain or discomfort being experienced, but requires extended study of individual dogs over time. It is neither practical nor easily quantifiable. An alternative approach is necessary for quantitative studies and for characterization of the pain/discomfort experienced by canines.

The use of activity monitors designed for humans has been shown to successfully capture both spontaneous and programmed level of activity in dogs. The purpose of this chapter is to provide a forecast of baseline activity levels for dogs throughout the day (midnight until midnight). This forecast will provide quantifiable baseline activity levels to distinguish from activity levels experienced by dogs experiencing pain or discomfort. The ultimate goal is the improvement of diagnostic capabilities for more effective treatment.

The first section of this chapter focuses on the literature within the areas of activity monitors and time series forecasting using autoregressive integrated moving average (ARIMA) techniques. The activity data is characterized in the second section, including descriptive statistics and frequency distribution. Regression and ARIMA models are presented in conjunction with model results in the third section. The final section presents conclusions and future research.

LITERATURE

The literature is presented in discrete sections, each addressing one aspect of the chapter. The first section addresses the validation of the use of activity monitors, originally designed for human use, in dogs. The second section addresses studies in which the data from activity monitors has been used in evaluations of pain and discomfort. These studies have also validated appropriate data collection intervals. The final section examines the use of various forecasting techniques that may be useful in predicting activity levels in dogs. The primary emphasis is on applications of ARIMA. Note that the use of activity monitors on dogs is a recent development resulting in limited research in the specifically related areas.

Validate Activity Monitors

The omnidirectional accelerometer-based devices used to record activity levels in dogs were Actical Activity Monitors (AAM) and were initially produced for use in humans by the Respironics Mini Mitter division in Bend, Oregon. The monitors were watch-sized, placed in waterproof housings, and attached to the collars of the dogs. The AAMs continuously record intensity, frequency, and duration of movement and were set to record data at 60-second epochs (intervals), 24 hours every day.

Validation of the use of activity monitors in dogs was first studied in conjunction with videographic measurements of movement and mobility in health dogs (Hansen, Lascelles, Keene, Adams, & Thomson, 2007). Monitors were placed at locations on the dogs to test their output in order to determine the most effective location. Movement and mobility of dogs was recorded with a computerized videography system for 7-hour sessions, while also wearing activity monitors. Accelerometer values were combined into 15-minute intervals and compared with videographic measures (distance traveled, time spent walking, and time spent changing position). When comparing accelerometers with the greatest disparity, 96% of all values compared were within two standard deviations of the mean. All monitor placement locations provided acceptable correlation with the videographic data, but the ventral collar (front of the dog's neck) was determined to be most convenient.

Once activity monitors were determined to provide accurate results, the optimal or most appropriate sampling interval was evaluated (Dow, Michel, Love, & Brown, 2009). Dogs in this study wore monitors for two weeks. Variation between dogs and within dogs was evaluated on a day-to-day basis and then evaluated between week 1 and week 2, comparing for weekdays, weekends, and full weeks. Significant variation in activity counts between dogs was detected as well as variation within dogs over the course of a full week. The study determined that monitors should be worn for 7-day intervals in order to follow activity over time.

Body conformation and signalment (medical history dealing with a dog's age, sex, and breed) were examined in the use of activity monitors (Brown, Michel, Love, & Dow, 2010). A sample of 104 companion dogs was led through a series of standard activities to determine whether signalment and body conformation had an impact on activity counts. It was determined with 95% confidence that activity counts decreased with increased body weight. Activity counts also decreased with increases in age.

The GT3-X accelerometer has been studied for validity as well as practical utility and reliability in measuring activity in pets (Yam et al., 2011). The validation study examined 30 dogs for one day, filming them while they wore the monitors. Data and film were synchronized to reflect variations in activity levels of a habitual nature. Reliability and practical utility were evaluated on 20 dogs who wore the monitors for one week. The data was supplemented by owner questionnaires. In support of validity, activity levels differed significantly and compared directly to activity intensity. The devices were also found to be well-tolerated (practical utility) and to have minimal data loss (reliability), supporting the conclusions that the devices are valid, practical, and reliable way to collect habitual activity data in dogs.

Differentiation among activities of differing intensities and delineation of the times spent in these activities was completed in a two-phase study (Michel & Brown, 2011). During the first phase, dogs were led through a series of activities, at differing levels of intensity. Characteristic curves were developed and used to determine the most prevalent activity counts when predicting the intensity of these activity levels. Dogs wore the monitors at home for two weeks during the second phase of the study. The outcome of the first phase was used to classify intensity of activity during the 14-day period. Distinguishing sedentary activity from walking activity was highly significant as was distinguishing trotting activity from walking activity.

The cumulative outcomes of the validity studies have strongly supported the use of activity monitors in assessing activity levels in dogs at varied levels of intensity of activity.

Studies Utilizing Activity Monitors

Once the use of activity monitors was determined to be effective, examining treatment responses followed. Researchers had found a way to evaluate levels of pain and discomfort in dogs that could be used to support other anecdotal and clinical measurements.

Discomfort in dogs takes many forms; pruritus (itching) in dogs is one such form of discomfort. It impacts quality of life and is difficult to assess objectively. Atopic dermatitis in dogs was studied using Actiwatch® collar-mounted activity monitors (Nuttall & McEwan, 2006). Activity levels of five normal dogs were compared to six dermatitis dogs, with controls for defined periods of exercise, playing, etc. Data was collected over 7 days, with 15-second epochs. Overall, interquartile ranges for daytime activity were similar during the day and evening, while lower during the night. Using the Mann–Whitney test, the authors found that mean activity during the epochs was significantly higher in atopic dogs, compared to healthy dogs during all three periods.

Activity monitors have been used to compare differences in activity level of dogs undergoing three laparoscopic surgical techniques (LAG, hand suture TLG, and Endostitch™ TLG) in preventative treating of gastric dilation and volvulus (Mayhew & Brown, 2009). This condition is commonly referred to as bloat, and occurs most frequently in large and giant breed dogs. The surgical procedure attaches the dog's stomach (gastric antral wall) to their right body wall to prevent rotation. Monitors were placed on dogs for 7 days before surgery and 7 days after surgery. The activity counts gathered were used to compare recovery rates of dogs between the two laparoscopic procedures. The result of the analysis showed Lag to result in more greatly reduced activity levels than either TLG procedure. No differences in activity levels were demonstrated between TLG techniques.

A similar study examined activity levels in small (< 10 kg) female dogs undergoing sterilization (Culp, Mayhew, & Brown, 2009). A laparoscopic surgical procedure (LapOVE) was compared to the traditional open procedure (OOVE). Activity data was collected 24 hours prior to surgery and 48 hours after surgery, with the removal and return of the dog to her housing run marking the bounds for collection of data. As expected, activity levels in dogs in the OOVE group were substantially lower (62% decrease compared to baseline) than those in the LapOVE group (25% decrease compared to baseline).

Evaluation of osteoarthritis treatment in dogs has traditionally been completed by the use of gait analysis and descriptions of activity provided by owners. Activity monitors have offered an alternative to descriptive data and gait analysis in evaluating the efficacy of medications. A study of 70 dogs with osteoarthritis was completed to evaluate the efficacy of carprofen (Brown, Boston, & Farra, 2010). Dogs were monitored for 21 days; no treatment was given for the first 7 days. During days 8–21, dogs were either given a placebo (control group) or carprofen. Changes in activity level were evaluated between the first 7 days and the remaining 14 days for each group. Linear regression was used to determine associations between treatments and percentage change in activity counts while controlling for conformation and signalment variables. With 95% confidence, an increase of 20% in median activity count was found, suggesting that carprofen was effective in treating osteoarthritis.

Canine Hyperactivity (Hyperkinesis Syndrome a.k.a HS) has been studied in Beagles. Accelerometers have been used to assist in determining the effectiveness of dextroamphetamines in treatment of HS (Stilesa, Palestrinib, Beauchampa, & Franka, 2011). In dogs with HS, oral dextroamphetamines have demonstrated a paradoxically effect and therefore do not elevate activity levels. This study demonstrated the same findings with lower doses. Beagles wore collar-mounted AAMs and recorded 180 minutes of activity recorded at 15-second epochs. Monitor data was compared to video collected during the same time and found to be consistent with the videos. Results also showed no significant effects of treatment on the dogs' activity level.

Accelerometry was used in an assessment of the ability to reduce doses of non-steroidal anti-inflammatory drugs (NSAID) in dogs, yet still control pain resulting from osteoarthritis (Wernham et al., 2011). A number of dogs dropped out of the study because their owners determined that the pain control was insufficient. Among the remaining 59 dogs, activity monitoring was maintained during the duration of the study. Posthoc Bonferoni analysis was used to determine that there was no evidence of effects for the percentage of time above upper thresholds for activity.

The final study in this area has the specific purpose of measuring daily activity, using activity monitors, in health adult Labrador retrievers as a predictor of maintenance energy requirements (MER) (Wrigglesworth, Mort, Upton, & Miller, 2011). Dogs wore the monitors for two-week period. Activity counts in conjunction with data on daily activity levels and body weight were characterized as independent variables in a multiple linear regression to predict daily MER. A second regression excluding activity counts was also completed. Dietary energy intake at a stated body weight was used as a proxy variable for MER. Inclusion of the activity levels significantly improved the predictive capabilities of the multiple linear regression model.

Activity monitors proved to be useful and significant in studying various conditions and determining energy needs for dogs. As this area of study expands, it is important to develop a method of prediction for baseline activity levels in dogs. This baseline may then be used to further assess the impact of pain and discomfort on activity levels.

Forecasting and Nonstationary Data

Predicting activity levels in animals has typically been handled in an anecdotal fashion. Descriptive statistics, confidence intervals, and linear regressions are used to compare changes in activity levels based on matched pairs (pre and post treatment). These analyses have been helpful, but fall short of reaching a goal of characterization of a polynomial activity count time series. To date, establishment of base expectations for activity levels in dogs has not been explored. This section of the literature presents applications of time series methods and our intended approach, ARIMA methods from different fields of study. The common thread among all of these studies is the existence of potentially nonstationary, seasonal data.

Time series forecasting methods have been applied extensively to supply chain and inventory problems. These range from Bayesian methods (Yelland, Kim, & Stratulate, 2010) to linear state space forms (Aviv, 2003) to random walks (Graves, 1999) and to stationary data methods. Of particular interest in this research is the application of stationary techniques to non-stationary time series data. Stationary methods can be successfully used to model nonstationary data (Neale & Willems, 2009). In this case, the planning horizon is divided into intervals, each of which represents a stage of the product life cycle. Demand within each phase is assumed to be stationary allowing the use of models with stationary data assumptions.

The use of ARIMA in supply chain modeling, particularly in modeling consumer demand and the bullwhip effect has been successful (Gilbert, 2005). The general class of ARIMA models was used to model demand, orders, and inventory. Demand is assumed to be stationary, but with predictable (regular) seasonal components.

A popular use of ARIMA is call center forecasting. Data again exhibits nonstationary characteristics due to a seasonal trend, but the seasonal trend is typically well defined allowing for the use of ARIMA. Call center forecasting at L.L. Bean has used ARIMA to model seasonal patterns strongly influenced by independent variables such as holidays and advertising (Andrews & Cunningham, 1995). A survey of approaches to call center forecasting documents many different approaches including time series and ARIMA-based models (Gans, Koole, & Mandelbaum, 2003).

ARIMA has been successfully applied to the Nevada gaming industry and as an economic indicator for the state of Nevada (Cargill & Eadington, 1978). Revenues are subject to seasonal fluctuations in which the amplitude of the fluctuations diminished over time. ARIMA was applied due to the systematic time varying characteristics of the data without applying causal characteristics. The model is not specified ahead of time, but is suggested by the data.

The variation of dates for holidays results from the use of different calendars. Forecasting demand centered on these holidays presents a unique challenge as the dates of some holidays change each year. ARIMA models require intervention to be adequate to forecast these demands (Liu, 1980).

The variety of applications using ARIMA for nonstationary data provides a basis for the use of ARIMA for the canine activity level data.

DATA CHARACTERISTICS

Activity data has been collected from 118 normal dogs. Normal dogs are considered to have no illnesses or conditions that might otherwise impact their activity levels. The dogs range in age from 1 to 13 years and range in weight from 5 to 62 pounds. Activity counts have been collected every minute of the day, typically over two to three weeks for each dog. In total, 4,004 days of activity data have been collected using the activity monitors.

Upon examination of the data, there are clear cases of anomalies in the activity counts. We have no basis for exclusion of these anomalies and presume they are specifically related to the monitors. Lacking the ability to definitively establish sources for the anomalies, they have remained in the analysis.

The overriding goal of the data analysis is to characterize the distribution of the time series in a manner that may be used for comparison. Once the baseline has been appropriately defined, it will improve the diagnostic abilities of veterinarians, rather than having to rely on owner judgment and comparative analysis during illness or disease progression.

The data was first aggregated and averages were calculated for activity counts every minute of the day. The following descriptive data applies to these 1,440 data points.

Using the distribution fitting capabilities in JMP, the activity count averages have been examined to determine whether an appropriate distribution may be fitted. A frequency histogram of the data is shown in Table 1. After attempting to fit continuous distribution models to this histogram, based on the Akaike Information Criteria (AIC) we concluded that the most likely fit was a mixture of normal distributions. The parameters for these distributions are presented in Table 2.

The probabilities within Table 2 show that the first normal distribution fits 24.15% of the data and is truncated on the right. The second normal

Table 1. Best Fit Multiple Regression Output.

Response Ln Average

Summary of fit

R^2	0.784224
R^2 Adj.	0.78332
Root mean square error	0.186067
Mean of response	4.889981
No. of observations (or Sum Wgts)	1439

Analysis of Variance

Source	DF	Sum of Squares	Mean^2	F Ratio
Model	6	180.18515	30.0309	867.4172
Error	1432	49.57729	0.0346	Prob$>F$
C. Total	1438	229.76244		$<.0001^*$

Parameter Estimates

Term	Estimate	Std. Error	t Ratio	Prob$>|t|$
Intercept	9.2191043	0.297543	30.98	$<.0001^*$
Root	1.7885557	0.125674	14.23	$<.0001^*$
Cube root	-7.128479	0.557679	-12.78	$<.0001^*$
Minute^2	$-6.361e{-}6$	4.354e-7	-14.61	$<.0001^*$
Minute^3	1.8223e-9	1.66e-10	10.98	$<.0001^*$
Ln minute	2.205151	0.231923	9.51	$<.0001^*$
ave(t) − ave$(t-1)$ $t=1,...,1,440$	0.0037696	0.000682	5.53	$<.0001^*$

*Statistically significant terms.

Table 2. Parameters of the Normal 2 Mixture Distribution Fitting.

Type	Parameter	Estimate	Lower 95%	Upper 95%
Location	μ_1	71.068646	70.119484	72.017809
Location	μ_2	165.53903	163.75055	167.3275
Dispersion	σ_1	9.0304447	8.1260676	10.035473
Dispersion	σ_2	30.157882	28.427571	31.993513
Probability	π_1	0.2414748	0.2170097	0.2677549
Probability	π_2	0.7585252	0.7107484	0.8006242

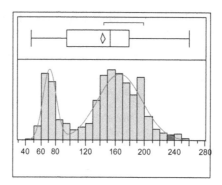

Fig. 1.   Histogram of Average Activity Count.

distribution specified fits the remaining 75.85% of the data and is truncated on the left. By its nature, the frequency histogram eliminates the time series represented in the data and the application of the normal 2 mixture is impractical since we cannot determine which portion of the data should be fit to normal distribution 1 and which should be fit to normal distribution 2 (Fig. 1).

Distributions

Average
A time series plot of the average activity count per minute is provided in Fig. 2. Minute 1 refers to 12:01 am, minute 700 signals noon, and minute 1,440 is the final moment of a single day, representing 12:00 am the next day. We can easily see that there is a pattern to canine activity levels and that these levels are most elevated during the early morning and afternoon. Overall activity levels are also higher during the day than during the night.

FORECASTING

The activity data presents a significant challenge in the development of forecasts. Though it appears that a seasonal pattern may exist in the data, seasonal models provide a poor fit. Regression models and ARIMA models both provide strong fit and each have their own advantages in modeling the activity data.

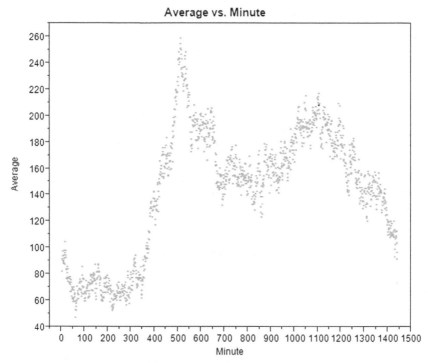

Fig. 2. Time Series Plot of Average Activity Counts.

Multiple Polynomial Regression

Time series methods such as multiple regression were appealing in this case due to their ability to predict an indeterminate number of time periods into the future. Given the shape of the average activity level data presented in Fig. 2, appropriate models were most likely to include polynomial terms and may also have benefited from transcendental transformations. The lack of supporting data also incited the exploitation of the time period (minute of the day) within the regression variables. Since activity levels in dogs are not expected to change simply based on the passage of time, we did not seek to model any trend behavior in the regression.

The multiple regression with the best fit to the data had an adjusted R^2 of 0.78. The significant independent variables included $(minute)^2$, $(minute)^3$, $(minute)^{1/2}$, $(minute)^{1/3}$, $ln(minute)$ as well as a one period difference term.

The linear variable *minute* was eliminated from the model due to a lack of significance. The regression output is presented in Table 1.

The graph of the predicted activity levels versus actual activity levels is presented in Fig. 3. The graph represents activity each minute over the course of an average day (1,440 minutes). Though the coefficient of determination showed that 78% of the variation in activity level was explained by the independent variables, the most significant extremes are under-represented in the predicted activity levels. The regression does offer a viable method for prediction of activity levels across the day, but may not provide an appropriate baseline for comparison when evaluating the existence of disease and degree of disease experienced by a dog.

Given the results of the multiple regression, alternative methods with higher predictive capability were explored.

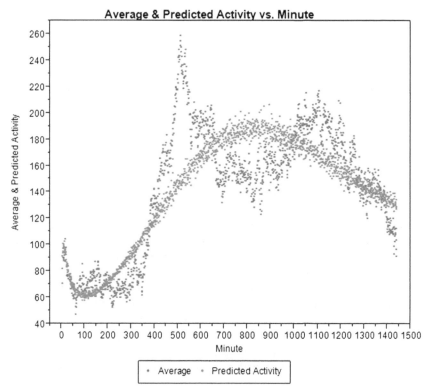

Fig. 3. Predicted versus Actual Activity Levels.

Arima

The forecasting method that offered the greatest potential in examining the data is ARIMA. In this model, there is an assumption that the data is stationary and this assumption is typically met.

> If arbitrary snapshots of the time series we study exhibit similar behavior in central tendency and spread, we will proceed with our analysis assuming that the time series is indeed stationary. (Bisgaard & Kulahci, 2011)

Based on the overall appearance of the data in Fig. 2, it is highly unlikely that it would be considered stationary. The average activity counts for the 1,440 minutes of the day do not visually appear to exhibit similar behavior in central tendency and spread when arbitrary snapshots of data are chosen. Table 3 shows mean, standard deviation, and range for two snapshots of data: 100–200 minutes and 1,100–1,200 minutes. Note that all three measures demonstrate significant differences. We concluded that the data was likely to be non-stationary and in addition to forecasting activity levels, we calculated single lag differences.

In many applications with non-stationary data, the change in an observed value between lagged time periods will serve to produce stationary data. We examined this transformation and used a lag of one time period. The resulting calculation was:

$$\Delta Avg = Avg_t - Avg_{t-1} \tag{1}$$

The plot resulting from this transformation is shown in Fig. 4. Table 4 shows the revised mean, standard deviation, and range for the transformed change data. The change in activity counts initially appeared to produce more stationary data when examining raw differences. When considering these differences relative to the magnitude of the data, the results were inconclusive in determining whether the differences were stationary. Despite this, the data plot did have a more stationary appearance than the original

Table 3. Variation between Snapshots of "Average Activity Counts".

	Minutes 100–200	Minutes 1,100–1,200	Difference
Mean	71.22	189.08	−117.86
Standard deviation	7.08	12.04	−4.96
Range	28.00	49.61	−21.61

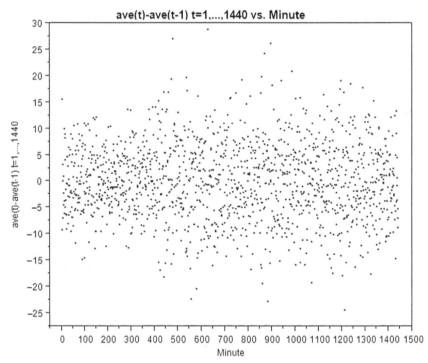

Fig. 4. Time Series Plot of Change in Average Activity Counts (1-period lag).

Table 4. Variation between Snapshots of "Change in Average Activity Counts".

	Minutes 100–200	Minutes 1,100–1,200	Difference
Mean	0.08	−0.46	0.54
Standard deviation	5.44	8.14	−2.70
Range	24.93	37.01	−12.08

data. As a result, we performed ARIMA model analysis on both the average activity counts and the single lag based differences.

The ARIMA models performed poorly on the lagged differences but produced better results for the average activity counts. Due to this improved performance, the assumption of stationary data was relaxed. Results were again measured using AIC, as a measure of the relative goodness of fit.

The models with the best fit are mixed models: ARIMA (1,1,1), ARIMA(1,1,2), ARIMA(2,1,1), ARIMA(2,1,2), and ARIMA(1,2,2). Mixed models are prone to overfitting the data and can result in coefficients that are not unique. Because of the potential to over fit and a negligible difference in AIC (0.04%) between the best mixed and the best non-mixed models, a non-mixed model has been selected to offer the best fit: the ARIMA (0,1,2) model, also known as IMA(1,2). This model contains no autoregressive terms, one seasonal difference, and two lagged forecasting errors in the prediction equation. In other words, the data is differenced once and a second order moving average term is included. The results are presented in Table 5; both constants for MA(1) and MA(2) were found to be significant.

The resulting plot of predicted versus actual activity averages is shown in Fig. 5. Clearly the fit is superior to the fit achieved by the multiple regression

Table 5. ARIMA(0,1,2) Output Report Differenced.

Model: IMA(1, 2)

Model summary

DF	1436
Sum of squared errors	67753.8094
Variance estimate	47.1823185
Standard deviation	6.86893867
Akaike's 'A' information criterion	9632.79806
Schwarz's Bayesian criterion	9648.61317
R^2	0.97993711
R^2 Adj.	0.97990917
MAPE	4.18577139
MAE	5.45358793
-2 log likelihood	9626.79806
Stable	Yes
Invertible	Yes

Parameter Estimates

Term	Lag	Estimate	Std. Error	t Ratio	Prob$>|t|$	Constant Estimate
MA1	1	0.30196653	0.0260575	11.59	$<.0001^*$	0.00406478
MA2	2	0.12999600	0.0273083	4.76	$<.0001^*$	
Intercept	0	0.00406478	0.0149028	0.27	0.7851	

*Statistically significant terms.

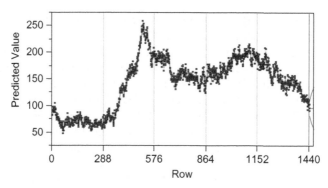

Fig. 5. ARIMA(0,1,2) Plot of Actual and Predicted Values.

model, though the ability to forecast into future time frames is limited. This approach is therefore considered to be superior because it does produces a characterization of the average activity levels that may be used in establishing the degree of disease being experienced by a dog. Diagnostic improvements are significant and crucial elements in the treatment of animals.

CONCLUSIONS AND FUTURE RESEARCH

Canine activity count averages were poorly represented when trying to fit statistical distributions to them. Time series methods such as multiple polynomial regression with transcendental transformations and ARIMA were found to be superior models in characterizing the activity data. Regression provided a good fit with the ability to predict broadly into the future while ARIMA provided a superior fit with limited ability to project into the future. Since the most important aspect of the analysis was the complete characterization of baseline levels of activities for dogs over the 1,440 minutes of the day, the ARIMA(0,1,2) model was found to be valid and preferred over the regression model.

The ability to characterize a full day of canine activity is only the first step in the use of activity data. Future research includes analysis of dogs with osteoarthritis, dermatitis, and sarcoma, in determining the existence and progression of these diseases. The ultimate goal is the determination of the level of pain or discomfort being experienced by a dog in support of assigning appropriate levels of medication. This will avoid over-treating dogs with possibly increased complications, or under-treating dogs resulting in excess pain and discomfort.

REFERENCES

Andrews, B. H., & Cunningham, S. M. (1995). L.L. Bean improves call center forecasting. *Interfaces, 25*(6), 1–13.

Aviv, Y. (2003). A time-series framework for supply-chain inventory management. *Operations Research, 51*(2), 210–227.

Bisgaard, S., & Kulahci, M. (2011). *Time series analysis and forecasting by example.* Hoboken, NJ: Wiley.

Brown, C. D., Boston, R. C., & Farrar, J. T. (2010). Use of an activity monitor to detect response to treatment in dogs with osteoarthritis. *Journal of the American Veterinary Medical Association, 237*(1), 66–70.

Brown, C. D., Michel, K. E., Love, M., & Dow, C. (2010). Evaluation of the effect of signalment and body conformation on activity monitoring in companion dogs. *American Journal of Veterinary Research, 71*(3), 322–325.

Cargill, T. F., & Eadington, W. R. (1978). Nevada's gaming revenues: Time characteristics and forecasting. *Management Science, 24*(12), 1221–1230.

Culp, W. T. N., Mayhew, P. D., & Brown, C. D. (2009). The effect of laparoscopic versus open ovariectomy on postsurgical activity in small dogs. *Veterinary Surgery, 38,* 811–817.

Dow, C., Michel, K. E., Love, M., & Brown, C. D. (2009). Evaluation of optimal sampling interval for activity monitoring in companion dogs. *American Journal of Veterinary Research, 70*(4), 444–448.

Gans, N., Koole, G., & Mandlebaum, A. (2003). Telephone call centers: Tutorial, review, and research prospects. *Manufacturing & Service Operations Management, 5*(2), 79–141.

Gilbert, K. (2005). An ARIMA supply chain model. *Management Science, 51*(2), 305–310.

Graves, S. C. (1999). A single-item inventory model for a nonstationary demand process. *Manufacturing & Service Operations Management, 1*(1), 50–61.

Hansen, B. D., Lascelles, B. D. X., Keene, B. W., Adams, A. K., & Thomson, A. E. (2007). Evaluation of an accelerometer for at-home monitoring of spontaneous activity in dogs. *American Journal of Veterinary Research, 68*(5), 468–475.

Liu, L. M. (1980). Analysis of time series with calendar effects. *Management Science, 26*(1), 106–112.

Mayhew, P. D., & Brown, C. D. (2009). Prospective evaluation of two intracorporeally sutured prophylactic laparoscopic gastropexy techniques compared with laparoscopic-assisted gastropexy in dogs. *Veterinary Surgery, 38,* 738–746.

Michel, K. E., & Brown, C. D. (2011). Determination and application of cut points for accelerometer-based activity counts of activities with differing intensity in pet dogs. *American Journal of Veterinary Research, 72*(7), 866–870.

Neale, J. J., & Willems, S. P. (2009). Managing inventory in supply chains with nonstationary. *Interfaces, 39*(5), 388–399.

Nutall, T., & McEwan, N. (2006). Objective measurement of pruritus in dogs: A preliminary study using activity monitors. *European Society of Veterinary Dermatology,* 348–351.

Signalment. (n.d.). *In the free dictionary by Farlex*. Retrieved from http://medical-dictionary. thefreedictionary.com/signalment. Accessed on November 5, 2012.

Stilesa, E. K., Palestrinib, C., Beauchampa, G., & Franka, D. (2011). Physiological and behavioral effects of dextroamphetamine on Beagle dogs. *Journal of Veterinary Bahavior, 6*, 328–336.

Wernham, B. G. J., Trumpatori, B., Lipsett, J., Davidson, G., Wackerow, P., Thomson, A., et al. (2011). Dose reduction of meloxicam in dogs with osteoarthritis-associated pain and impaired mobility. *Journal of Veterinary Internal Medicine., 25*, 1298–1305.

Wrigglesworth, D. J., Mort, E. S., Upton, S. L., & Miller, A. T. (2011). Accuracy of the use of triaxial accelerometry for measuring daily activity as a predictor of daily maintenance energy requirement in healthy adult Labrador Retrievers. *American Journal of Veterinary Research, 72*(9), 1151–1155.

Yam, P. S., Penpraze, V., Young, D., Todd, M. S., Cloney, A. D., Houston-Callaghan, K. A., et al. (2011). Validity, practical utility and reliability of actigraph accelerometry for the measurement of habitual physical activity in dogs. *Journal of Small Animal Practice, 52*, 86–92.

Yelland, P. M., Kim, S., & Stratulate, R. (2010). A Bayesian model for sales forecasting at Sun Microsystems. *Interfaces, 40*(2), 118–129.

FORECASTING PATIENT VOLUME FOR A LARGE HOSPITAL SYSTEM: A COMPARISON OF THE PERIODICITY OF TIME SERIES DATA AND FORECASTING APPROACHES

Kristin Kennedy, Michael Salzillo, Alan Olinsky and John Quinn

ABSTRACT

Managing a large hospital network can be an extremely challenging task. Management must rely on numerous pieces of information when making business decisions. This chapter focuses on the number of bed days (NBD) which can be extremely valuable for operational managers to forecast for logistical planning purposes. In addition, the finance staff often requires an expected NBD as input for estimating future expenses. Some hospital reimbursement contracts are on a per diem schedule, and expected NBD is useful in forecasting future revenue.

Two models, time regression and autoregressive integrated moving average (ARIMA), are applied to nine years of monthly counts of the

Advances in Business and Management Forecasting, Volume 9, 33–44
Copyright © 2013 by Emerald Group Publishing Limited
All rights of reproduction in any form reserved
ISSN: 1477-4070/doi:10.1108/S1477-4070(2013)0000009006

NBD for the Rhode Island Hospital System. These two models are compared to see which gives the best fit for the forecasted NBD. Also, the question of summarizing the time data from monthly to quarterly time periods is addressed. The approaches presented in this chapter can be applied to a variety of time series data for business forecasting.

Keywords: Time series; ARIMA modeling; periodicity; forecasting; hospital bed-days; regression analysis

INTRODUCTION

Upper management of municipal hospitals must delicately balance care for the public while making sound decisions to keep the hospital financially solvent. One significant piece of information that should be carefully monitored is the number of bed days (NBD). Bed days represent the number of patients who are occupying a bed for each day in the hospital over a specific time period. For example, the NBD for January 2011 is the sum of all overnight stays for every patient discharged in January 2011. Not only are operational managers concerned with predicting the NBD, but the finance staff too can require an expected NBD as input for estimating future expenses. In fact, some hospital reimbursement contracts are on a *per diem* schedule, and expected NBD is useful in forecasting future revenue. This chapter will address the issue of how an operational or financial manager can forecast NBD for logistical planning. The chapter examines the appropriate level of periodicity in the time series that should be represented, that is, whether a monthly model or a quarterly model would produce a better prediction to forecasting NBD. Furthermore, the chapter tests two predictive models, namely the autoregressive integrated moving average (ARIMA) model and time regression analysis, to determine which can better forecast the NBD.

The data consist of nine years of monthly counts of NBD for the Rhode Island Hospital System. There are several questions that are addressed. First, what level of summarization by time period (e.g., monthly or quarterly) will provide the best estimates for future periods? If the goal is to predict the volume of NBD for the next quarter, should a monthly time series be used or should the data be summarized as quarterly data? Second, when is information lost by summarizing? Finally, which basic forecast methodology should be applied to attain the best prediction? A comparison of time regression models and ARIMA is presented and summarized.

LITERATURE REVIEW

Linden and Schweitzer (2001) remarked that hospital spending consumes the largest portion of the healthcare dollar, and the number of bed days for any given hospital should remain an area of continued intense scrutiny for anyone involved with controlling costs. They suggest that hospitals should use mathematical models based on previous data to forecast hospitalization rates, rather than simply using benchmarks or subjective valuation. They used an ARIMA model to forecast NBD in a Medicare HMO, and they found their predictive model to be quite accurate when compared to the subjectively derived budget of bed day goals established yearly by the HMO. Also, the model identified a seasonal trend in hospitalizations occurring every December in senior populations.

Furthermore, Corke, de Leeuw, Lo, and George (2009) used time series analysis to show that the senior population is driving demand of bed days in ICUs in Australia. They found that the greatest demand of bed days in ICUs is for the 65–79 age group, and they predict that this age group will also account for the greatest increase in future demand. They also recognized that total number of bed days is a recognized costing unit for all hospitals and that the NBD can be estimated with reasonable accuracy using a time series model.

Farmer and Emami (1990) reviewed two forecasting models: (1) using a structural model and (2) using a time series approach. They state that healthcare managers require access to good models for predicting future hospital needs such as predicting the NBDs. They also used data from the acute sector, and they found that the time series approach to predict future NBD offered greater scope to the predicting model.

Earnest, Chen, Ng, and Sin (2005) employed an ARIMA model to predict NBD needed in a real time capacity during an outbreak of an infectious disease such as SARS. They found that the ARIMA model was able to describe and predict the NBD fairly well. "The mean absolute percentage error for the training set and validation set were 5.7% and 8.6% respectively." Also they found that the three-day forecasts provided a reasonable prediction of the NBD required during the outbreak of SARS.

There has been a concern for the overcrowding and lack of supplies in emergency rooms in Korea. To help address this problem, Kam, Sung, and Park (2010) utilized several models, including a univariate seasonal ARIMA as well as a multivariate seasonal ARIMA, to predict the daily number of patients using emergency room services in a Korean hospital. The multivariate ARIMA model had the smallest mean absolute percentage error (7.4%) and was selected as the final model to predict the number of daily patients.

In another study, Joy and Jones (2005) applied both neural networks and ARIMA models to predict the demand for hospital beds by emergency patients in a South London hospital. There is a serious duty for hospital bed managers, which is to determine how many beds should be allocated for elective admissions and how many for emergency admissions. Setting aside too many beds for either target group presents problems. The main focus of the chapter was to predict the maximum emergency demand for one week in the future, an example of short-term forecasting, which would be most helpful for the hospital bed managers. The neural network modeling utilized the prediction errors from the linear model, in order to handle the nonlinearity inherent in the data. In a similar investigation, Abraham, Byrnes, and Bain (2009) applied both regression and a seasonal ARIMA model to predict emergency occupancy for at most one week into the future for a hospital in Melbourne, Australia. They also studied emergency admissions but found that they were essentially random and unpredictable.

THE DATA

The Department of Health for the State of Rhode Island tracks hospital data for the major hospitals in the state. The data set utilized in this analysis covers information from 2003 to 2011. This is a large data set, with well over 1 million records, and there exists a plethora of analytical questions that could be studied.

It should be noted that we decided to hold out the data for 2011 so that we could validate the forecasting ability of our models. Therefore, the data used in the forecasting models includes the years 2003–2010. Software that was used included SAS™ Enterprise Guide (2011) for the data manipulation and Minitab (2010) for the regression and ARIMA analysis.

ANALYSIS

The first question to address was the issue of how the model would improve by changing the periodicity in the data. The entire data set was used to run a regression on (1) using month as the seasonal period and (2) using calendar year quarters as the seasonal period. The results are provided in

Table 1. Monthly Regression ($R^2 = .564598$).

Source	DF	Sum of Squares	Mean Square	F Value	Pr > F
Model	12	345288307.7	28774025.6	10.27	< .0001
Error	95	266276039.7	2802905.7		
Corrected total	107	611564347.4			

Table 2. Quarterly Regression ($R^2 = .243214$).

Source	DF	Sum of Squares	Mean Square	F Value	Pr > F
Model	4	148740916.7	37185229.2	8.28	< .0001
Error	103	462823430.7	4493431.4		
Corrected total	107	611564347.4			

Tables 1 and 2. The one dependent variable was NBD, and that variable was regressed on two independent variables: time and an indicator variable that captures the seasonal impact. Thus Table 1, which represents monthly data, has an indicator for January, February, March, etc. Table 2, which represents quarterly data, has an indicator value to signify the different quarters each year.

Using a monthly time variable, the R^2 value was 0.56 compared to an R^2 value of 0.24 for the quarterly regression. Based on comparison of the two R^2 values, it appears that using monthly data would significantly increase accuracy for this data set. Moving forward, all analysis below is based on a time value in months.

Thus, using time in months on the x-axis and NBD on the y-axis, Fig. 1 provides a time series graph of all of the data from January 2003 to December 2011. There are a couple of peaks with outliers, but the NBD appears to be decreasing as time goes on. This may be explained by the fact that hospitals do try to send patients home as soon as they can, and many procedures today are done on an outpatient basis. Some downward trends could be expected over a long period of time for NBD.

The autocorrelation function (acf) and partial autocorrelation function (pacf) are very important at the identification stage of ARIMA modeling. They measure the statistical relationship between observations in a single data series. They are used to infer the structure of the underlying pattern that has given rise to the data being studied. The acf and pacf are most

KRISTIN KENNEDY ET AL.

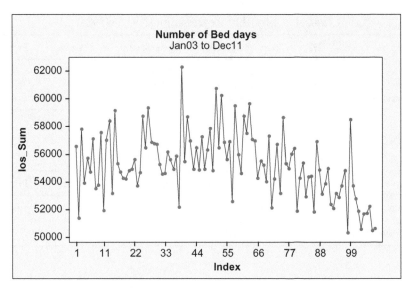

Fig. 1. Number of Bed Days from January 2003 Until December 2011.

useful when presented in graphical form. Some data series show very clear and obvious patterns while others do not. The next two graphs represent the autocorrelation function (Fig. 2), and the partial autocorrelation function (Fig. 3), for NBD. Both graphs show spikes outside the confidence limits, for lags are of 2 and 3 months, and a third spike for a lag of 12 months. This seems to suggest that the NBD are highly correlated for different lag periods. Likewise, the partial autocorrelation function shows similar characteristics with respect to spikes outside the confidence limits. These two graphs taken together indicate that both an autoregressive term and moving average term, as provided for in the ARIMA model, would be appropriate to use for this analysis.

Both ARIMA analysis and Regression analysis were performed, and the complete output of both are listed in Fig. 4.

The ARIMA model has three independent variables – autoregression with a lag of 1 (AR), seasonal autoregression with a lag of 12 (SAR), and moving average (MA). Although the AR variable was not significant with a p-value of 0.283, starting with an AR with a lag of 1 is a good benchmark place to start. The SAR with a 12-month lag and the MA were both found to be significant, which was expected with the spikes that occurred in Figs. 2 and 3.

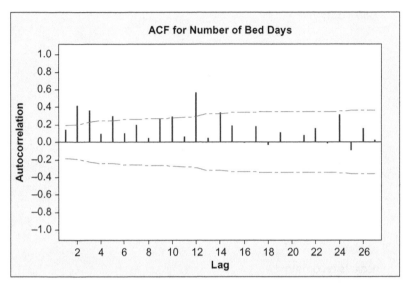

Fig. 2. Autocorrelation Function for Number of Bed Days.

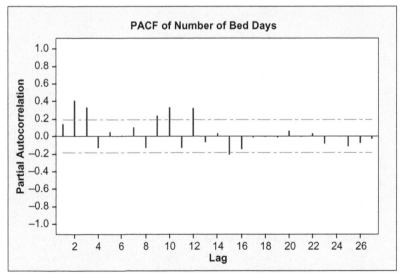

Fig. 3. Partial Autocorrelation Function for Number of Bed Days.

ARIMA OUTPUT

```
Final Estimates of Parameters

Type         Coef  SE Coef       T      P
AR    1   -0.1249   0.1157   -1.08  0.283
SAR  12    0.7284   0.0784    9.29  0.000
MA    1    0.8750   0.0543   16.11  0.000
Constant   -5.92     19.88   -0.30  0.767


Differencing: 1 regular difference
Number of observations:  Original series 96, after differencing 95
Residuals:    SS =  215423139
              MS =    2367287  DF = 91


Period  Forecast     Lower    Upper
    97   53360.2   50343.9  56376.4
    98   51496.9   48480.6  54513.2
    99   55181.8   52142.1  58221.5
```

REGRESSION OUTPUT

```
Coefficients

Term         Coef  SE Coef        T      P
Constant  56113.9  325.465  172.412  0.000
new         -11.3    5.838   -1.931  0.057
C13-T
    1      1531.7  533.325    2.872  0.005
   10       958.7  532.750    1.800  0.076
   11     -1757.5  533.005   -3.297  0.001
   12      -537.3  533.325   -1.007  0.317
    2     -1823.5  533.005   -3.421  0.001
    3      3704.9  532.750    6.954  0.000
    4        54.2  532.558    0.102  0.919
    5       807.4  532.430    1.517  0.133
    6      -123.2  532.366   -0.231  0.818
    7       -64.4  532.366   -0.121  0.904
    8     -1097.1  532.430   -2.061  0.042


Summary of Model

S = 1572.69         R-Sq = 53.99%        R-Sq(adj) = 47.33%
PRESS = 274763229   R-Sq(pred) = 38.41%


Analysis of Variance

Source      DF      Seq SS      Adj SS     Adj MS        F          P
Regression  12   240845465   240845465   20070455  8.11468  0.0000000
   new       1    15054475     9225133    9225133  3.72981  0.0568627
   C13-T     11  225790990   225790990   20526454  8.29905  0.0000000
Error       83   205288065   205288065    2473350
Total       95   446133530
```

Fig. 4.   ARIMA and Regression Models for Predicting Number of Bed Days.

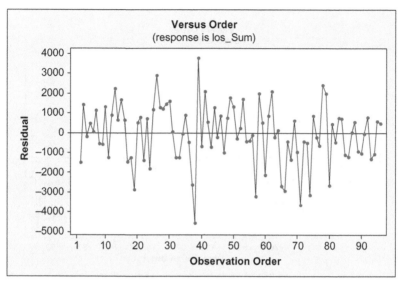

Fig. 5. ARIMA Residuals.

The independent time variable for the regression analysis represents months and can be considered significant, but not highly so. The variables under the column C13-T are dummy variables that are used to identify each individual data value with a month, for example, Jan = 1, Feb = 2, etc. Under the ANOVA output for the Regression analysis, the C13-T was significant with a *p*-value of 0.0.

The ARIMA model has a mean square error (MS) of 2,367,287, whereas the mean square error for the regression analysis is a little larger with a value of 2,473,350, indicating that ARIMA is a slightly better fit for the data.

Finally, in the process of comparing ARIMA to Regression, graphs of the residuals for both models were examined. In Fig. 5, which represents the ARIMA model, the residuals are randomly scattered, with a few notable spikes clearly visible. However, in Fig. 6, which represents the regression model, the residuals appear to be significantly correlated with the model overpredicting for some periods and underpredicting for others.

RESULTS

Comparing the mean square error term for both models shows the ARIMA model with a slightly lower error term than the Regression analysis

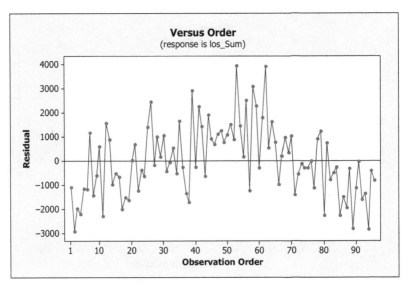

Fig. 6.   Regression Residuals.

(2,367,287 compared to 2,473,350). Also the graph of the residuals for ARIMA was a graph that the authors expected as a fit, rather than the graph of residuals for the Regression model. It appears that there is some indication that the ARIMA model is a better fit for the NBD data than the Regression model. However, the results are marginally different.

Data for the year 2011 were held out at the beginning of the analysis for validation purposes. The actual NBD that was recorded for the first quarter of that year was 163,647. Within the ARIMA output, there is a block of data for "period" and "forecast." The periods of 97, 98, and 99 correspond to January, February, and March of 2011, so the forecast column is stating the forecast for the first quarter. The approximate forecast then is the summation of those three forecasts which is 160,039 for the first quarter. The regression equation predicted 168,442 NBD for that same quarter (Table 3).

The predicted NBD for each model differs slightly from the actual value. The ARIMA model underpredicts the true value by 2.2%, whereas the regression analysis overpredicts the first quarter NBD by 2.9%. The ARIMA prediction is a little closer to the actual NBD than that estimated by the regression model.

Table 3. Comparison of Models for Predicting 1st Quarter in 2011.

1st Quarter 2011 Actual = 163,647
ARIMA Predicted 1st Quarter 2011 = 160,039 (2.2%) Diff. vs. Actual
Regression Predicted 1st Quarter 2011 = 168,442 (2.9%) Diff. vs. Actual

CONCLUSIONS

Would a financial manager or an operational manager of a hospital want to predict slightly over or slightly under the actual number needed? Perhaps the answer to that question would depend on the manager. It could be argued that both predictions are close, and perhaps the average of the two would be a safe benchmark to use.

Statistically speaking, the ARIMA model showed better results with a lower mean square error, with a graph of residuals that were more randomly scattered, and a predicted result that was closer to the actual NBD rather than the regression model. As more current data are collected, the models could be used again to examine if the ARIMA model continued to outperform the regression model.

Both models are generally good for predicting on a short-term basis. It was not surprising that using a monthly periodicity for the data was significantly better than using a quarterly one. In today's world, managers should certainly be utilizing short-term forecasting.

In conclusion, the authors were able to analyze a real world hospital data set in order to predict the key variable of bed days. However, this data set is rich in variables that will allow for much deeper analysis. We hope to present additional results in the future.

REFERENCES

Abraham, G., Byrnes, G. B., & Bain, C. A. (2009). Short-term forecasting of emergency inpatient flow. *IEEE Transactions on Information Technology in Biomedicine*, 1–9. IEEE TITB-00211-2007.R1.

Corke, C., de Leeuw, E., Lo, S. K., & George, C. (2009, December 4). Predicting future intensive care demand in Australia. *Critical Care and Resuscitation*, *11*, 257–260.

Earnest, A., Chen, M. I., Ng, D., & Sin, L. Y. (2005). Using autoregressive integrated moving average (ARIMA) models to predict and monitor the number of beds occupied during a SARS outbreak in a tertiary hospital in Singapore. *BMC Health Services Research*, *5*(36).

Farmer, R. D. T., & Emami, J. (1990). Models for forecasting hospital bed requirements in the acute factor. *Journal of Epidemiology and Community Health, 44*(4), 307–312.

Joy, M. P., & Jones, S. (2005). Predicting bed demand in a hospital using neural networks and arima models: A hybrid approach. *ESANN 2005 Proceedings, 13th European Symposium on Artificial Neural Networks,* Bruges, Belgium, April 27–29, 2005, pp. 127–132.

Kam, H. J., Sung, J. O., & Park, R. W. (2010, September). Prediction of daily patient numbers for a regional emergency medical center using time series analysis. *Healthcare Informatics Research, 16*(3), 158–165.

Linden, A., & Schweitzer, S. (2001). Using time series ARIMA modeling for forecasting bed-days in a Medicare HMO. In AHSRHP 18th Annual Meeting (Vol. 18, p. 25). Washington, DC: Academy for Health Services Research and Health Policy.

Minitab 16 Statistical Software. (2010). *Computer software.* State College, PA: Minitab, Inc. www.minitab.com

SAS Institute Inc. (2011). *SAS enterprise guide.* Cary, NC: SAS Institute Inc.

PART II
FINANCIAL

ESTIMATION OF PENALTY COSTS IN SERVICE INDUSTRIES

Amitava Mitra and Jayprakash G. Patankar

ABSTRACT

The service sector comprises a dominant segment of the economy. Customer satisfaction, a measure of quality, is based on the degree of difference between expected quality and the actual level of quality experienced. Expected level of quality is influenced by customer perception of quality, which in turn is impacted by external and internal factors. In service industries, the interaction between the service provider and the customer may also influence quality. Thus quality may consist of tangible and intangible factors. In this chapter we consider the measurable attributes associated with quality in the service sector. Based on a specified guarantee level associated with the attribute, for example, service time, a penalty function is used to determine the impact of deviating from the guarantee level. With service time being a stochastic random variable, expected penalty costs to the service provider are found under a variety of conditions.

Keywords: Customer satisfaction; penalty function; service guarantee time; service time distribution; Taguchi loss function

Advances in Business and Management Forecasting, Volume 9, 47–57
ISSN: 1477-4070/doi:10.1108/S1477-4070(2013)0000009007

INTRODUCTION

The service industry is a sizeable segment of the United States economy. Consequently, consumer satisfaction in this sector is an important attribute in impacting market share. With competition for service increasing, both in the domestic market and the global market, industries are challenged to retain existing customers as well as identify new customers. The key to increasing market share is to satisfy the customer. Growth in market share is usually associated with exceeding the expectations of the customer. Customer satisfaction in the service industry may be interpreted as the difference between the expected level of quality and actual level of quality. Attributes of quality may be tangible and intangible. Specific variables, such as delays in providing a service, are measurable. On the other hand, the nature of interaction between the service provider and the customer, such as the behavior and attitude of the service provider to the customer, can only be observed qualitatively. Furthermore, expected level of quality is based on customer perception, which may be influenced by external or internal factors. External factors comprise the competitor's offerings, social values and changes in lifestyle, knowledge explosion, among others. Under internal factors, the degree of client management, depth of advertising, operational performance of the company as disseminated publicly via annual and quarterly reports and shareholder reports are examples.

In this chapter we focus on the tangible aspects of service performance. Hence, a performance metric that is measurable is selected to determine the level of performance of the service organization. A common example is the time to provide a service to the customer. For instance, this could be the transportation time to deliver goods via trucks between an origin and a destination. It could also be the processing time to repair a machine or an equipment or the time between the placement of a web-based order and the actual receipt of goods by the customer. Another example could involve the scheduling of multiple jobs in a computer processor, where the performance measure is the time to complete a given job.

Taniguchi and Thompson (2002) consider the problem of optimizing urban freight transportation by minimizing total costs. The model solves a vehicle routing and scheduling problem while incorporating stochastic transportation times. The total cost involves three major components, that is, fixed costs of vehicles, operating costs of vehicles that are proportional to travel time and time spent waiting at customer sites, and a penalty cost for missing designated pickup or delivery time at customer sites. A designated time window, indicating an early arrival time and a late arrival time, is incorporated in the model. In the paper, the authors consider a penalty for early arrival and that for a late arrival. Both of these penalty functions increase linearly as a function of the deviation from the respective designated times.

A review of service network designs and associated formulations using a mathematical programming approach has been considered by Crainic (2000). The paper focuses on freight transportation using railways, or less-than-truckload (LTL) motor carriers, or intermodal container shipping lines, as possible examples. Further, network design addresses the issues of selection and scheduling of services to operate, specifications of the terminal operations, and the routing of freight. The functionality of the formulation is stressed rather than the transportation mode to which it is applied. As a measure of service quality, delays incurred due to congestion or existing operational policies in terminals are used. A penalty function is modeled using expected delay. A review paper on optimization models for long-haul freight transportation (Crainic, 2002) considers deterministic models. It analyzes multimodal, multi-commodity transportation systems at the regional, national, or global level. Operational models that consider the allocation and repositioning of resources such as empty vehicles are also included in the study.

Given a measurable variable, which serves as an index to the quality level of performance, a threshold must be defined to determine the degree of conformance to customer expectations. Typically, this threshold may be a "guarantee level" as agreed upon by the service level agreement (SLA). For example, a transportation company that delivers goods between two locations, the agreed upon guarantee level may be five days. This threshold may be a hard deadline. Alternatively, depending on the nature of the SLA, it could be a soft deadline. In any event, the larger the deviation from the threshold, the larger the penalty to the service organization.

Here, we consider a penalty function that increases at an increasing rate based on the deviation from the guarantee level. Such functions are more realistic as the "loss" to the customer does increase at a steeper rate as the delay in providing the service increases. Alternatively, in most instances, there is no incentive for the service provider to complete the service prior to the guarantee date. Thus, we consider the situation where the organization incurs a penalty only when the time to provide the service exceeds the stipulated guarantee level.

MODEL DEVELOPMENT

The following notation is used in the chapter:

$P(t)$: Penalty function associated with service delay
t: Instant of time
w: Guaranteed period for service time
$s(t)$: Service time density function
T: Maximum time for completing the service

Penalty Function in Service Delay

For many service industries, time delay in providing or completing the service, is of interest to the customer. Customer expectations are formed on the acceptable time for providing the service in many instances based on contractual obligations or published information. For example, for delivery of goods from one destination to another by trucks, a delivery due date is specified. For passenger travel using airlines, scheduled departure and arrival times indicate the expected travel time. For processing of information technology tasks in a cluster computing environment, SLAs may specify the time to complete the task. In such cases there could be a hard deadline or a soft deadline for completion. However, for jobs that are not completed within the hard deadline, the contract value may decrease till the soft deadline, using a chosen functional form that could be linear. Beyond the soft deadline, further penalties may accrue, which may be at an increasing rate.

A simple form of the penalty function could be a discretized version, where the delay time is measured in discrete units, say days. For every unit of time that is delayed beyond the guarantee period for the service, a jump takes place in the penalty function. The jumps need not be equal to each other. In other words, the jump that arises from being 5 to 6 days late could be much more than that from being 2 to 3 days late. Fig. 1 shows the discrete version of the penalty function. A continuous version of the penalty function using a quadratic form is shown in Fig. 2. This version is more realistic and supports the notion of a loss function proposed by Taguchi (Taguchi, 1986; Taguchi & Wu, 1979). The penalty increases quadratically as the deviation from the guarantee period increases. However, there is no incentive to complete the service earlier than the specified guarantee.

The penalty function is given by

$$P(t) = C_1(t - w)^2, \quad \text{for } w \leq t \leq T$$
$$= 0, \qquad\qquad \text{otherwise} \tag{1}$$

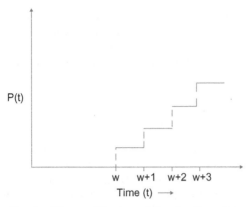

Fig. 1. Discrete Version of Penalty Function.

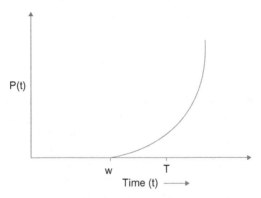

Fig. 2. Quadratic Penalty Function.

where C_1 is a constant based on the relative degree of severity imposed by the customer on deviation from the specified guarantee. It is assumed that the maximum time to complete the service is given by T.

Service Time Distribution

The time to complete the service is a stochastic random variable. Many unforeseen events may have an impact on the completion of service. In the transportation of goods by trucks, there could be breakdown of trucks, delays due to road construction/improvement, unavailability of drivers at the required time, weather-related delays, etc. Hence, even for known distances between the origin and destination and known loads, completion of the service is not always a fixed amount of time. We model the service distribution by a Gamma density function with parameters α and β given by

$$S(t) = \frac{\alpha^\beta}{\Gamma(\beta)} e^{-\alpha t} t^{\beta-1}, \quad t \geq 0 \tag{2}$$

There are several reasons for the selection of a Gamma distribution. Depending on the choice of the parameters α and β, the shape of the Gamma density function can vary quite a bit, enabling one to model a wide variety of situations. In the special case when $\beta = 1$, the Gamma distribution reduces to the exponential distribution. It is known that the service rate is constant for an exponential distribution. In general, the mean and the variance of the Gamma random variable are given by

$$\mu_s = \frac{\beta}{\alpha} \tag{3}$$

$$Var(s) = \frac{\beta}{\alpha^2} \tag{4}$$

The nature of costs incurred by a service organization to reduce the average service time or the variability in service time may be quite different. For instance, increasing the fleet size of trucks could be one way of reducing the mean service time. On the contrary, reduction in the variability of service times could deal with many other issues such as availability of operators when needed, stable distribution in the quantity of goods to be transported, uniform availability of standard routes, uniform weather conditions, and so forth. Through an adequate choice of the parameters α and β, and a selection of the corresponding guarantee period w, several situations are explored. Theoretically, while it is possible for the service time (t) to be very large, in practice the maximum service time (T) is typically constrained within certain bounds. Hence, a truncated form of the service distribution may occur in practice.

Consider, for example, the exponential distribution which is a special case of the Gamma distribution when $\beta = 1$. Denoting T to be the maximum time for completion of the service, the truncated exponential distribution has the form

$$s(t) = \frac{1}{R}[\alpha e^{-\alpha t}] \tag{5}$$

$$\text{where} \quad R = \int_{t=0}^{T} \alpha e^{-\alpha t} dt \tag{6}$$

Frequently, in practice, hypothesized distributions, for example, as in service time, must be estimated from sample data observed from the process. In this context, using the sample data, the method of least squares or the method of maximum likelihood estimation (Neter, Wasserman, & Kutner, 1990) may be used to estimate the parameters of a selected distribution. To determine the goodness-of-fit of the sample data to a selected distribution, one possible statistical test is the Kolmogorov–Smirnov goodness-of-fit test (Pfaffenberger & Patterson, 1981). Using the sample information, of size n, let the observations be denoted by $X_1, X_2, ..., X_n$. Let the hypothesized population cumulative distribution function be denoted by $F_0(x)$, assumed to be continuous, while the sample cumulative distribution function (CDF), based on the ordered sample observations, be denoted by $S(x)$. Note that the sample CDF is a discrete step function. The Kolmogorov–Smirnov test statistic is based on the maximum absolute difference between the hypothesized cumulative distribution function and the sample cumulative distribution function. It is given by

$$KS = \sup_{x} \left| F_0(x) - S(x) \right| \tag{7}$$

The test statistic (KS) is compared to critical values that are tabulated based on the level of Type I error and the sample size. If the test statistic does not exceed the critical value, the null hypothesis of the theoretical distribution being $F_0(x)$ is not rejected.

Expected Penalty Cost

The expected penalty cost, in general, may be expressed as:

$$EPC = \int P(t)s(t)dt \tag{8}$$

However, since a penalty occurs only when the service time exceeds the guarantee period w, and considering a truncated form of the service time distribution, we obtain

$$EPC = \int_{t=w}^{T} P(t)s(t)dt \tag{9}$$

For the quadratic penalty function given by Eq. (1), and the truncated exponential distribution of service time, we have

$$EPC = \frac{\alpha}{R} \int_{t=w}^{T} C_1(t - w)^2 e^{-\alpha t} dt$$

Upon simplification, we obtain

$$EPC = \frac{C_1}{\alpha^2\{1 - e^{-\alpha T}\}} \left[2e^{-\alpha w} + e^{-\alpha T}\{\alpha^2 T^2 + \alpha^2 w^2 + 2)(1 + \alpha T)(1 - \alpha w\} \right]$$

$$(10)$$

RESULTS

Some results are shown for the truncated exponential distribution for service time, a special case of the general Gamma distribution. The value of T (for truncation) was chosen to be 20, while the constant C_1, in the penalty function, was 10. Note that for realistic situations, a customer may estimate the loss to its business functions based on the degree of lateness in providing the service. For example, if these are components used in an assembly, for being late by a day, there could be a downtime in production, resulting in a loss of say \$5,000, say. This information may be used in Eq. (1) to estimate the constant C_1.

Several values of the service rate (α) are used to calculate expected penalty costs for values of the guarantee period (w) being 1, 2, 3, 4, 5, and 6 time units, respectively. Table 1 shows expected penalty costs for small values of the service rate, $\alpha = 0.1$, 0.2, 0.3, 0.4, and 0.5, respectively. The mean service time is proportional to the inverse of the service rate while the variance of service time is proportional to the inverse of the square of the service rate.

Table 1. Expected Penalty Costs for Truncated Exponential
Distribution with Small Service Rate.

Service Guarantee (w)	Service Rate (α)				
	$\alpha = 0.1$	$\alpha = 0.2$	$\alpha = 0.3$	$\alpha = 0.4$	$\alpha = 0.5$
1	620.090	304.872	152.365	82.246	48.323
2	510.137	238.051	110.676	54.754	29.248
3	416.007	184.560	80.023	36.365	17.686
4	335.897	141.913	57.534	24.076	10.678
5	268.174	108.078	41.080	15.874	6.434
6	211.361	81.389	29.082	10.409	3.865

As expected, for a given service rate, as the guarantee time increases, the expected penalty costs decease. Further, as the service rate increases, the expected penalty costs decrease, for a given guarantee time. Table 2 shows expected penalty costs for large values of the service rate, $\alpha = 0.6$, 0.7, 0.8, 0.9, and 1.0, respectively. The expected penalty costs, as expected, are much smaller than those associated with small service rates, for a chosen level of guarantee time. Similar patterns of results, as in the previous table, are observed here.

To visualize the results two graphs are created based on the results. Given the order of difference in the magnitude of the expected penalty costs, for small and large values of the service rate, separate graphs are created for each. Fig. 3 shows the expected penalty costs as a function of the service

Table 2. Expected Penalty Costs for Truncated Exponential Distribution with High Service Rate.

Service Guarantee (w)	Service Rate (α)				
	$\alpha = 0.6$	$\alpha = 0.7$	$\alpha = 0.8$	$\alpha = 0.9$	$\alpha = 1.0$
1	30.463	20.265	14.041	10.039	7.358
2	16.709	10.062	6.309	4.081	2.707
3	9.162	4.995	2.835	1.659	0.996
4	5.021	2.480	1.274	0.675	0.366
5	2.749	1.230	0.572	0.274	0.135
6	1.503	0.610	0.257	0.112	0.050

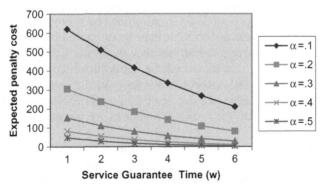

Fig. 3. Expected Penalty Costs for a Truncated Exponential Service Time Distribution for Small Service Rates.

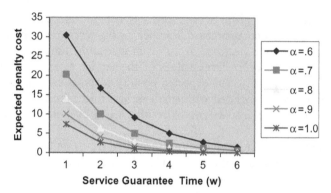

Fig. 4. Expected Penalty Costs for a Truncated Exponential Service Time Distribution for Large Service Rates.

guarantee for small values of the service rate, while Fig. 4 shows similar graphs for large values of the service rate.

Note that the rate of decrease in the expected penalty costs, as the service guarantee time increases, will be influenced by the guarantee time as well as the constant C_1, in the service penalty function. Graphs corresponding to large values of the service rate dominate those for smaller values of the service rate.

CONCLUSIONS

The chapter has considered estimation of penalty costs in the context of service operations. A probabilistic situation has been modeled whereby the form of the service time distribution may be estimated based on observed data. Additionally, a truncated service time distribution is used for demonstration purposes since, in most realistic applications, completion time for a service is bounded. The concept of a penalty in the form of an impact to the customer, influenced by the degree of delay or lateness in completing the service, is incorporated. Such penalty functions are not necessarily linear in the degree of delay.

The results demonstrate the impact of the service rate on the expected penalty costs, as a function of the service guarantee time. The managerial implications of the choice of the service rate and the service guarantee level are quite important. Increasing the service rate has cost implications. One avenue to accomplish this may be to increase the availability of operators and/or equipment that are necessary to provide the service, thus increasing the cost of providing the service. On the other hand, selection of a service guarantee level is influenced not only by the capability of the organization to provide the service, but also by external factors such as the degree of guarantee level provided by competitors. Increasing market share may be quite influenced by the latter factor. Hence, management faces a balancing act in weighing the cost increases along with the contemplated increase in market share, based on a chosen policy.

REFERENCES

Crainic, T. G. (2000). Service network design in freight transportation. *European Journal of Operational Research, 122*(2), 272–288.

Crainic, T. G. (2002). A survey of optimization models for long-haul freight transportation. In R. W. Hall (Ed.), *Handbook of transportation science*. Norwell, MA: Kluwer.

Neter, J., Wasserman, W., & Kutner, M. H. (1990). *Applied linear statistical models – Regression, analysis of variance, and experimental designs* (3rd ed.). Homewood, IL: Richard D. Irwin, Inc.

Pfaffenberger, R. C., & Patterson, J. H. (1981). *Statistical methods for business and economics* (Revised ed.). Homewood, IL: Richard D. Irwin, Inc.

Taguchi, G. (1986). *Introduction to quality engineering: Designing quality into products and processes*. Hong Kong: Asian Productivity Organization.

Taguchi, G., & Wu, Y. I. (1979). *Introduction to off-line quality control*. Nagoya: Central Japan Quality Control Association.

Taniguchi, E. & Thompson, R. G. (2002). *Modeling city logistics*. Transportation Research Record 1790, Paper No. 02-2649, pp. 45–51.

PRICE DYNAMICS ON EARNING ANNOUNCEMENT

Xuan Huang and Nuo Xu

ABSTRACT

In this chapter, we argue that under- and over-reaction are both parts of the price dynamics caused by investor's naïve judgmental extrapolation. We propose to use the Holt–Winters model, a parsimonious model with two parameters, to represent investor's conservatism (anchoring) and representativeness (trending). The complexity of earning information, which is broken down into a drift, a transitory shock, and an auto-correlated permanent shock, add further volatility to the price. We explain the price dynamics caused by the interplay of the earning model and investor's naïve belief. It is further argued that empirical "underreaction" and "overreaction" differ from true under- and overreaction. The simulated results with the proposed model confirm with empirical findings on under- and overreaction.

Keywords: Behavioral finance; Holt–Winters model; ARIMA model; momentum strategy; contrarian strategy

INTRODUCTION

Empirical studies (Bernard & Thomas, 1989, 1990; De Bondt & Thaler, 1985; Jegadeesh & Titman, 1993) have found short-term momentum and

Advances in Business and Management Forecasting, Volume 9, 59–75
Copyright © 2013 by Emerald Group Publishing Limited
ISSN: 1477-4070/doi:10.1108/S1477-4070(2013)0000009008

long-term reversal in security prices. One explanation of this phenomenon is that the market underreacts to news over short horizons and overreacts to those over longer horizons. Earning news provides a natural avenue to study this problem. Bernard and Thomas (1989, 1990) find evidence that an incomplete response to earning news leads to post-announcement drift of stock prices. However, Chan, Jegadeesh, and Lakonishok (1996) find little evidence of subsequent reversals in the returns of high earnings momentum. Does earning announcement lead to both under- and over-reaction or only contribute to one of them? Barberis, Shleifer, and Vishny (1998) propose a regime-switching model of investor sentiment and shed light on how earning announcement can lead to both over- and underreaction. This chapter provides an alternative model based on investor's naïve judgmental extrapolation and discusses the impact of earning dynamics to under- and over-reaction.

The second section presents and discusses several earning models and provides a careful anatomy of earning components. It explains how observed accounting earnings are different from fundamental earnings. The third section proposes a parsimonious model which unifies investor's cognitive limits such as conservatism and representativeness. The fourth sections demonstrates price dynamics and the fifth section provides empirical implications of the model. The sixth section discusses the difference of this model with existing models, the implication of this model in relation to empirical evidence, and concludes the paper.

THE EARNING PROCESS

For an investor to correctly determine the fundamental price, he has to disentangle the informative signal from noise signals, accurately model the earning dynamics, and hence predict future earning stream. If the latter task can be achieved by one's best effort through advanced time-series modeling, as many researchers have attempted (Brown & Rozeff, 1979; Foster, 1977; Grifin, 1977), the former task is hard if not impossible, given that the investor only has an access to the public earning information. In fact, it is hard to believe that the investor achieves the latter task either. Evidence (Abarbanell & Victor, 1992; Bernard & Thomas, 1990) shows that investors, even analysts, often use naïve model to predict future earnings. Thus in a simplified economy, with only one representative investor who determines stock price through discounting his expectation of future earning stream, it is hard to believe that he gets the fundamental price correct.

Although the focus of this paper is to understand how the investor's belief affects the price dynamics, a careful look on the earning models only helps our understanding of the price dynamics.

Fully interpreting earning is hard at best. A simple yet useful model to start with is the random walk model $X_t = X_{t-1} + a_t$. This model assumes that at each period there is a permanent shock to the earning level and the shock is totally unpredictable.

However, Beaver (1981) suggests that there is an atypical (transitory) component in earnings, which we will later refer to as transitory shock η_t on top of the accumulated permanent shocks $\sum_{j=0}^{\infty} \varepsilon_{t-j}$. The fundamental earning level is the accumulated permanent shocks $\bar{X}_t = \bar{X}_{t-1} + \varepsilon_t = \sum_{j=0}^{\infty} \varepsilon_{t-j}$. The observed earning is contaminated by transitory shock η_t,

$$X_t = \bar{X}_t + \eta_t = \bar{X}_{t-1} + \varepsilon_t + \eta_t = X_{t-1} - \eta_{t-1} + \varepsilon_t + \eta_t \qquad (1)$$

If both permanent and transitory components are i.i.d., it can be shown that Eq. (1) is equivalent to an IMA(1,1) model,

$$(1 - B)X_t = (1 - \theta B)a_t \qquad (2)$$

The differenced earning is negatively autocorrelated at lag 1, through the transitory shock $-\eta_{t-1}$.

Early research (Foster, 1977; Griffin, 1977) shows that there is a seasonal component and an adjacent quarter-to-quarter component in earning series. It is shown that autocorrelation of seasonally differenced quarterly earnings are positive and tapers off in the first three quarters and becomes negative at the fourth quarter.

Brown and Rozeff (1979) propose a model that generates more accurate out-of-sample earnings forecasts than other univariate time-series models based on 240 NYSE firms over period of 1962–1977:

$$(1 - \phi B)(1 - B^4)X_t = (1 - \theta B^4)a_t \qquad (3)$$

The year-to-year earnings (observations four quarters apart) resemble an IMA process and the seasonal differenced earnings are autocorrelated quarter-to-quarter. Observing its resemblance to an IMA process in the yearly level, let us take a bold step to expand the permanent and transitory earning idea to this model.

We conjecture that at the year-to-year level, earnings are exposed to both permanent and transitory shocks,

$$X_t = \bar{X}_t + \eta_t = \bar{X}_{t-4} + \varepsilon_t + \eta_t = X_{t-4} - \eta_{t-4} + \varepsilon_t + \eta_t \qquad (4)$$

Further, the permanent shock follows an AR(1) model quarter-to-quarter instead of being i.i.d.,

$$\varepsilon_t = \phi\varepsilon_{t-1} + e_t \tag{5}$$

Intuitively, permanent shocks may occur due to companies' operations (launching a new product, cost-saving projects) and are reasonable to be followed by permanent shocks (of the same sign and diminishing size) in the following quarters. The accumulated permanent shocks $\bar{X}_t$ follows

$$(1 - \phi B)(1 - B^4)\bar{X}_t = e_t \tag{6}$$

Hence the observed earning X_t

$$\begin{aligned}(1 - \phi B)(1 - B^4)X_t &= (1 - \phi B)(1 - B^4)(\bar{X}_t + \eta_t) \\ &= e_t + (1 - \phi B)(1 - B^4)\eta_t\end{aligned} \tag{7}$$

Under model (7), the seasonal differenced earning $(1 - B^4)X_t$ can be represented by

$$\begin{aligned}(1 - \phi B)^{-1}e_t + (1 - B^4)\eta_t &= (e_t + \eta_t) + \phi e_{t-1} + \phi^2 e_{t-2} + \phi^3 e_{t-3} \\ &\quad + (\phi^4 e_{t-4} - \eta_{t-4}) + \ldots \\ &\cong (e_t + \eta_t) + \phi e_{t-1} + \phi^2 e_{t-2} + \phi^3 e_{t-3} - \eta_{t-4}\end{aligned} \tag{8}$$

This explains the positive and attenuating autocorrelation at the first three lags and negative autocorrelation at the fourth lag.

Note the moving average part of Eq. (7) is $e_t + (1 - \phi B - B^4 + \phi B^5)\eta_t$. The autocorrelation at the first and fifth lag are $\mp\phi\sigma_\eta^2/(\sigma_a^2 + 2(1 + \phi^2)\sigma_\eta^2)$ respectively, small and only ϕ times of the autocorrelation at the fourth lag. With the lagged transitory shocks at the first and fifth lag dropped from the moving average part, Eq. (7) becomes ARIMA $(1, 0, 0) \times (0, 1, 1)_{s=4}$ model, which is what Brown and Rozeff (1979) have also identified. The evidence above confirms to some extent our conjecture that at the year-to-year level, earnings are exposed to i.i.d. transitory shocks and permanent shocks that is autocorrelated quarter-to-quarter.

Ball and Watts (1972) find that earning process is a submartingale process, or there is a constant positive drift term in the model (Foster, 1977). The Brown--Rozeff model can be easily augmented to include the drift term,

$$(1 - \phi B)(1 - B^4)X_t = \delta + (1 - \theta B^4)a_t \tag{9}$$

Alternatively, we could think of a permanent shock to have a positive mean $\delta/(1 - \phi)$. It is reasonable in light that the company is making effort to grow and average permanent shock should be positive rather than 0. The model will end up the same as Eq. (9).

In summary, the analysis in this section reveals that earning has several important components: (1) autocorrelated permanent shocks, (2) i.i.d. transitory shocks, (3) a drift. We acknowledge that seasonality is also an important feature of the earning process, however, research shows that investors account for seasonality in their naïve model and thus seasonality should not be a contributing factor for price misperception.

A UNIFIED MODEL OF CONSERVATISM AND REPRESENTATIVENESS

At time $t-1$, new earning announcement X_{t-1} is made; the investor tries to estimate the current fundamental earning level S_{t-1} (different than observed X_{t-1} because X_{t-1} is contaminated by transitory shocks), make predication of future earning stream $E_{t-1}X_{t+j}$ ($j=0$, 1, 2,...), determine the stock price through discounting his predictions. Note that $E_{t-1}X_{t+j} = E_{t-1}S_{t+j}$ because the expected transitory shock is 0. Once time t comes, X_t is observed. The investor then compares it with his expectation $E_{t-1}S_t$ and updates his belief on the fundamental earning level. A simple model can describe this updating process,

$$S_t = E_{t-1}S_t + \alpha(X_t - E_{t-1}S_t) = E_{t-1}X_t + \alpha\underbrace{(X_t - E_{t-1}X_t)}_{\text{earning surprise}} = \alpha X_t + (1-\alpha)E_{t-1}X_t$$

$$(10)$$

Similar models have been used to model belief updating (Anderson, 1959, 1965, 1981).

Anchoring (Conservatism)

If the earning surprise is positive, the investor adjusts his estimation of the earning level upward, however, only by a degree of α. The smaller the alpha, the more the investor is anchoring on his previous knowledge. When the investor believes that the earning is an IMA model without drift, his best prediction of future earnings E_tX_{t+j} would be the estimated current earning level S_t. Model (10) becomes an exponential smoothing model. In fact, Muth (1960) shows that the best forecast of an IMA process is an EWMA smoother

$$E_t y_{t+1} = \sum_{j=0}^{\infty} \theta(1-\theta)^j y_{t-j} = E_{t-1} y_t + \theta(y_t - E_{t-1} y_t) \tag{11}$$

with θ determined by $\theta = \dfrac{1}{2}\dfrac{\sigma_\varepsilon^2}{\sigma_\eta^2} - \dfrac{\sigma_\varepsilon}{\sigma_\eta}\sqrt{1 + \dfrac{1}{4}\dfrac{\sigma_\varepsilon^2}{\sigma_\eta^2}}.$

Parameter θ is an increasing function of the standard deviation ratio $\sigma_\varepsilon/\sigma_\eta$. $\theta = 0$ when $\sigma_\varepsilon/\sigma_\eta = 0$ and $\theta = 1$ when $\sigma_\varepsilon/\sigma_\eta \to \infty$. Intuitively, when σ_η is 0, the process is essentially a random walk and the best estimate would be the last observation; when σ_ε is 0, there is no permanent shock and the process is white noise, thus the best estimate would be the average of the past observations. Optimally, the investor should use $\alpha = \theta$ in his belief updating model; however, the investor tends to think that the earning process is more stationary than it actually is. In another words, he underestimates σ_ε in relative to σ_η. He believes that shocks are more transitory. Such conservatism makes him underestimate the ratio $\sigma_\varepsilon/\sigma_\eta$ and use a value $\alpha < \theta$ to update his belief about the process level. A small α reflects the investor anchors his previous belief and tends to underreact to earning news to begin with.

Trending (Representativeness)

De Bondt (1993) uses classroom experiments to show that naïve investors bet on trend. Andreassen and Kraus (1990) have also shown that investors chase after salient trend and they further propose to use the Holt–Winters model to represent investors' naïve judgmental extrapolation:

$$\begin{aligned}
S_t &= \alpha X_t + (1-\alpha)(S_{t-1} + T_{t-1}) \\
T_t &= \beta(S_t - S_{t-1}) + (1-\beta)T_{t-1} \\
F_t(m) &= S_t + mT_t
\end{aligned} \tag{12}$$

X_t is the current observation; S_t is the estimated level of the time series; T_t is the estimated trend of the time series. When new earning X_t is announced, the investor updates his belief in the level and trend by employing model (12). The two parameters in this model, α and β, represent the investor's anchoring and trending. The smaller the α, the heavier the investor is anchoring (as is discussed in section "Anchoring (Conservatism)"); the larger the β, the more inclined the investor is to trend. Note that when $\beta = 0$, Eq. (12) becomes Eq. (11).

It is worth noting that there is some relationship between β and representativeness. If investor observes one salient level shift $S_t - S_{t-1}$, T_t may not change much due to a small β. However, if the level shift has been going on for a while, that is, a streak of positive $S_t - S_{t-1}$, T_t could grow large gradually. And later it will be shown that T_t has a bigger role than S_t in determing the perceived price. Thus a streak of positive $S_t - S_{t-1}$ could lead investor to believe in a salient trend T_t and overestimate the price. T_t reflects the salience of the information while β reflects the sensitivity of the investor to trend information. Later it will be shown that with any $\beta > 0$, the investor extrapolates his way to overshoot the target.

It is possible that investor adjusts β upon the salience of the trend (Andreassen & Kraus, 1990) or other collaborating facts (Andreassen, 1987). However, in this paper, both parameters are assumed to be constant to make the problem more tractable.

WHAT MAKES UNDERREACTION AND OVERREACTION?

If the investor can read the permanent earning shocks and their implications correctly, he should be able to determine the fundamental price. However, several factors contribute to his misperception of the earning information. First and foremost, anchoring makes him underreact to permanent shocks in short run and trending makes him overreact in the long run. Second, Bernard and Thomas (1990) present evidence that investors ignore the implication of future same-sign shocks by the current earning shock. Third, although on average the transitory shock should not bias the investor's perception of price, it confuses the investor and adds excessive volatility to the price dynamics. Since investor's judgmental extrapolation model (12) is a linear model, we can consider the three factors separately. In this section, we break down these confounding factors in parts. But before we proceed, an expression of $F_t(m)$ in terms of exogenous earning series X_t is useful and can be obtained from Eq. (12):

$$
F_t(m) = \begin{cases}
\alpha(1+m\beta)X_t + \dfrac{1}{\sin\theta}\displaystyle\sum_{k=1}^{\infty}\alpha D^{k-1}(D(1+m\beta)\sin(k+1)\theta \\
\quad - (1-\beta+m\beta)\sin k\theta)X_{t-k} & \phi_1^2 - 4\phi_2 < 0 \\[2ex]
\alpha(1+m\beta)X_t + \displaystyle\sum_{k=1}^{\infty}(\alpha(1+m\beta)(a_1^k + ka_2^k) \\
\quad - \alpha(1-\beta+m\beta)(a_1^{k-1} + (k-1)a_2^{k-1}))X_{t-k} & \phi_1^2 - 4\phi_2 = 0 \\[2ex]
\alpha(1+m\beta)X_t + \displaystyle\sum_{k=1}^{\infty}(\alpha(1+m\beta)(A_2a_1^k + A_1a_2^k) \\
\quad - \alpha(1-\beta+m\beta)(A_2a_1^{k-1} + A_1a_2^{k-1}))X_{t-k} & \phi_1^2 - 4\phi_2 > 0
\end{cases}
$$

$$\tag{13}$$

where

$$
\begin{aligned}
\phi_1 &= -(2 - \alpha - \alpha\beta) \\
\phi_2 &= (1 - \alpha) \\
D &= \sqrt{\phi_2} \\
\cos\theta &= -\frac{\phi_1}{2\sqrt{\phi_2}} \\
a_{1,2} &= \frac{-\phi_1 \pm \sqrt{\phi_1^2 - 4\phi_2}}{2} \\
A_{1,2} &= \frac{\mp a_2}{a_1 - a_2}
\end{aligned}
\tag{14}
$$

We then can proceed in light of Eq. (13).

Pricing of Permanent Shocks and Transitory Shocks

Consider a permanent shock X_t. The pricing of it alone is X_t/ρ with ρ being the expected return. Because permanent shocks are autocorrelated, it implies a (expected) shock of ϕX_t at time $t+1$, the pricing of which is $\phi X_t/\rho(1 + \rho)$, a shock of $\phi^2 X_t$ at time $t+2$, the pricing of which is $\phi^2 X_t/\rho(1 + \rho)^2$, so on and so forth. Thus the pricing of X_t and its implication of future permanent shocks is

$$
\frac{X_t}{\rho} \sum_{i=0}^{\infty} \left(\frac{\phi}{1 + \rho} \right)^i = \frac{(1 + \rho)X_t}{\rho(1 + \rho - \phi)}
\tag{15}
$$

The median value of φ, as found in Bernard and Thomas (1990), is 0.36.

The pricing of transitory shock should be 0 because it does not imply future earning stream.

Investor's pricing of earning shocks, no matter permanent or transitory, is through discounting his expectation of future earnings (13),

$$
P_t = \sum_{m=0}^{\infty} \frac{F_t(m)}{(1 + \rho)^m} = \sum_{m=0}^{\infty} \frac{S_t + mT_t}{(1 + \rho)^m} = \frac{S_t}{\rho} + \frac{1 + \rho}{\rho^2} T_t = \frac{1}{\rho} F_t \left(\frac{1 + \rho}{\rho} \right)
\tag{16}
$$

Note that S_t affects the perceived price P_t through a factor $1/\rho$ while T_t does so through $1 + \rho/\rho^2$. Thus the investor's estimate of the trend has a much bigger impact in the price than his estimate of the level.

The step response of this function, corresponding to the impact of a permanent shock, and the impulse response of this function, corresponding to the impact of a transitory shock, are shown in Fig. 1. In plotting Fig. 1(a) it is assumed that $\phi = 0$ (no residual effects), however, the response function with $\phi \neq 0$ is not hard to plot either.

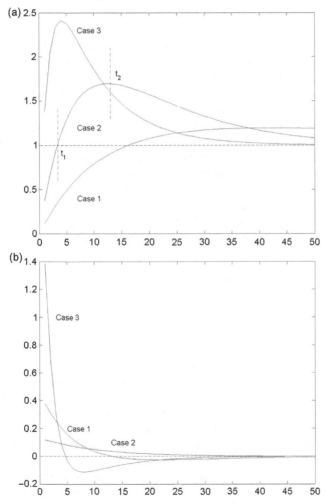

Fig. 1. Security Price Response to (a) Permanent (b) Transitory Shocks. Case 1: $\alpha = 0.1$, $\beta = 0.01$; Case 2: $\alpha = 0.2$, $\beta = 0.05$; Case 3: $\alpha = 0.5$, $\beta = 0.1$. (a) Response to Permanent Shock of Unity and (b) Response to Transitory Shock of Unity.

For both Case 1 and Case 2, where α and β take relatively small numbers, the investor gradually absorbs the information (underreaction), overshoots the target (overreaction), and then gradually tapers down to the correct level. It is interesting to point out, in Case 2 for example, the response underreacts to begin with, exceeds 1 (the correct level) at time t_1, nevertheless continues to increase until t_2. The true underreaction only continues until t_1, however, empirical studies will consider response between t_1 and t_2 as underreaction as well. More interestingly, for Case 3, the initial response exceeds 1, which indicates overreaction to begin with, however, its dynamics will still suggest "underreaction" empirically because the early positive return predicts short-term positive return.

Response to permanent shocks eventually stabilizes around 1 and response to transitory shocks eventually dies out.

Although the expected impact of transitory shocks to price should be 0, it is not necessarily true in extreme cases. De Bondt and Thaler (1985) find extreme winners underperform extreme losers. One explanation could be the transitory shocks. Conditioning on extreme winners (losers) who have continuous good (bad) earning surprises, the average transitory shock in its winning (losing) period is probably more positive (negative), thus the overreaction caused by the transitory shocks should be reversed in the long run, causing these winners (losers) to underperform (outperform).

Underreaction and Overreaction

Fig. 2 shows the contour map of the initial response as percentage of the accurate response (provided by Eq. (15)) in relate to α and β. The larger the parameters, the larger the initial response. In fact, only the area to the left of the curve labeled "100%" is true underreaction. However, all the area to the left of the dashed curve would exhibit empirical underreaction (like Case 3 in Fig. 1). Note 300%, for example, does not mean return level; instead, it means that a permanent shock which brings 1% (or x%) return is perceived as 3% (or $3x$%) return at its arrival.

Fig. 3 shows the contour map of the response peak as percentage of the accurate response in relate to α and β. The response peak is more sensitive to β than to α. With any $\beta > 0$, the investor will eventually overreact.

Another result of interest is how long (in quarters) it takes for the response to peak. Fig. 4 shows the parameter regions for peaking time equal to 4, 12, and 20 (quarters) respectively. As it is shown and can be intuitively

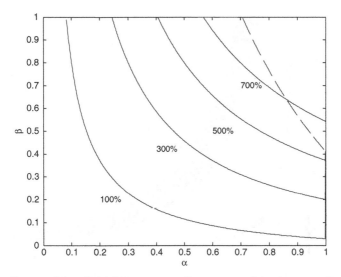

Fig. 2. Contour Map: Initial Response as Percentage of the Accurate Response.

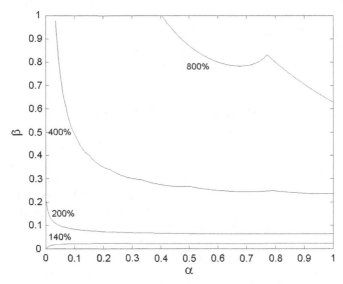

Fig. 3. Contour Map: Response Peak as Percentage of the Accurate Response.

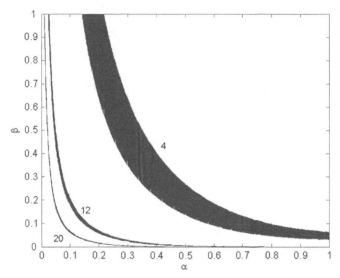

Fig. 4.   Time (in Quarters) Taken to Reach the Peak.

expected, the smaller the parameters, the longer it takes to reach its peak. This is also obvious in Fig. 1(a).

In general, the smaller the parameters, the smaller the initial response and the overshoot, and the longer it takes to reach its peak and settle down to the target level. The overshoot is very sensitive to β.

EMPIRICAL IMPLICATION

Empirical study of the proposed model roughly follows the strategy proposed by Jegadeesh and Titman (1993). $N=1,000$ earning series are simulated. Each series is generated by a white-noise transitory shock process and an AR(1) permanent shock process with $\phi = 0.36$ (the median value estimated by Bernard & Thomas, 1989). The starting value of the earning process is set to be high enough to avoid becoming negative during simulation. Each series is simulated for $J + K$ periods (quarters). Price series (perceived by the investor) are computed correspondingly based on Eq. (12) with $\alpha = 0.5$ and $\beta = 0.1$. At the end of quarter J, stocks are ranked into deciles based on their returns in the first J quarters. At the end of quarter $J + K$, stocks are ranked again into deciles based on their return from quarter $J+1$ to quarter $J+K$. For example, stock i $(i=1 \sim N)$ is ranked into decile D_i^J and D_i^K $(D_i^J, D_i^K = 1,2,\ldots 10)$ for J- and K-period correspondingly. R_d, an average of the decile rank of the later K-quarter returns of all stocks in decile d of the first J-quarter returns is computed. In another words, $R_d = \sum_i D_i^K \cdot 1_{\{D_i^J=d\}} / \sum_i 1_{\{D_i^J=d\}}$, $d=1,2,\ldots 10$. If there is an increasing relationship between d and R_d, it implies that high past J-quarter return is followed by high future K-quarter return; otherwise it implies that high past J-quarter return will be reversed in the future K-quarter. Table 1 presents the results. The first three rows of each table show that the relative strength strategy work in short horizon (notice J, K are both in quarters) and the rest

Table 1. Empirical Implication on Relative Strength Strategy and Contrarian Strategy.

					d					
	1	2	3	4	5	6	7	8	9	10
(a) R_d vs. d – no transitory shocks, autocorrelated permanent shocks										
$J=1$ $K=2$	2.93	3.432	4.21	4.766	5.326	5.876	6.268	6.884	7.312	7.996
$J=1$ $K=4$	3.852	4.272	4.822	4.672	5.306	5.816	5.982	6.298	6.702	7.278
$J=2$ $K=4$	4.25	4.776	4.826	5.178	5.104	5.71	5.914	6.288	5.962	6.992
$J=12$ $K=12$	6.788	6.292	6.366	5.964	5.234	5.438	4.742	5.174	5.066	3.936
$J=20$ $K=20$	7.14	6.686	5.636	5.726	5.376	5.516	5.482	4.822	4.604	4.012
(b) R_d vs. d – transitory and permanent shocks, $\sigma_\varepsilon : \sigma_\eta = 1:1$, autocorrelated permanent shocks										
$J=1$ $K=2$	3.674	4.410	5.122	5.244	5.416	5.884	5.824	6.094	6.534	6.798
$J=1$ $K=4$	4.608	4.978	4.914	4.932	5.548	5.966	5.784	5.876	6.070	6.324
$J=2$ $K=4$	4.540	5.040	5.320	5.196	6.078	5.220	5.846	5.596	5.920	6.244
$J=12$ $K=12$	6.774	6.516	5.980	5.452	5.896	5.598	5.174	5.042	4.782	3.786
$J=20$ $K=20$	7.174	6.340	5.580	5.942	5.766	5.228	5.444	5.136	4.498	3.892

d: the decile rank of the first J-quarter returns; $R_d = \sum_i D_i^K \cdot 1_{\{D_i^J=d\}} / \sum_i 1_{\{D_i^J=d\}}$.

two rows of each table show that the contrarian strategy work in longer horizon (3 year/3 year; 5 year/5 year). The simulated result confirms with empirical studies (Bernard & Thomas, 1989, 1990; De Bondt & Thaler, 1985; Jegadeesh & Titman, 1993).

DISCUSSION AND CONCLUSION

The Holt–Winters Model and Beyond Earning News

Several behavioral models have been proposed to study the phenomenon of under- and overreaction. Notably, the psychology aspects of the Holt–Winters model (namely, conservatism and representativeness) have been carefully studied in Barberis et al. (1998) through a regime-switching model. As an alternative model, the Holt–Winters model generally functions similarly yet still deserves some study. First, this model is intuitively friendly. If naive investors, who are not mathematically sophisticated, do employ some model in forecasting, this model is simple and appealing. Further, it can be used by the investor in face of continuous-valued time series earning model, such as the ARIMA(1,1,1) model, the one studied in this paper (modification needed on the Holt–Winters model to accommodate seasonality). Last but not least, there is difference between this model and the regime-switching model, although their predictions are largely aligned. With Holt–Winters model the investor either believes in significant trend or no trend. He never believes in short-term (next period) mean reverse. While with the regime-switching model, the investor assigns a higher probability to Model 1 of mean-reversal if he observes a sequence of sign-flipping shocks. The underreaction in the Holt–Winters model is due to an incomplete response (i.e., a smaller α) to the shocks while in the regime-switching model it is due to investor believing in mean reverting of a random walk process. However, overreactions in the two models are both due to investor extrapolating too far into the future.

   An alternative explanation for overreaction is the participation of momentum-trader (Hong & Stein, 1999) and positive feedback investor (De Long, Shleifer, Summers, & Waldmann, 1990) who purposefully feed and ride the trend. Although in this paper I studied a simplified economy with one investor, it could actually be an economy with two groups of investors, one naively and subconsciously using the Holt–Winters model to update their belief and the other purposefully and speculatively using the model to chase after the trend.

In a larger picture, the Holt–Winters model can be applied beyond the earning stream to, for example, stock prices. In fact De Bondt (1993) finds evidence that investors do trend on stock prices. In essence the Holt–Winters model has a built-in negative feedback mechanism through comparing the expected value with a reference – the observed value. While next observed earning provides a reasonably accurate reference to stabilize the model prediction, the next observed price is a much noisier reference and may cheat itself to ungrounded trends through irrational exuberance before it settles back to the true level. With such noisy reference the model behaves much like a positive feedback system and eventually collapses, much like a price bubble.

α, β *Different for Different Stocks?*

It is possible that to different stocks with different public exposure, the investor responses differently. For glamour stocks, for example, the investor responses more promptly (larger α) and more eager to follow the trend (larger β). For value stocks, the investor response more sluggishly (smaller α). Interestingly, Chan et al. (1996) point out that it takes time for extreme losers to shake off the unfavorable opinions that investors have accumulated, which indicates small α and β for these stocks (more discussion follows in section "Does Earning Surprise Predict Long-Term Reversal"). If it is true that α, β are different for different stocks, it is implicated that different stocks could have different length of mean-reverting cycles.

Previous Earning News versus Previous Returns

Two approaches have been taken to empirically study the market under- and overreaction. One approach conditions on previous returns (Chopra, Lakonishok, & Ritter, 1992; De Bondt & Thaler, 1985; Jegadeesh & Titman, 1993) while the other conditions on previous earning surprises (Bernard & Thomas, 1989; Chan et al., 1996). Previous returns may comprise a more comprehensive set of information than that from earning surprises. Chan et al. (1996) show that underreaction to quarterly earning surprises is a more short-lived phenomenon than the underreaction to past returns. In reflecting upon the earning model, it is possible that earning surprises alone could be due to transitory shocks while previous return (during as long as six months as studied in Chan et al., 1996) has more reliable information about fundamental permanent shocks.

Does Earning Surprise Predict Long-Term Reversal?

Chan et al. (1996) claim that they find little evidence of subsequent reversals in the returns of high earnings momentum. More specifically, they find that the losers tend to persist than to reverse. However, they provide possible reasons such as that people less inclined to take account of new information for extreme losers (i.e., small α and β). As was discussed in section "Underreaction and Overreaction", small α and β lead to a prolonged cycle, thus may only be captured if the study period in Chan et al. (1996) was longer.

For winners, they find the excessive return evaporates in the second and third year. Especially when past return is not corroborated with positive earning surprise, the return is below average. It is of no surprise because conflicting earning news with previous return indicates the peak of the overshoot and hence the beginning of the reversal.

On the contrary, De Bondt and Thaler (1985), Chopra et al. (1992) find evidence of return-reversal. The difference is that they use accumulated long-term past return (over 3–5 years) while Chan et al. (1996) use accumulated short-term past return (6 months) or last period earning surprise. Positive (negative) accumulated long-term past return is probably the result of a streak of positive (negative) earning surprises while that of short-term is not necessarily. Therefore, Chen et al. (1996) does not find long-term reversal with accumulated short-term past return; neither is it expected.

REFERENCES

Abarbanell, J. S., & Victor, L. B. (1992). Tests of analysts' overreaction/underreaction to earnings information as an explanation for anomalous stock price behavior. *Journal of Finance, 47*, 183–198.

Anderson, N. (1959). Test of a model for opinion change. *Journal of Abnormal and Social Psychology, 59*, 371–381.

Anderson, N. (1965). Primacy effects in personality impression formation using a generalized order effect paradigm. *Journal of Personality and Social Psychology, 2*, 1–9.

Anderson, N. (1981). *Foundations of information integration theory.* Boston, MA: Academic Press.

Andreassen, P. B. (1987). On the social psychology of the stock market: Aggregate attributional effects and the regressiveness of prediction. *Journal of Personality and Social Psychology*, *53*, 490–496.

Andreassen, P. B., & Kraus, S. J. (1990). Judgmental extrapolation and the salience of change. *Journal of Forecasting*, *9*, 347–372.

Ball, R., & Watts, R. (1972). Some time series properties of accounting income. *Journal of Finance*, *27*, 663–682.

Barberis, N., Shleifer, A., & Vishny, R. (1998). A model of investor sentiment. *Journal of Financial Economics*, *49*, 307–343.

Beaver, W. (1981). *Financial reporting an accounting: Revolution* (1st ed.). Englewood Cliffs, NJ: Prentice-Hall.

Bernard, V. L., & Thomas, J. (1989). Post-earning-announcement drift: Delayed price response or risk premium? *Journal of Accounting Research* (Suppl. 27), 1–36.

Bernard, V. L., & Thomas, J. K. (1990). Evidence that stock prices do not fully reflect the implications of current earnings for future earnings. *Journal of Accounting and Economics*, *13*, 305–340.

Brown, L. P., & Rozeff, M. (1979). Univariate time-series models of quarterly accounting earnings per share: A proposed model. *Journal of Accounting Research*, *21*, 21–47.

Chan, L. K., Jegadeesh, N., & Lakonishok, J. (1996). Momentum strategies. *Journal of Finance*, *51*, 1681–1713.

Chopra, N., Lakonishok, J., & Ritter, J. (1992). Measuring abnormal performance: Do stocks overreact? *Journal of Financial Economics*, *31*, 235–268.

De Bondt, W. F. (1993). Betting on trends: Intuitive forecasts of financial risk and return. *International Journal of Forecasting*, *9*, 355–371.

De Bondt, W. F., & Thaler, R. (1985). Does the stock market overreact? *Journal of Finance*, *40*, 793–805.

De Long, J. B., Shleifer, A., Summers, L., & Waldmann, R. (1990). Positive feedback investment strategies and destabilizing rational speculations. *Journal of Finance*, *45*, 375–395.

Foster, G. (1977). Quarterly accounting data: Time-series properties and predicative-ability results. *The Accounting Review*, *52*, 1–21.

Griffin, P. A. (1977). The time-series behavior of quarterly earnings: Preliminary evidence. *Journal of Accounting Research*, *15*, 71–83.

Hong, H., & Stein, J. C. (1999). A unified theory of underreaction, momentum trading, and overreaction in asset markets. *Journal of Finance*, *54*, 2143–2184.

Jegadeesh, N., & Titman, S. (1993). Returns to buying winners and selling losers: Implications for stock market efficiency. *Journal of Finance*, *48*, 65–91.

Muth, J. F. (1960). Optimal properties of exponentially weighted forecasts. *Journal of the American Statistical Association*, *55*, 299–306.

HOW TO LESSEN THE DISPOSITION EFFECT? IT PAYS TO STUDY BEFORE INVESTING

Min-Hua Kuo, Shaw K. Chen and Shao-Shing Chen

ABSTRACT

In this chapter, we demonstrate that studying relevant investment information helps reduce individual investors' disposition effect. It is prevalent that many individual investors in stock market do not form their own opinion about the investments; instead they mimic investment strategies of others. This research shows that the intention of making easy money only worsens the disposition effect. We collect 2,632 individual stock investors through nationwide surveys in Taiwan. Using regression models, we examine the effects of study on reducing investors' inclination of holding-losers/selling-winners and the disposition effect. The findings show that investors realize losses sooner and significantly reduce the disposition effect if they choose to learn about their investments. The results also demonstrate that if the investors are willing to learn about firms in which they invest, they become more rational about their investment decisions. They are no longer influenced by the sentiment of regret resistance or misperception of the stock trend, which in turn reduces the disposition effect. This study supports that investors make

Advances in Business and Management Forecasting, Volume 9, 77–90

ISSN: 1477-4070/doi:10.1108/S1477-4070(2013)0000009009

*better investment decisions if they perform necessary due diligence prior
to investing.*

Keywords: Disposition effect; the investment study hypothesis

INTRODUCTION

Ever since Shefrin and Statman (1985) extended the Kahneman and
Tverskey's Prospect Theory to the field of investments and proposed the
disposition effect (DE thereafter), the DE has been widely documented in
the capital market studies (e.g., Ferris, Haugen, & Makhija, 1988; Kuo &
Chen, 2012; Kuo, Kuo, Chiu, & Fang, 2005; Lakonishok & Smidt, 1986;
Odean, 1998; Weber & Camerer, 1998). The DE indicates that investors
have a tendency to hold losers too long and sell winners too soon. What
dispose investors to such effect? Besides the asymmetry of risk preference
over gains and losses as argued by Kahneman and Tversky (1979) in their
prospect theory, several other conjectures were suggested, such as cognitive
dissonance (Goetzmann & Peles, 1997), quasi-magical thinking (Shiller,
1999), insufficient self-control (Glick, 1957; Shefrin & Statman, 1985), mental
accounting, pride seeking, regret averse (Shefrin & Statman, 1985), and
others. The aforementioned theories can be classified into two kinds of
psychological biases: perceptional and emotional.

Benartzi and Thaler (1995), Odean (1998), and Grinblatt and Keloharju
(2001) have studied disadvantages of the disposition effect on the investment
performance. However, the results to the earlier research provide little
advice on how the investors can identify and avoid shortcomings of the
disposition effect. Simply advising investors to hold winners longer or to sell
losers sooner is ineffective if the DE is driven by psychological factors. We
search for certain mechanisms to overcome the psychological forces and to
encourage correct actions.

Very frequently, individual investors base their investment decisions on
the opinion of other investors, experts, or acquaintances in their social
networks. Kuo (2006) reports that more than 56% of individual investors in
Taiwan admit that they did not know anything about stock performance of
the firms in which they invest and 47.9% did not know anything about
business nature of the firms.

People change behaviors when they gain new information and thus
modify their expectations (Beaver, 1968; Grossman, 1976). Accordingly,

relevant information equips investors with better judgment about price trend and future stock performance, and helps them become more rational and subject to less disposition effect.

HYPOTHESIS

We argue that knowledge about investment opportunities is valuable to investors because it reduces perception errors and sense of uncertainty. Those who are willing to devote time and effort to learn about investments would gain greater perception about stock value. Investors would tend to realize smaller losses if they "learn" that the losers are likely to devalue further; they would be willing to hold on to the winners for longer period of time if they believe that the winners are likely to appreciate. Therefore, the more effort the investors put into studying about investments, the less disposition effect they would experience. Based on this reasoning, we propose the investment study hypotheses as follows.

H1. If the investors are more inclined toward investment time and effort in learning about investment opportunities, they would have a tendency of selling losers before incurring greater losses.

H2. If the investors are more inclined towards investment time and effort in learning about investment opportunities, they would have a tendency of keeping winners to realize all possible gains.

H3. If the investors are more inclined towards investment time and effort in learning about investment opportunities, they would experience smaller disposition effect.

DATA SOURCES AND VARIABLE DEFINITIONS

To test the hypotheses, we use the databank of Individual Investors Sentiment Index in Taiwan, a nationwide survey targeting individual stock investors. The databank offers three surveys on the disposition effect, investigated in August 2004, April, and June 2005, respectively, resulting in 2,632 responses. The surveys are administered via phone by the representatives at the Professional Survey Center of Shih Hsin University, Taiwan. The sampling error is below 3% in 95% confidence level.

The disposition effect represents "selling winners too quickly and holding losers too long" assumption (Shefrin & Statman, 1985). Various techniques are used to measure the DE, such as selling proportion of winners versus that of losers (Odean, 1998; Weber & Camerer, 1998), comparison of holding periods (Odean, 1998; Shapira & Venezia, 2001), and price changes of losers and winners (Kuo, 2009). For example, Odean (1998) finds that holding period for losers (median 124 days) is longer than that for winners (median 104 days) and that proportion of winner realization is 24%, compared to 15% in losers. Kuo (2009) reports that nearly one-third of individual investors refuse to sell losers in their investment portfolio, which leaves the average absolute return of losers significantly greater than that of winners. This study adopts the same measure used by Kuo (2009), which includes two questions and is constructed as follows:

• On an average, how much do you earn when you sell stocks at gain?
  □0–5% □6–10% □11–20% □ 21–30% □ 31–50% □ More than 51%
  □I do not sell.
• On an average, how much do you lose when you sell stocks at loss?
  □0–5% □6–10% □11–20% □ 21–30% □ 31–50% □ More than 51%
  □I do not sell.

We construct the DE measure as a difference between the price changes of losses and gains. We take the median of each bracket above as the proxy measure. For example, we take 8% to represent the region of 6%–10% and 15.5% to represent the region of 11%–20%, etc. We take 60% and 100% to represent "more than 51%" and "I do not sell," respectively. Thus,

DE_i = price change of losers to be realized for investor i– price change of winners to be realized for investor i.

If $DE > 0$, it indicates that the investor i is more willing to hold losers than winners, in terms of the price changes, before realizing the gains/losses, consistent with the disposition effect.

If $DE < 0$, it indicates that the investor i is more willing to hold winners than losers, in terms of the price changes, before realizing the gains/losses, which is a reversed disposition effect in Kuo (2009).

And if $DE = 0$, it indicates that the investor i has no significant preference to dispose of winners or losers, in terms of the price changes.

As for the study measurement, there are two questions in the databank:

- If possible, how many hours a week at most will you spend on studying investment information?
- If possible, how many media resources at most will you access a week to get investment information? (For instance, five media outlets are used if you access one magazine, two TV channels, and two newspapers.)

The first question is included in all three surveys, but the second is part of only one survey. Both questions are of subjective willingness, instead of objective actions. It is more plausible to inquire about the subjective intention than if an interviewee was asked an open-end question. The latter may involve greater estimation error, because some methods of acquiring knowledge about investments such as reading/listening to relevant information (say, reading/listening on the way home or to work) may be counted in by some interviewees while not by others. Therefore, there are at least two advantages to inquire about the subjective intention. First, the measurement error is more limited. Second, it reflects the interviewees' intention or motivation of devoting themselves to studying of investments, which is relevant in exploring investing behaviors. Higher motivation usually represents better quality of actions. When only limited time is available for acquisition of information, a dedicated knowledge seeker will try to enhance his/her study quality via alternative routes, such as interpersonal networks that are frequently utilized for discussions about investments.

In the following empirical analysis sections, we examine the differences of study efforts among different disposition patterns and the estimation results of multi-regression analysis on observing the effects of study on reducing investors' inclination of holding-losers/selling-winners and the disposition effect. The conclusion follows in the last section.

EMPIRICAL ANALYSIS

Sample Distributions

From our sample, the distribution of male and female is about the same (51.1% and 48.9% respectively); most of the interviewees are between 30 and 59 years old (81.7%), live in northern Taiwan (56.7%), are highly educated (40.9%), and have yearly income between NT$200,000 and 1 million dollars (see Table 1).

Table 1. Sample Distributions.

Variables		Samples	Percent	Variables		Samples	Percent
Gender	Male	1,344	51.1	Income	Less than $0.2M	524	22.0
	Female	1,286	48.9	(NT$)	$0.2–1M	1477	62.0
	Total	2,630	100		More than $1M	380	16.0
					Total	2,381	100.0
Age	Less than 29	290	11.1				
	30–39	717	27.3	Education	Low	884	33.9
	40–49	768	29.3		Middle	658	25.2
	50–59	632	24.1		High	1,067	40.9
	More than 60	215	8.2		Total	2,609	100.0
	Total	2622	100.0				
Location	Northern TW	1492	56.7				
	Middle TW	540	20.5				
	Southern TW	600	22.8				
	Total	2632	100.0				

The samples come from three nationwide surveys targeting on the individual stock investors. The total samples of each demographic variable may be different due to missing data.

Table 2. Sample Distributions of Investment Study Intention: Time and Media.

Time (T, hours)	0	$0 < T \leq 3$	$3 < T \leq 10$	$T > 10$	Total
Samples	332	934	946	420	2,632
Percent	12.6%	35.5%	35.9%	16.0%	100.0%

No. of media (M)	0	$0 < M \leq 2$	$2 < M \leq 5$	$M > 5$	Total
Samples	44	399	291	117	851
Percent	5.2%	46.9%	34.2%	13.7%	100.0%

The data of study time are from three surveys and those of study media are from one survey.

Investment Study

Regarding the intention to make investment study, the individual investors would spend an average of 7.1 hours per week. Amongst the investors, 12.6% of them do not spend any time on studying about the investments, while 16% of them spend more than 10 hours a week on studying. They would access on average 3.76 media sources to get related information (including financial newspaper, magazines, and TV programs). Most investors choose 1 or 2 media (46.9%) (Table 2).

Disposition Patterns

Observing the average price changes of gains (or losses), we find that three-fourth of investors will realize their gains before the prices rise by 20%; to our surprise, about 40% of investors do not intend to realize any losses in hope for the prices to rise back, and about one-third realize their losses at the prices drop of up to 10% (see Fig. 1).

The distribution of individual's DE shows two peaks. One is at around zero with one-third of investors demonstrating the pattern of symmetry in terms of the price changes. The other peak of DE is at around $0.71 \sim 1$, with one-third of investors who are reluctant to realize any losses (see Fig. 2).

As a group, most individual investors (nearly 50%) demonstrate the disposition effect; that is, they hold losers longer than winners in terms of the price changes; 32.7% of investors are indifferent to the price changes when disposing of winners and losers; 18.5% of individual investors reveal reversed disposition effect, keeping winners longer than losers in terms of the price changes (see Fig. 3).

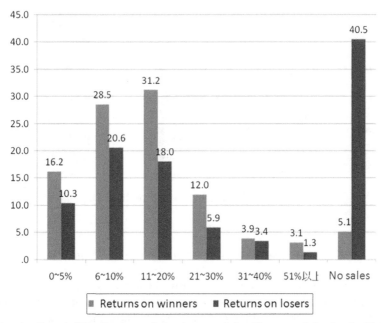

Fig. 1. Sample Distributions of the Average Price Changes of the Stocks Held.

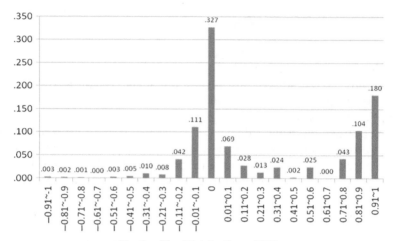

Fig. 2.   The Distribution of DE.

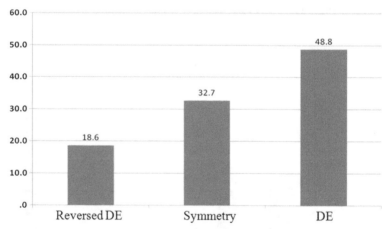

Fig. 3.   Sample Distributions of Disposition Patterns.

The Disposition Patterns and Investors Profiles

The disposition patterns are significantly related to gender, income, and education, according to the ANOVA results. The male investors with high income and high education are more inclined to show the reverse DE, while female investors with low income and low education are inclined to show the disposition effect (Table 3).

As for the DE value of each geographic sector, the average DE of female is 0.37, significantly higher than that of male (0.22), consistent with the

Table 3. Independent Test of Disposition Patterns and Demographic Variables.

Gender	Male	Female	Total				χ^2 (*p*-Value)
Reverse DE	253	144	397				52.222
	23.6%	13.5%	18.6%				(0.000)
Symmetry	369	328	697				
	34.5%	30.8%	32.6%				
DE	449	593	1042				
	41.9%	55.7%	48.8%				
Total	1,071	1065	2136				

Age	<30	30–39	40–49	50–59	>59	Total	
Reverse DE	46	121	115	92	21	395	11.004
	20.2%	20.4%	17.6%	18.7%	12.5%	18.5%	(0.201)
	80	185	229	148	55	697	
Symmetry	35.1%	31.3%	35.1%	30.1%	32.8%	32.7%	
DE	102	286	308	252	92	1040	
	44.7%	48.3%	47.2%	51.2%	54.8%	48.8%	
Total	228	592	652	492	168	2132	

Income	<$0.2M	$0.2–1M	>$1M	Total			
Reverse DE	62	221	82	365			12.572
	15.6%	18.0%	24.9%	18.7%			(0.014)
Symmetry	128	392	105	625			
	32.2%	32.0%	31.9%	32.0%			
DE	208	614	142	964			
	52.3%	50.0%	43.2%	49.3%			
Total	398	1227	329	1954			

Education	Low	Middle	High	Total			
Reverse DE	108	99	189	396			14.286
	16.2%	17.7%	21.1%	18.6%			(0.006)
Symmetry	203	179	310	692			
	30.4%	32.0%	34.6%	32.6%			
DE	356	282	397	1035			
	53.4%	50.4%	44.3%	48.8%			
Total	667	560	896	2123			

Table 4. ANOVA of DE and Demographic Variables.

Variable	Item	Samples	Average DE	F	p-Value
Gender	Male	1,071	.22	87.290	.000
	Female	1,065	.37		
Age	Less than 29	228	.19	8.194	.000
	30~39	592	.27		
	40–49	652	.28		
	50–59	492	.35		
	More than 60	168	.41		
Location	Northern TW	1224	.28	2.469	.085
	Middle TW	439	.29		
	Southern TW	476	.34		
Income	<$0.2M	398	.36	7.808	.000
	$0.2–1M	1227	.30		
	>$1M	329	.23		
Education	Low	667	.36	17.136	.000
	Middle	560	.32		
	High	896	.24		

previous empirical findings (e.g., Feng & Seasholes, 2005; Kuo et al., 2005). From the ANOVA results, there are significant differences among different age groups, income, and education ($p < 0.05$), and they are linearly related. Older investors with low income and low education demonstrate higher DE. In addition, the disposition effect is more pronounced for those investors living in the southern Taiwan than those in the north (Tables 4 and 5).

The Impacts of Investment Study on the Price Changes of Winners and Losers

From previous analysis we find a great variation on the tendency of the disposition. We use regression models to analyze the impact of the intention to study the investments on the disposition tendency. Table 6 summarizes estimation results of the effect of amount of time spent on studying investments that was obtained from the three surveys (1,672 samples) and

Table 5. The Difference Test on Study Time among the Demographic Sectors.

Average Studying Time (I)	Average Studying Time (J)	Mean Difference (I–J)	p-Value	Average Studying Time (I)	Average Studying Time (J)	Mean Difference (I–J)	p-Value
Age				Location			
<30	30–39	−.08404	.014	Northern	Middle	−.00813	.741
	40–49	−.09269	.006	Taiwan	Southern	−.05254	.028
	50–59	−.15761	.000	Middle	Northern	.00813	.741
	>59	−.21580	.000	Taiwan	Southern	−.04441	.128
30–39	<30	.08404	.014	Southern	Northern	.05254	.028
	40–49	−.00866	.728	Taiwan	Middle	.04441	.128
	50–59	−.07358	.006	Yearly income			
	>59	−.13176	.001	<0.2M	0.2–1M	.06244	.014
40–49	<30	.09269	.006		>1M	.12932	.000
	30–39	.00866	.728	$0.2~1M	<0.2M	−.06244	.014
	50–59	−.06492	.013		>1M	.06688	.014
	>59	−.12310	.001	>$1M	<0.2M	−.12932	.000
50–59	<30	.15761	.000		0.2~1M	−.06688	.014
	30–39	.07358	.006	Education			
	40–49	.06492	.013	Lower	Middle	.04885	.052
	>59	−.05818	.138		Higher	.12862	.000
>59	<30	.21580	.000	Middle	Lower	−.04885	.052
	30–39	.13176	.001		Higher	.07977	.001
	40–49	.12310	.001	Higher	Lower	−.12862	.000
	50–59	.05818	.138		Middle	−.07977	.001

Table 7 presents both study time and information media from one of the surveys (593 samples).

According to the estimation results, all models show statistically good fitness except for the model of price changes for winning stocks. Moreover, the study intention has good explanatory power on the disposition effect. Despite the insignificance of the study coefficients in models 2 and 5 (where study does not make investors keep winners longer), we find the DE value and the price changes of holding losers to be negatively related to the investment study time and the number of information media. The less effort the investors are willing to put into studying investments, the more disposition effect they are subjected to. The intention to study helps to mitigate the disposition effect, which in turn promotes the loss realizations. We believe it is because the

Table 6. The Impacts of Investment Study Intention (Time) on the
Disposition Effects: Regression Models.

	Y = DE		Y = Return on Gains		Y = Absolute Return on Losses	
	Coeff.	p-Value	Coeff.	p-Value	Coeff.	p-Value
Intercept	0.292	0.000	0.176	0.000	0.473	0.000
Time of studying	−0.004	0.000	0.000	0.549	−0.003	0.001
Gender (1 = male, 0 = female)	−0.127	0.000	0.011	0.288	−0.112	0.000
Age	0.004	0.000	0.000	0.926	0.004	0.000
Location (1 = northern Taiwan, 0 = southern Taiwan)	−0.051	0.059	−0.007	0.590	−0.060	0.022
Location (1 = middle Taiwan, 0 = southern Taiwan)	−0.033	0.318	0.016	0.284	−0.018	0.566
Income (NT$M)	−0.040	0.031	0.007	0.394	−0.034	0.055
Education (1 = middle, 0 = lower)	−0.003	0.921	−0.010	0.471	−0.012	0.674
Education (1 = higher, 0 = lower)	−0.033	0.219	−0.026	0.037	−0.061	0.018
Survey (1 = #2?0 = #?)	−0.001	0.978	0.011	0.354	0.011	0.661
Survey (1 = #3?0 = #1)	0.005	0.860	0.001	0.904	0.007	0.773
Adjusted R^2	0.053		0.001		0.055	
F-statistic	10.292		1.143		10.644	
Prob. (F-statistic)	0.000		0.326		0.000	
No. of samples: 1,672						

knowledge gained from studying effectively reduces the uncertainty about stock value and thus reduces the resistance to realize losses. Hypotheses 2 and 3 are supported by the empirical evidences while Hypothesis 1 is not.

The regression models also show the influences of demographical variables. Female and older investors with lower income and living in the southern Taiwan demonstrate significantly higher disposition effect. The data are from three surveys; we control for the potential influence of investigation timing, so we assign a dummy variable to each survey. The coefficients are insignificant. In other words, the effects of investment study weakening the disposition effect are robust.

Table 7. The Impacts of Investment Study Intention (Time and Media) on the Disposition Effects: Regression Models.

	Y = DE		Y = Return on Gains		Y = Absolute Return on Losses	
	Coeff.	*p*-Value	Coeff.	*p*-Value	Coeff.	*p*-Value
Intercept	0.330	0.000	0.211	0.000	0.541	0.000
Time of studying	−0.004	0.027	0.000	0.676	−0.004	0.016
Channels of studying	−0.005	0.012	−0.001	0.236	−0.006	0.002
Gender (1 = male, 0 = female)	−0.155	0.000	0.038	0.018	−0.117	0.001
Age	0.003	0.015	0.000	0.561	0.003	0.029
Location (1 = northern Taiwan, 0 = southern)	−0.023	0.597	−0.044	0.026	−0.067	0.124
Location (1 = middle Taiwan, 0 = southern)	−0.014	0.781	0.008	0.733	−0.006	0.901
Income (NT$M)	−0.007	0.822	0.001	0.932	−0.006	0.851
Education (1 = middle, 0 = lower)	−0.044	0.337	−0.014	0.491	−0.058	0.202
Education (1 = higher, 0 = lower)	−0.065	0.126	−0.022	0.254	−0.087	0.040
Adjusted R^2	0.065		0.020		0.065	
F-statistic	5.567		2.317		5.575	
Prob. (*F*-statistic)	0.000		0.015		0.000	
No. of samples: 593						

CONCLUSION

Existing studies on the disposition effect are mainly of a descriptive nature. The empirical evidences consider the DE to be a disadvantage to the investment performance. The DE can be reduced in many different ways, leaving it a research gap to be filled. We propose that studies help reduce the stock value uncertainty and thus decrease investors' resistance to realize losses or to keep winners longer. Through the nationwide surveys in Taiwan, we collected 1,672 effective observations to conduct the empirical analysis and found that the study hypothesis is significantly supported. That is, if investors attempt investment study, their disposition effects lessens. This change is mainly due to the study effect on promoting loss realizations; the intention to study investments promotes investors to keep winners longer. We suggest that study leads investors to become more rational and less driven by the sentiment regret averse. In short, investment study weakens the disposition effect.

REFERENCES

Beaver, W. H. (1968). The information content of annual earnings announcements. *Journal of Accounting Research, 6*, 67–92.

Benartzi, S., & Thaler, R. (1995). Myopic loss aversion and the equity premium puzzle. *Quarterly Journal of Economics, 110*, 75–92.

Feng, L., & Seasholes, M. (2005). Do investor sophistication and trading experience eliminate behavioral biases in financial markets? *Review of Finance, 9*(3), 305–351.

Ferris, S. P., Haugen, R. A., & Makhija, A. K. (1988). Predicting contemporary volume with historic volume at differential price levels: Evidence supporting the disposition effect. *Journal of Finance, 43*(3), 677–697.

Glick, I. (1957). *A social psychological study of futures trading.* Ph.D. dissertation, University of Chicago, IL.

Goetzmann, W. N., & Peles, N. (1997). Cognitive dissonance and mutual fund investors. *Journal of Financial Research, 20*(2), 145–158.

Grinblatt, M., & Keloharju, M. (2001). What makes investors trade? *Journal of Finance, 56*, 589–616.

Grossman, S. J. (1976). On the efficiency of competitive stock markets where traders have diverse information. *Journal of Finance, 31*(2), 573–584.

Kahneman, D., & Tversky, A. (1979). Prospect theory: An analysis of decision under risk. *Econometrica, 47*, 263–291.

Kuo, M.-H. (2006). Down-to-earth is the secret to happy investment? In T. C. Huang, N. F. Kuo & C. C. Chen (Eds.), *Industrial development and management: New thinking and new methodology* (pp. 259–279). ISBN 978-957-8462-54-0.

Kuo, M.-H. (2009). Does the prospect theory necessarily mean disposition effect? An extension of disposition effect. *Annual meeting of the Northeast Decision Sciences Institute,* March 26–28, Alexandria, VA, USA.

Kuo, M.-H., & Chen, S. K. (2012). Prospect theory and disposition patterns: Evidence from Taiwan investors. *Studies in Economics and Finance, 29*(1), 43–51.

Kuo, M.-H., Kuo, N. F., Chiu, Y. C., & Fang, P. H. (2005). Gender and investment behavior: On Taiwanese individual investors. *Journal of Financial Studies, 13*(2), 1–28.

Lakonishok, J., & Smidt, S. (1986). Volume for winners and losers: Taxation and other motives for stock trading. *Journal of Finance, 41*, 951–974.

Odean, T. (1998). Are investors reluctant to realize their losses? *Journal of Finance, 53*, 1775–1798.

Shapira, Z., & Venezia, I. (2001). Patterns of behavior of professionally managed and independent investors. *Journal of Banking and Finance, 25*, 1573–1587.

Shefrin, H., & Statman, M. (1985). The disposition to sell winners too early and ride losers too long: Theory and evidence. *Journal of Finance, 40*, 777–790.

Shiller, R. J. (1999). Human behavior and the efficiency of the financial system. In J. B. Taylor & M. Woodford (Eds.), *Handbook of macroeconomics* (1st ed., Vol. 1, pp. 1305–1340, Chap. 20). Netherlands: Elsevier.

Weber, M., & Camerer, C. F. (1998). The disposition effect in securities trading: An experimental analysis. *Journal of Economic Behavior and Organization, 33*(2), 167–184.

FORECASTING U.S. COTTON PRICES IN A CHANGING MARKET

Olga Isengildina-Massa and Stephen MacDonald

The purpose of this study is to analyze structural changes that took place in the cotton industry and develop a statistical model that reflects the current drivers of U.S. upland cotton prices. This study concludes that a structural break in the U.S. cotton industry occurred in 1999, and that world cotton supply has become an important determinant of U.S. cotton prices. The model developed here forecasts changes in U.S. cotton price based on changes in U.S. cotton supply, changes in U.S. stocks-to-use ratio (S/U), changes in China's net imports as a share of world consumption, the proportion of U.S. cotton engaged in the loan program, and changes in world supply of cotton.

Keywords: Forecasting; cotton; price; supply; trade; structural change

INTRODUCTION

Agricultural prices are notoriously difficult to forecast due to shocks from weather events around the world, the influence of government policy in the marketplace, and changing tastes and technology. Nevertheless, significant

Advances in Business and Management Forecasting, Volume 9, 91–113
ISSN: 1477-4070/doi:10.1108/S1477-4070(2013)0000009010

resources across multiple public and private agencies are devoted to this task. These forecasts are believed to provide information to the market and assist in price discovery and efficient asset allocation (Vogel & Bange, 1999). There is considerable evidence that USDA reports that contain government forecasts move the markets (e.g., Adjemian, 2012; Baur & Orazem, 1994; Colling & Irwin, 1990; Fortenbery & Sumner, 1993; McKenzie, 2008; Sumner & Mueller, 1989) and these reports are usually widely anticipated. Recent years have proved to be particularly more challenging for agricultural price forecasting as wheat, rice, corn, and cotton prices have each spiked at least once since 2005, increasing risks for low-income consumers in developing countries, and livestock and clothing producers around the world. Furthermore, with relatively low reserve stocks of commodities around the world, new information from many sources now drives markets with much greater speed than in the past. In this environment, concerns have surfaced about USDA's ability to reliably provide markets with information needed to find equilibrium quickly, hence minimizing the need for costly corrections along the food supply chain. In December 2011, the *Wall Street Journal* reported that over the last two years, USDA's monthly forecasts of how much farmers will produce has been, "off the mark to a greater degree than any other two consecutive years in the last 15 [years]."

Particular challenges have been found in cotton price forecasting. Treated differently from other agricultural commodities, cotton price forecasts by USDA were banned until 2008.[1] Cotton price forecasts were available each month from the International Cotton Advisory Committee (ICAC) and – with less frequent updates – from the Food and Agricultural Policy Research Institute (FAPRI), the Australian Bureau of Agricultural and Resource Economics (ABARE), and the World Bank. However, because of the rapid on-going structural changes in the cotton industry, most forecasts have tended to overestimate cotton prices in recent years. For example, the International Cotton Advisory Committee (ICAC), which provides forecasts for the Cotlook A-Index (the accepted measure of the world price and a factor in determining U.S. loan deficiency payments), released a new forecasting model in 2007 after having to rely solely on judgment for months, when their previous forecasting model had been projecting "unrealistic" prices as cotton prices have consistently been low not only with respect to forecasts, but also in comparison with other commodities. Cotton prices have risen since 2006, but relative to most other commodities remained well below historical levels (Meyer, MacDonald, & Skinner, 2008).

Given the poor predictive capability of existing cotton price forecasting models, the importance of price forecasts for the cotton industry and the renewed public access to USDA cotton price forecasts, the goal of this study was to analyze structural changes that took place in the cotton industry in the recent years and develop a forecasting model that accurately accounts for the current drivers of U.S. cotton prices. A cotton price model was developed based on our revision of the traditional framework for structural price forecasting using annual data from 1974 through 2006. The analysis of structural change based on statistical tests developed by Hansen (2001) identified a structural break in 1999. The increased export orientation of the U.S. cotton industry in post-1999 period is modeled through a world supply variable. The accuracy and the forecasting performance of the proposed price forecasting model are subsequently evaluated. The results of this study can be used by the USDA and cotton market participants to help obtain accurate cotton price forecasts.

USDA COTTON PRICE FORECASTS

Similar to other commodities, cotton prices are forecasted by USDA on a marketing year average basis for farm level price. As shown in Fig. 1, the U.S. marketing year for cotton lasts from August to July and the average price is computed based on prices received by farmers throughout the marketing year weighted by the amount marketed at each price. Most marketing takes place from October to March. Even though the marketing year is later than for other main agricultural commodities, the first USDA forecast of the marketing year average price (and the other variables for

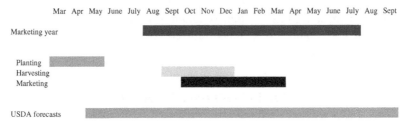

Fig. 1. U.S. Upland Cotton Crop Calendar. *Source*: USDA National Agricultural Statistics Service, Foreign Agricultural Service, World Board.

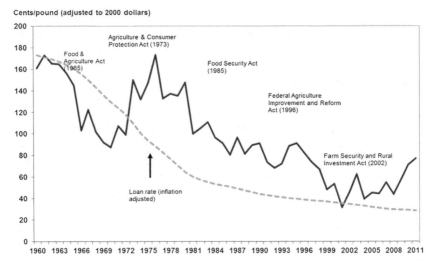

Cents/pound (adjusted to 2000 dollars)

Fig. 2. U.S. Marketing Year Average Farm Price, Upland Cotton. *Source*: ERS Calculations Based on Data from NASS and the U.S. Department of Commerce.

the marketing year) is released in May prior to the marketing year. This forecast is revised each month thereafter until it is finalized by November following the marketing year. The prices used for this analysis are obtained from the various issues of World Agricultural Supply and Demand Estimates and the internal records of USDA's Interagency Commodity Estimates Committee for cotton. Fig. 2 shows that the U.S. cotton price has been highly variable over time under the pressure of various economic and political factors. This figure also demonstrates that the annual U.S. cotton price is a low frequency variable, which limits the use of new time series forecasting techniques developed for high frequency data (see Elliot & Timmermann, 2008). Therefore, our approach in this study was to start with a traditional structural model that is commonly used for agricultural price forecasting and update it to reflect current determinants of supply and demand in this market.

FORECASTING MODEL

Traditionally, in agricultural commodity forecasting models, price is specified as a function of the stocks-to-use ratio (e.g., Goodwin, Schnepf, & Dohlman,

2005; MacDonald, 2006; Meyer, 1998; Westcott & Hoffman, 1999) and a set of supply and demand shifters.

$$p_t = f(r_t, z_t, y_t) \tag{1}$$

where p_t is the real average farm level price of upland cotton for marketing year t, r_t is the ratio of ending stocks to total use for marketing year t, and z and y are supply and demand shifters.

The dependent variable (p_t) in this study is the season-average price reported by USDA's National Agricultural Statistics Service deflated by the U.S. Department of Commerce's gross domestic product price index.[2] A broad measure of inflation was chosen since cotton products compete with a broad range of products for consumer demand. Since time-series data are often nonstationary, most variables in this study are measured in percent changes from the previous year's level. Historical cotton supply and demand data are drawn from the "Production, Supply and Distribution Online" database maintained by USDA's Foreign Agricultural Service (U.S. Department of Agriculture, Foreign Agricultural Service, 2012). Thus, the base model for cotton price forecasting used in this study is:

$$\frac{(p_t - p_{t-1})}{p_{t-1}} = \alpha_0 + \alpha_1 \frac{(r_t - r_{t-1})}{r_{t-1}} \tag{2}$$

The remainder of this section describes the demand and supply shifters included in this model.

One of the most significant demand shifters in U.S. and world cotton markets is export demand changes associated with China's trade policy. The strong correlation between world cotton prices and China's net trade was noted as early as 1988 by the ICAC, and the level of China's net trade was included in the ICAC's world price forecasting model for the 1974/1975–1986/1987 period (International Cotton Advisory Committee, 1988). Similarly, MacDonald (1997) adjusted the world (minus China) stocks-to-use variable by the amount of China's net trade in another world price model, estimated using the 1971/1972–1995/1996 data. In 2001, researchers at USDA's Economic Research Service highlighted how China's domestic cotton policy drove its cotton trade, with significant impacts on world markets:

> Stocks rose after 1994/95 as China raised its farm prices while maintaining an open trade regime ... Stocks reached a staggering 106 percent of use in 1998/99, and China accounted for 47 percent of the entire world's cotton ending stocks. Then, starting in 1998/99, the government began applying quantitative restrictions to cotton imports and subsidizing exports. In 1999/2000 the government effectively cut farm prices by refusing

to guarantee procurement, and ... [b]y 2000/01, China had cut its ending stocks by nearly 10 million bales, mostly from government stocks. (U.S. Department of Agriculture, Economic Research Service, Market and Trade Economics Division, 2001)

This demand shifter is measured in this study as an absolute change[3] from the previous 2-year average of China's net imports as a share of world consumption:

$$CNI_t = \frac{Imports_t^{China} - Exports_t^{China}}{Consumption_t^{World}} \qquad (3)$$

Another factor affecting the relationship between U.S. ending stocks and prices is the U.S. government policy (see Meyer, MacDonald, & Foreman, 2007, for a summary of U.S. farm programs affecting cotton). Before 1986, U.S. commodity programs sometimes served to establish a price floor for U.S. crops. USDA's Commodity Credit Corporation (CCC) acquired large stocks of cotton (and other commodities) during the early 1980s as market prices in the United States fell toward U.S. loan rates (Table 1). Stocks owned by CCC were not available to the market, and prices were higher than if the stocks could have been drawn upon to satisfy demand. Furthermore, even cotton that had not yet been acquired by CCC, but was still being used as collateral in the loan program, was also not freely available for spinning, export, or private stockholding.

The shift of U.S. cotton policy to a marketing loan program meant that CCC acquisition of cotton was significantly reduced, and in 2006 CCC instituted a policy of immediately selling any forfeited cotton, ensuring negligible CCC stocks at the end of the marketing year. However, the ability of producers to place their cotton in the loan program affected prices after 1986, and the volume of cotton remaining as collateral in the loan program at the end of the marketing year was often significant, even in recent years. Until 1996, producers had the option of keeping their cotton under loan as long at 18 months. Therefore, a variable was created representing the amount of cotton under CCC loan relative to total U.S. cotton use:

$$CCC_t = \frac{Loan_t^{us}}{Consumption_t^{us} + Exports_t^{us}} \qquad (4)$$

Changes in this variable were included as a demand shifter reflecting the impact of the U.S. marketing loan program.

Another U.S. government policy that affected cotton markets is the Step 2 program, which was introduced in the 1990 and continued until 2006. The Step 2 program offered payments to U.S. textile mills and U.S. exporters

Table 1. Season-Ending U.S. Commodity Program Cotton Stocks.

Marketing Year	CCC Loans Thousand bales	Inventory as Share of Use Percent
1974/1975	901	9
1975/1976	110	1
1976/1977	309	3
1977/1978	1209	10
1978/1979	614	5
1979/1980	501	3
1980/1981	626	5
1981/1982	3643	31
1982/1983	4267	40
1983/1984	444	4
1984/1985	1597	14
1985/1986	5965	73
1986/1987	2914	21
1987/1988	3164	23
1988/1989	4119	30
1989/1990	430	3
1990/1991	215	1
1991/1992	297	2
1992/1993	558	4
1993/1994	179	1
1994/1995	165	1
1995/1996	312	2
1996/1997	311	2
1997/1998	61	0
1998/1999	326	2
1999/2000	68	0
2000/2001	1460	10
2001/2002	665	4
2002/2003	668	4
2003/2004	1371	7
2004/2005	301	1
2005/2006	1185	5
2006/2007	857	5
2007/2008	3819	22
2008/2009	195	1
2009/2010	417	3
2010/2011	536	3
2011/2012	573	4

Source: Stultz et al., Farm Service Agency (FSA), and ERS calcuations based on data from FSA and WASDE.

when the price of U.S. cotton in Northern Europe exceeded the world price of cotton, also measured in Northern Europe. A World Trade Organization (WTO) panel found in 2005 the program in violation of the General Agreement on Trade and Tariffs (GATT), in large part because the payments to U.S. mills were exclusively for the consumption of U.S. cotton rather than either U.S. or imported cotton (see Schnepf, 2007, for a summary of the dispute). The subsidies were nontrivial, averaging 5 percent of the value of U.S. cotton use during 1991–2006. Since U.S. cotton accounted for about 20 percent of global cotton use during this time, the program likely had an impact on the world price as well as the U.S. price. The Step 2 program was terminated in August 2006 as part of the United States' efforts to comply with the WTO panel's findings.

Since Step 2 will no longer be a factor in U.S. prices, and since it influenced past prices, the forecasting model was estimated with data for the dependent variable adjusted to remove the past impact of Step 2. Data on expenditures for the U.S. User Market Certificate Program ("Step 2") were obtained from FSA. Data on spending for Step 2 payments in each year were divided by the value of U.S. cotton use to determine the relative subsidy provided each year (Table 2). An adjustment variable (λ_t) was constructed so that each year's price adjustment was proportional to that year's subsidy, while the average for the adjustment variable over 1991–2006 was 2.9 percent.[4] Thus, if Z_t equals a given year's subsidy, then $\lambda_t = 0.029 \times Z_t/(\Sigma Z_t/T)$, where $T =$ number of years between 1991 and 2006. This variable was used to adjust the U.S. season-average upland farm price to remove the impact of Step 2:

$$p_t^* = (1 - \lambda_t)p_t \tag{5}$$

Finally, it is necessary to take into account the fact that cotton markets have experienced rather dramatic changes in supply due to the spread of genetically modified varieties and other technologies over the last 20 years. Changes in supply from the previous marketing year are included in the model to reflect these trends. Supply includes beginning stocks, domestic production, and imports. Raw cotton imports have historically been close to zero in the United States. This approach assumes that supply is largely predetermined in the beginning of the marketing year.[5] Thus, the cotton price model including the demand and supply shifters is:

$$\frac{(p_t^* - p_{t-1}^*)}{p_{t-1}^*} = \alpha_0 + \alpha_1 \frac{(S_t - S_{t-1})}{S_{t-1}} + \alpha_2 \frac{(r_t - r_{t-1})}{r_{t-1}} + \alpha_3 \left(CNI_t - \frac{CNI_{t-1} + CNI_{t-2}}{2} \right)$$
$$+ \alpha_4 (CCC_t - CCC_{t-1}) \tag{6}$$

Table 2. Step 2 Expenditures and Price Adjustment Variable.

Marketing Year	Payments[a]	Payments/Cotton Use	Subsidy (S_t)	Adjustment (λ_t)[b]
	$ Million	$/pound	Percent	Percent
1991/1992	140	0.02	2.9	1.6
1992/1993	114	0.02	2.7	1.5
1993/1994	149	0.02	2.5	1.5
1994/1995	88	0.01	1.0	0.6
1995/1996	34	0.00	0.5	0.3
1996/1997	6	0.00	0.1	0.1
1997/1998	416	0.05	6.4	3.7
1998/1999	280	0.04	6.7	3.9
1999/2000	445	0.05	10.4	6.0
2000/2001	236	0.03	5.5	3.2
2001/2002	182	0.02	4.9	2.8
2002/2003	455	0.05	8.9	5.1
2003/2004	363	0.04	5.5	3.1
2004/2005	582	0.06	10.7	6.2
2005/2006	397	0.04	6.2	3.6
Average	259	0.03	5.0	2.9

[a]Fiscal year.
[b]Derived from annual subsidy so that 1991–2005 average adjustment is 2.9 percent and each year is proportional to that year's subsidy.
Source: Farm Services Agency, and ERS calculations based on data from the Farm Services Agency, WASDE, and Cotlook.

where all variables are as defined above and refer to U.S. values unless otherwise stated.[6] Since supply is predetermined, changes in supply have an inverse effect on price. Changes in stocks-to-use ratio are inversely related to price. Increases in China's net cotton imports represent a greater export demand for U.S. cotton and thus have a positive relationship with price changes. CCC stocks describe the amount of cotton not available to the market, thus a positive relationship between these stocks and prices is expected.

Other factors that may have an important effect on cotton prices include energy prices. Previous work (e.g., Barsky & Kilian, 2002) has indicated how oil price shocks can affect prices in general. More recently, policy changes – like those regarding ethanol – have linked energy and grain prices (Baffes & Haniotis, 2010). Energy market shocks occurred in the 1970s and again after 2004. In an effort to develop a model that is robust to both high and low energy prices, and to a variety of policy environments, this study concentrates on cotton price movements starting from the 1974/1975 marketing year and extending to 2011/2012. Since the proposed model is estimated in reduced form, the impact of energy prices is included implicitly through the supply variable. A similar argument can be made about other supply-inducing variables, such as the price of cotton seed.

Structural Change Test

Stability of a forecasting model specified in Eq. (6) was tested using the Quandt-Likelihood Ratio (QLR) (Hansen, 2001). The QLR test consists of calculating Chow breakpoint tests at every observation, while ensuring that subsample points are not too near the end points of the sample. The QLR test was applied to the model with 20 percent trimming. The structural break was found in 1999 based on the values of the F-statistic (at the 95 percent level), log likelihood ratio, and Wald statistic (at the 99 percent significance level).

This structural break was likely caused by a combination of factors. Besides significant changes in international trade discussed earlier, which have been transitory in nature, this period coincided with some permanent fundamental regime changes in China's supply due to the end of guaranteed procurement prices. Some permanent changes also took place in China's consumption sector due to its growing textile industry. These regime changes in China's cotton sector are likely associated with China's accession to the WTO at the end of 2001. China joined the WTO just as the textile trade liberalization provisions of the Uruguay Round Agreement were having an impact. The phasing-out of developed country textile trade protection (commonly referred to as Multifiber Arrangement, or MFA) was an important factor behind the rapid increased export orientation of the U.S. cotton industry. Fig. 3 shows that in the early 2000s, export demand surpassed domestic use of the U.S. upland cotton. As the export share of U.S. cotton use rose to levels not seen since the 19th century, the importance of world supply and demand to U.S. cotton prices increased. In addition to policy changes in China, 1999 marked the first year that foreign cotton supplies (excluding China) surpassed 75 million bales. As a liberalizing global economy began an accelerated expansion in 1999, foreign cotton supplies began rising to meet this demand.

To correct for the structural change detected in the estimated model (Eq. (6)), an additional shift variable was added to reflect the increased export orientation of the U.S. cotton industry. World market signals are assumed to be transmitted to the U.S. market through foreign supply, which

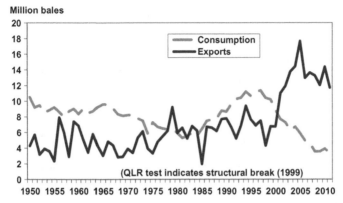

Fig. 3. U.S. Cotton Exports, Consumption, and Structural Change, 1950–2011. *Source*: Production, Supply and Distribution Online.

was constructed, excluding China's supply but including China's net contribution to the global availability of cotton (net exports)[7]

$$Supply_t^{Foreign} = Supply_t^{Foreign} - Supply_t^{China} + Exports_t^{China} - Imports_t^{China} \quad (7)$$

Foreign supply is an important factor for U.S. cotton prices. The United States is one of the largest producers and exporters of cotton and directly competes with cotton coming from other countries. With this variable included, no structural break was detected and the specification of the model was complete. Thus, the final model specification is

$$\frac{(p_t^* - p_{t-1}^*)}{p_{t-1}^*} = \alpha_0 + \alpha_1 \frac{(S_t - S_{t-1})}{S_{t-1}} + \alpha_2 \frac{(r_t - r_{t-1})}{r_{t-1}} + \alpha_3 \left(CNI_t - \frac{CN_{t-1} + CN_{t-2}}{2} \right)$$
$$+ \alpha_4 (CCC_t - CCC_{t-1}) + \alpha_5 \frac{\left(S_t^{Foreign} - S_{t-1}^{Foreign} \right)}{S_{t-1}^{Foreign}}$$

$$(8)$$

All data used for the empirical estimation of this equation are presented in Table 3. Estimation was conducted using E-views software.

Specification Tests

Stationarity of each series in Eq. (8) was assessed using the Augmented Dickey Fuller (ADF) test. ADF regressions, with and without a constant,

Table 3.   Model Data 1974/1975 through 2011/2012 Marketing Years.

Marketing Year	Price	Supply	Stocks/Use	China Net Imports	CCC	Foreign Supply
1974/1975	−12.0	−10.8	114.1	−2.1	7.5	8.5
1975/1976	11.6	−8.5	−41.6	−0.8	−4.4	−4.3
1976/1977	17.7	1.6	−26.4	−0.2	−2.4	−6.3
1977/1978	−23.5	21.2	82.2	1.6	8.2	2.6
1978/1979	3.4	−6.5	−34.8	1.7	−1.5	0.9
1979/1980	−1.4	14.9	−37.7	3.3	−4.3	−2.6
1980/1981	9.3	−24.0	7.9	0.7	1.3	−0.1
1981/1982	−32.4	29.9	179.9	−2.4	26.6	−0.6
1982/1983	5.1	1.3	34.0	−3.0	21.8	2.1
1983/1984	5.7	−15.8	−68.3	−2.6	−31.8	−4.3
1984/1985	−13.0	0.2	46.6	−1.9	−8.1	18.8
1985/1986	−5.6	11.4	226.9	−3.0	62.7	13.6
1986/1987	−11.6	8.6	−68.7	−1.4	−21.8	−1.3
1987/1988	19.8	3.2	13.7	1.1	−23.6	0.3
1988/1989	−15.8	7.1	33.8	3.0	8.1	0.1
1989/1990	10.2	−10.9	−69.2	2.6	−23.3	−1.9
1990/1991	1.8	−3.1	−24.2	1.0	−14.8	0.5
1991/1992	−19.0	8.6	82.5	−0.1	−0.1	2.6
1992/1993	−7.5	−1.0	24.3	−1.9	2.0	−3.4
1993/1994	6.0	4.8	−30.0	−0.3	−1.7	−5.1
1994/1995	22.5	12.0	−35.3	4.8	−1.5	−4.6
1995/1996	3.0	−9.4	14.3	1.0	0.8	14.4
1996/1997	−9.5	4.1	55.4	0.0	0.5	−0.8
1997/1998	−10.6	3.8	−6.1	−1.7	−1.4	3.5
1998/1999	−9.1	−20.1	14.3	−3.4	1.2	2.2
1999/2000	−28.2	13.9	−3.6	−2.5	−0.9	5.7
2000/2001	11.5	1.4	54.4	0.8	8.0	0.4
2001/2002	−41.0	24.5	11.0	1.1	−1.3	0.5
2002/2003	43.0	−7.2	−29.3	2.5	−3.0	−3.8
2003/2004	38.2	−2.9	−36.0	7.6	3.3	−5.1
2004/2005	−36.8	12.8	51.7	0.2	−3.7	23.3
2005/2006	14.1	11.0	−8.5	9.2	0.9	−6.4
2006/2007	−1.9	−6.7	123.1	−2.7	1.6	7.9
2007/2008	24.4	3.1	5.8	−3.2	16.0	−3.1
2008/2009	−20.6	−19.4	−41.6	−2.6	−11.7	−2.6
2009/2010	30.1	−20.0	−42.9	1.4	−8.4	−1.7
2010/2011	25.0	15.2	−21.1	2.7	1.0	4.7
2011/2012	8.3	−15.7	29.2	13.9	1.0	1.3

Note: Price is percent change in the real U.S. season-average upland cotton farm price from year *t*–1 to year *t*, Supply is percent change in U.S. supply from year *t*–1 to year *t*, S/U is percent change in U.S. stocks-use-ratio from year *t*–1 to year *t*, China net imports is the absolute change in China's net imports as a proportion of world demand from their average over the preceeding two years, and CCC is the change from year *t*–1 to year *t* in the stocks of cotton under loan with USDA's Commodity Credit Corporation as proportion of U.S. consumption. Foreign supply is the percent change in world minus U.S. cotton supply (minus China's supply and plus China's net exports) from year *t*–1 to year *t*.
Source: USDA National Agricultural Statistics Service, and World Agricultural Supply and Demand Estimates (various issues).

with optimal number of lags selected based on Schwarz Information Criterion (SIC) were computed. For all variables the null hypothesis of unit root was rejected at 1-percent level,[8] which was not surprising since most variables are measured in first differences.

According to Pearson correlation coefficients, significant correlation exists between *stocks/use* and several other variables in the model. Multicollinearity caused by this variable may inflate standard errors and the R^2 statistic of the model. The variance inflation factor for stocks/use was 4.1, below the generally accepted cut-off level of 5, but high, and well above the average of 2.2 for all the variables. This issue was investigated by dropping *stocks/use*, which resulted in very minor changes (in the second decimal) in the standard errors and the R^2 and no changes in the signs of the coefficients. Thus, it was concluded that multicollinearity did not cause significant problems in this model.

Another potential statistical problem in the model is endogeniety. Goodwin et al. (2005) point out the presence of endogeniety between soybean prices and stocks-to-use ratio, which may lead to biased results of the OLS estimation. Another potential source of endogeniety is the supply variable if our assumption of predetermined supply is violated and supply and price are jointly determined. Potential endogeniety is evaluated in this study using a two-stage residual inclusion (2SRI) version of the Hausman test proposed by Terza, Basu, and Rathouz (2008). To conduct this test, the lagged values of the variables in question were used as instrumental variables. The test was conducted in two steps. In the first step the variable in question was regressed against all exogenous variables and the instruments to obtain the residuals. In the second step, Eq. (8) was re-estimated with the residuals from the auxiliary regression as additional regressors. In both cases, the coefficients on the first stage residuals were not significantly different from zero, thus failing to reject the hypothesis of consistent OLS estimates.

Finally, we test whether residuals of the OLS estimator of Eq. (8) are homoscedastic and i.i.d. White's heteroscedasticity test failed to reject the null hypothesis of homoscedasticity. The presence of autocorrelation is rejected by both the Durbin Watson test and the Breusch–Godfrey test. Thus we conclude that OLS assumptions are not violated and the estimation results are best linear unbiased estimates.

EMPIRICAL RESULTS

Table 4 presents the results of cotton price model estimation, Eq. (8), over the 1974/1975–2011/2012 period. The estimated model explains about 59 percent

Table 4. Estimation Results for Cotton Price Model, 1974/1975–2011/
2012 Marketing Years.

Variable or Statistic	Coefficient	Std. Error	t-Statistic	Prob.
Constant	0.040	0.025	1.600	0.119
Supply	−0.536	0.187	−2.871	0.007
Stocks/use	−0.189	0.062	−3.073	0.004
China net imports	1.032	0.670	1.540	0.133
CCC stocks	0.786	0.214	3.667	0.001
Foreign supply	−0.707	0.399	−1.771	0.086
R^2	0.590	–	–	–
Adjusted R^2	0.526	–	–	–
Regression	–	0.138	–	–
Sum squared resid	0.606	–	–	–
Log likelihood	24.696	–	–	–
F-statistic	9.209	–	–	0.000
Mean dependent var.	0.003	0.200	–	–
Akaike info criterion	−0.984	–	–	–
Schwarz criterion	−0.725	–	–	–
Hannan–Quinn criter.	−0.892	–	–	–
Durbin–Watson stat	2.170	–	–	–
Breusch–Godfrey Test	1.629	–	–	0.213
White's Heteroscedasticity test	0.437	–	–	0.944

Note: Price is percent change in the real U.S. season-average upland cotton farm price from year $t-1$ to year t, Supply is percent change in U.S. supply from year $t-1$ to year t, S/U is percent change in U.S. stocks-use-ratio from year $t-1$ to year t, China net imports is the absolute change in China's net imports as a proportion of world demand from their average over the preceeding two years, and CCC is the change from year $t-1$ to year t in the stocks of cotton under loan with USDA's Commodity Credit Corporation as proportion of U.S. consumption. Foreign supply is the percent change in world minus U.S. cotton supply (minus China's supply and plus China's net exports) from year $t-1$ to year t.

of the variation in U.S. upland cotton price. All coefficients, except the *China Net Imports* variable, are significant at the conventional levels and have the expected signs. Since most variables are measured in percent changes, their coefficients are interpreted as elasticities. The one percent increase in the *stocks/use* will cause prices to drop by about 0.19 percent. Interestingly, foreign supply has a larger impact on the U.S. price than domestic supply, causing U.S. prices to drop by 0.707 and 0.536, respectively, due to a 1-percent increase in U.S. and foreign supply. An increase in CCC stocks equal to 1 percent of U.S. use would raise price by 0.786 percent.

The goodness of fit of the model in nominal prices is illustrated in Fig. 4. Nominal prices are calculated by removing the inflation adjustment from the real prices predicted by the model and adjusting them for Step 2 payments. Converting real prices into nominal terms makes it easier to compare model predictions against observed prices. The average forecast error for the entire sample is −1.2 cents/pound, which is not statistically different from zero (t-statistic = 0.916), suggesting that the model is unbiased. Mean absolute error is about 6.5 cents/pound and mean absolute percentage error is about 10 percent. The largest in-sample forecast error of 19 cents/pound occurred in 2008. This year was particularly challenging for commodity price forecasting as unusual circumstances associated with the global financial crisis affected prices in ways not accounted for in the structural models. Table 5 shows the 2×2 contingency table used for directional accuracy analysis, which demonstrates that the direction of forecast change was correctly estimated in 29 out of 38 cases or 76 percent of the time. The direction of forecast change was predicted incorrectly in

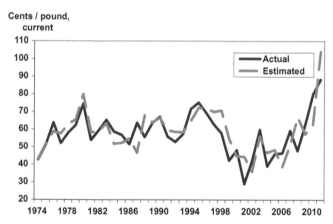

Fig. 4. Actual and Estimated U.S. Upland Cotton Farm Price, 1974/1975–2011/2012.

Table 5. Contingency Table for Directional Accuracy Analysis.

Actual	Estimated		
	$\Delta P > 0$	$\Delta P \leq 0$	Subtotal
$\Delta P > 0$	16	4	20
$\Delta P \leq 0$	5	13	18
Subtotal	21	17	38

9 out of 38 cases, nearly equally divided between failures to predict increases and decreases. A Pearson Chi-Square test of the independence between the rows and columns of the contingency data yielded a statistic of 10.450, which means that the null hypothesis of independence between actual and estimated price changes can be rejected at less than 1-percent level of significance. Interpreted in the framework described by Pons (2001), this result suggests that our model provides rational estimates of cotton prices.

The out of sample performance of the proposed model is very difficult to evaluate since the structural break occurred toward the end of the sample period. Nevertheless we attempt to assess the proposed model's out of sample performance relative to alternative forecasts over 2007–2011 period, since existing models demonstrated poor predictive capability in recent years as discussed in introduction. The first alternative is the cotton forecasting model developed by Meyer (1998) specified as:

$$ln(P) = f\left(ln\left(\frac{S}{U}\right), \ CHFSTKS, \ Index, \ DUM_{SU},\right.$$

$$\left.ln(LDP)^*DUM_{SU}, ln\left(1 + \frac{CCC}{Use}\right)\right) \qquad (9)$$

where P is the nominal U.S. season-average cotton price, CHFSTKS = change in foreign (excluding China) stocks, Index = product of the September average of the price of the December futures contract (National Cotton Council of America, 2012) and AMS's September estimate of the share of planted area already forward contracted (USDA-AMS, various years), DUM_{SU} = dummy valued at 1 when $stocks/use$ is less than or equal to 22.5 percent, LDP = the difference between the loan rate and effective loan repayment rate, and CCC = CCC inventory. Thus, the main difference between the proposed model and Meyer's model is that the latter does not take into account the changes in domestic and world supply (which was less relevant during the time that model was developed) but accounts for the impact of additional information through the index connected to futures prices.

The second alternative is the reduced-form model developed by USDA's World Agricultural Outlook Board (WAOB) in 2006 in an attempt to reflect the increased export orientation of the U.S. cotton industry (U.S. Department of Agriculture, World Agricultural Outlook Board, 2006). This model's specification is

$$P_t = f\left(WxC\frac{S}{U_t},\ WxC\frac{S}{U_{t-1}},\ \text{China net exports}_t \right) \qquad (10)$$

where P is the nominal U.S. season-average cotton price, WxC S/U = world, excluding China, *stocks/use*. The forecast from this model was used as one of the inputs in the USDA's cotton ICEC forecast. The biggest difference between the proposed model and the WAOB model is that the WAOB model focuses on international forces, while the proposed model includes both international and domestic components.

The proposed and alternative models were recursively estimated to construct one-year-ahead, out-of-sample forecasts for 2007/2008 through 2011/2012 using data that had been available in June of each year, starting with June 2007.[9] The analysis of these alternative forecasts shown in Table 6 demonstrates that the proposed model is an improvement over alternative models as it overcomes the bias (though not statistically significant in this small sub-sample) associated with the alternative models, and has lower variance relative to WAOB model. Parallel to the in-sample results the largest forecast error was observed in 2008 when our model failed to predict the impact of global financial crisis on cotton prices. The only model that avoided this shortcoming is Meyer's model since it includes observed futures prices. If 2008 is omitted from the evaluation sample, our model is superior

Table 6. Evaluation of the Out-of-Sample Performance of Our Model versus Alternative Price Forecasting Models, 2007/2008–2011/2012.

Model	Our Model	Meyer[a]	WAOB[b]
	Cents/lb	Error[c] cents/lb	Cents/lb
2007	9.0	2.7	−0.5
2008	−23.2	−2.0	−13.6
2009	2.3	2.4	27.6
2010	14.8	16.4	12.1
2011	5.4	12.2	31.2
Mean error (bias)[c]	1.7	6.3	11.3
Root mean squared error (RMSE)	13.2	9.3	20.3
	Percent	Percent	Percent
Mean absolute percent error (MAPE)	18.4	9.4	24.7

[a]Meyer (1998).
[b]Unpublished model developed by the World Agricultural Outlook Board.
[c]Error is computed as the difference between the actual realization of the price and the forecast.

to both alternatives in both the mean and the variance of its errors. Another indicator of the out of sample performance is parameter stability. If estimated parameters change significantly as new observations are added, the out-of-sample forecasts may become highly volatile and less accurate, and the model may be misspecified. Parameter estimates remain relatively unchanged when estimated using a 1974/1975–2006/2007 sample versus a 1974/1975–2011/2012 sample.[10] Furthermore, the out-of-sample forecasts of the model estimated with the 1974/1975–2006/2007 subsample are only slightly less accurate than the in-sample estimated prices of the model using the full dataset.

SUMMARY AND CONCLUSIONS

This study extended the traditional framework used for structural price forecasting models to account for structural changes in the cotton market and include the relevant factors that affect this market. The new model included several international demand shifters such as China's net trade as a proportion of world consumption, which was introduced to account for changes in export demand associated with China's commodity and trade policies. The impacts of U.S. farm policy were modeled by including a variable representing the amount of cotton in the marketing loan program as a share of use and by adjusting the dependent variable to reflect the historical impact of the User Marketing Certificate (Step 2) program, now discontinued. The proposed model also accounted for changes in supply to reflect dramatic changes in the supply of cotton in the last two decades due to the spread of genetically modified varieties and other new technologies.

Analysis of the cotton price forecasting model identified a structural break that occurred in the U.S. cotton industry in 1999. This structural break was likely caused by a combination of factors, including an increased export orientation of the U.S. cotton industry as the domestic textile industry contracted following the phasing out of the Multifibre Arrangement (for more information on the end of the MFA, see MacDonald & Vollrath, 2005). Thus, the model was modified to include the world supply of cotton, reflecting the increased role of exports and foreign cotton competition for the U.S. cotton industry and in the determination of prices. The final forecasting model was subjected to extensive in-sample testing to ensure its accuracy. The out-of-sample performance of the proposed model suggests that it overcomes the bias in alternative models, and has lower variance relative to WAOB model. Additionally, model's estimates and forecast errors do not change much between a full sample and reduced sample used for out-of-sample forecasting, indicating the stability of the model. This stability and accuracy is an improvement over past forecasting models that have been challenged by changing market conditions.

The out-of-sample evaluation of the price model does not include the consensus-based forecasts of USDA's Interagency Commodity Estimates Committee (ICEC) since they became publicly available in the WASDE reports only from June 2008 and may be partially based on the proposed model. The advantage that the ICEC will have in making its forecasts is the ability to incorporate additional information in its forecasting procedure that is hard to quantify within the framework of a statistical model. However, consensus forecasts are very specific to current events and difficult to replicate or adjust to changing circumstances. As such, they are of limited use when presenting policy-makers with alternative scenarios. A further advantage of the model developed in this study is the opportunity for consistency checking. USDA's ICEC sometimes adjusts its supply and demand outlook in response to prices, and this model provides an additional tool to aid in that process.

The model developed in this study is particularly informative in the environment of volatile commodity prices and an increased role of new players in futures markets. These developments and changing market institutions such as the rise of electronic trading have raised questions about the relationships among cash prices, futures prices, and supply/demand fundamentals. Specifically, there has been growing concern about changes in the relationship between futures prices and cash prices in the United States (Gilbert, 2010). While it would be irrational to ignore the information provided by futures markets when forecasting the U.S. farm price of cotton, it is also important to have forecasts such as the one developed in this study that are independent of that information.

Future avenues for research relate to both world cotton markets and to the characteristics of USDA's supply and demand forecasts. While this study identified some aspects of the structural change that has occurred in U.S. cotton markets since 1999, further examination of the sources of structural change and the channels through which it affects cotton prices is warranted. In addition, forecasts based on this model will depend not only on the parameters of the model, but will also be conditional on the forecasts of supply and demand used to derive any particular forecast of price. Intuitively, early-season forecasts are less reliable than late-season forecasts, but further research can inform these intuitions, and identify key points in the season with respect to the dynamics of forecast performance within the forecasting season. Furthermore, the accuracy of specific supply and demand variables and their potential contribution to price forecast errors should be examined with the goal of correcting for systematic errors in the cotton price forecasts.

ACKNOWLEDGMENT

The funding support of the Economic Research Service of U.S. Department of Agriculture under the Cooperative Agreement No. 58-3000-7-0063 is gratefully acknowledged. Any opinions, findings, conclusions, or recommendations expressed in this publication are those of the authors and do not necessarily reflect the view of the U.S. Department of Agriculture.

NOTES

1. In 1929, Congress passed legislation forbidding USDA from publishing cotton price forecasts (see Townsend, 1989 for a discussion of the circumstances surrounding this legislation).

2. Demand is almost invariably modeled as a function of real rather than nominal prices (Ferris, 1998).

3. Absolute changes from the previous 2-year average are used instead of percent change relative to previous year because of the sporadic changes in this variable, which cause small absolute changes to appear very large in percentage form.

4. Simulations by FAPRI (2005) and Mohanty, Pan, Welch, and Ethridge (2005) found similar impacts, with the removal of Step 2 to a U.S. price that was 2.9 percent lower, on average, and a world price that was slightly higher (less than 1 percent).

5. The U.S. marketing year for cotton begins in August when most of domestic production is ready for harvest and thus predetermined (Fig. 1). Planting decisions occur many months earlier and by biological necessity are unrelated to the price realized when the crop is marketed after harvest. Beginning stocks are also known at the beginning of the marketing year. Imports are not predetermined, but for the United States are trivially small compared with domestic production and beginning stocks.

6. The choice of percentage change as the functional form followed from the theoretical model's derivation in differences. Alternatives – such as using the variables in levels or logs – also resulted in less accurate out-of-sample forecasts.

7. China's stocks and production were excluded from this shift variable since the cotton stocks data are particularly unreliable (MacDonald, 2006). Stocks were regarded as a state secret in China for many years, and although the degree of secrecy has diminished profoundly even current stock estimates for China are highly conjectural. Production data in China are also considered less reliable than elsewhere, so China's impact on world supply comes through its net trade position.

With such problems in the data for the world's largest cotton consumer and stockholder, neither a world stocks-to-use (r_w) nor foreign stocks-to-use (r_f) ratio would be an appropriate variable. Exclusion of China's stocks is not uncommon in analysis of world grain prices (Wright, 2011), for similar reasons.

8. Results not presented here but available from the authors upon request.

9. A real-time data set was constructed, comprised for each vintage of: USDA historical PSD (USDA-FAS, various years) and outyear forecasts, U.S. Department of Commerce estimates of historical GDP deflator (UDOC-BEA, 2012), and IHS Global Insight forecasts of annual change in the GDP deflator. Both the proposed and alternate models' forecasts are conditional on forecasts of a few variables when forecasting in June: the September average of the closing value of the New York cotton contract expiring in December was forecast using the May average (National Cotton Council of America, 2012); the September estimate of forward contracted U.S. cotton plantings (USDA-AMS, various years) was based on a recursively estimated past relationship with the aforementioned May contract price; and the volume of cotton remaining under loan was based on vintage internal USDA forecasts.

10. Results not presented here but available from the authors upon request.

REFERENCES

Adjemian, M. (2012). Quantifying the WASDE announcement effect. *American Journal of Agricultural Economics, 94*(1), 238–256.

Baffes, J., & Haniotis, T. (2010). *Placing the 2006/08 commodity price boom into perspective.* Policy Research Working Paper No. 5371, The World Bank, Development Prospects Group.

Barsky, R. B., & Kilian, L. (2002). Do we really know that oil caused the great stagflation? A monetary alternative. In B. S. Bernanke & K. Rogoff (Eds.), *NBER Macroeconomics annual 2001* (Vol. 16, pp. 137–183). Cambridge, MA: MIT Press.

Baur, R. F., & Orazem, P. F. (1994). The rationality and price effects of USDA forecasts of oranges. *Journal of Finance, 49*, 681–696.

Colling, P. L., & Irwin, S. H. (1990). The reaction of live hog futures prices to USDA hogs and pigs reports. *American Journal of Agricultural Economics, 71*, 84–94.

Elliot, G., & Timmermann, A. (2008). Economic forecasting. *The Journal of Economic Literature, 46*, 3–56.

Ferris, J. N. (1998). *Agricultural prices and commodity market analysis.* WCB McGraw Hill.

Fortenbery, T. R., & Sumner, D. A. (1993). The effects of USDA reports in futures and options markets. *Journal of Futures Markets, 13*, 157–173.

Gilbert, C. (2010). How to understand high food prices. *Journal of Agricultural Economics, 61*(2), 398–425.

Goodwin, B. K., Schnepf, R., & Dohlman, E. (2005). Modelling soybean prices in a changing policy environment. *Applied Economics, 37*, 253–263.

Hansen, B. E. (2001). The new econometrics of structural change: Dating breaks in U.S. labor productivity. *The Journal of Economic Perspectives, 15*, 117–128.

International Cotton Advisory Committee. (1988). Where will cotton prices go? *Cotton Review of the International Situation, 41*(3), 3–5.

MacDonald, S. (1997). Forecasting world cotton prices. The ninth federal forecasters conference – papers and proceedings, National Center for Educational Statistics, U.S. Department of Education.

MacDonald, S. (2006). Cotton price forecasting and structural change. The 15th federal forecasters conference – papers and proceedings, U.S. Department of Veterans Affairs, Veterans Health Administration.

MacDonald, S., & Vollrath, T. (2005). The forces shaping world cotton consumption after the multifiber arrangement. U.S. Department of Agriculture, Economic Research Service, CWS-05C-01.

McKenzie, A. M. (2008). Pre-harvest price expectations for corn: The information content of USDA reports and new crop futures. *American Journal of Agricultural Economics*, *90*, 351–366.

Meyer, L. A. (1998). Factors affecting the US farm price of upland cotton. Cotton and wool situation and outlook, CWS-1998, U.S. Department of Agriculture, Economic Research Service.

Meyer, L., MacDonald, S., & Foreman, L. (2007). *Cotton backgrounder*. Outlook Report No. CWS-07B01, U.S. Department of Agriculture, Economic Research Service.

Meyer, L, MacDonald, S., & Skinner, R. (2008). *Cotton and wool outlook*. Outlook Report No. CWS-08a, U.S. Department of Agriculture, Economic Research Service.

Mohanty, S., Pan, S., Welch, M., & Ethridge, D. (2005). *The impacts of eliminating the Step 2 Program on the U.S. and World Cotton Market*. Briefing Paper CER-BR05-01. Cotton Economics Research Institute, Texas Tech University.

National Cotton Council of America. (2012). *Monthly prices*. Retrieved from http://www.cotton.org/econ/prices/monthly.cfm

Pons, J. (2001). The rationality of price forecasts: A directional analysis. *Applied Financial Economics*, *11*, 287–290.

Schnepf, R. (2007). *Brazil's WTO case against the U.S. cotton program*. CRS Report for Congress, No. RL32571. Retrieved from http://ncseonline.org/NLE/CRSreports/07Oct/RL32571.pdf

Sumner, D. A., & Mueller, R. A. E. (1989). Are harvest forecasts news? USDA announcements and futures market reactions. *American Journal of Agricultural Economics*, *71*, 127–134.

Terza, J. V., Basu, A., & Rathouz, P. J. (2008). Two-stage residual inclusion estimation: Addressing endogeniety in health econometric modeling. *The Journal of Health Economics*, *27*(3), 531–543.

Townsend, T. P. (1989). This was a high-powered instrument that sent its projectile to the vitals of the industry – Why USDA does not forecast cotton prices. *Proceedings of the Cotton Beltwide Conferences*, National Cotton Council.

U.S. Department of Agriculture, Agricultural Marketing Service. (various years). Weekly Cooton Market Review. Retrieved from http://search.ams.usda.gov/mnsearch/mnsearch.aspx

U.S. Department of Agriculture, Economic Research Service, Market and Trade Economics Division. (2001). Cotton and wool situation and outlook yearbook, CWS-2001.

U.S. Department of Agriculture, Foreign Agricultural Service. (2012). Production, supply and distribution online. Retrieved from http://www.fas.usda.gov/psdonline/

U.S. Department of Commerce, Bureau of Economic Analysis. (2012). Previously published estimates. Retrieved from http://www.bea.gov/histdata/

U.S. Department of Agriculture, World Agricultural Outlook Board. (2006). *Unpublished price model in ICEC current supply and demand summary.*

Vogel, F. A., Bange, G. A. (1999). Understanding USDA crop forecasts. Miscellaneous Publication No. 1554, U.S. Department of Agriculture, National Agricultural Statistics Service and Office of the Chief Economist, World Agricultural Outlook Board.

Westcott, P. C., & Hoffman, L. A. (1999). *Price determination for corn and wheat: The role of market factors and government programs. Technical Bulletin No. 1878.* U.S. Department of Agriculture, Economic Research Service. Retrieved from http://www.ers.usda.gov/publications/tb1878/tb1878.pdf

Wright, B. (2011). The economics of grain price volatility. *Applied Economic Perspectives and Policy, 33*(1), 32–58.

MACRO ECONOMETRIC MODELS TO PREDICT THE NAV OF AN ASSET ALLOCATION FUND, VWELX

Kenneth D. Lawrence, Gary Kleinman, Sheila M. Lawrence and Ronald K. Klimberg

ABSTRACT

This research examines the use of econometric models to predict the total net asset value (NAV) of an asset allocation mutual fund. In particular, the mutual fund case used is the Vanguard Wellington Fund (VWELX). This fund maintains a balance between relatively conservative stocks and bonds. The period of the study on which the prediction of the total NAV is based is the 24-month period of 2010 and 2011 and the forecasting period is the first three months of 2012. Forecasting the total NAV of a massive conservative allocation fund, composed of an extremely large number of investments, requires a method that produces accurate results. Achieving this accuracy has no necessary relationship to the complexity of the methods typically employed in many financial forecasting studies.

Keywords: Forecasting; macroeconomics; mutual funds; asset allocation; portfolio; econometrics

Advances in Business and Management Forecasting, Volume 9, 115–133
ISSN: 1477-4070/doi:10.1108/S1477-4070(2013)0000009011

INTRODUCTION

The purpose of this study is to develop a predictive regression model for the total net asset value (NAV) of a massive balance asset allocation mutual fund during a period of time when there is not a massive decline in the economy. The historical period chosen was the 24-month period beginning in January 2010 and running through December 2011. The forecasting period is the first three months of 2012.

The monthly explanatory variables used in the model are:

1. US National GDP (billions of dollars)
2. Dow average ($)
3. Standard & Poor average ($)
4. US unemployment rate (percentage of labor force unemployed but looking for work)
5. Price of oil per barrel ($)
6. Beta of VWELX
7. Average rate of return VWELX
8. Monthly price of VWELX
9. University of Michigan consumer confidence index

Macroeconomic data for this study was downloaded from the St. Louis Federal Reserve Bank (FRED) datasets available at http://research.stlouisfed.org/fred2/ as of November 2, 2012, with a description of the data collection methods available at http://www.bls.gov/opub/hom/). The appendix provides more detail on the FRED data elements. All data is monthly data except for Gross Domestic Product (GDP), which is reported on a quarterly basis. The GDP data used was seasonally adjusted. The data on VWELX performance was obtained from Dions Fidelity Advisor. The forecasting of mutual fund values with vast numbers of investments is certainly not the same as forecasting a single investment or a group of like-investments. Forecasting net asset values of an investment structure consisting of a massive asset allocation to stocks in various industry group and various types of bond investments, as well as both domestic and international investments, presents a specialized type of financial forecasting problem.

NAV OF A MUTUAL FUND

A mutual fund is an investment vehicle that operates as an investment pool. Initial investors put up pre-arranged amounts and issued shares of the mutual fund, with these shares representing their ownership interest. After the initial issuance, more investors can buy into the mutual fund by buying shares at the per share current net asset value, or total per share NAV. This may be more or less than the original per share NAV, depending on how the investments of the mutual fund have performed. NAV is simply the current total value of the assets of the fund minus any liabilities or management fees divided by the number of shares.

NAV = (current total value of assets − liabilities − management fees)/ number of shares

NAV mutual fund investors follow NAV closely, and some even use an investment strategy of investing in mutual funds, based on the trends in NAV over-time. The study of NAV history is a common practice among sophisticated investors and is considered by many to be one of the best metrics of mutual fund performance.

The value of mutual funds vary over time. Even the best mutual funds have occasionally declined. Many investors study these patterns and make investment decisions on the basis of NAV histories and others just look to invest in funds or managers with good track records in creating rising NAVs.

ASSET ALLOCATION FUND

On a historical basis, the performance of stocks has typically outperformed most of the other investments. However, stock investments carry more risk than many other investment types. Many tout the success of asset allocation in the investment process. Asset allocation investments cut across such investment classes, such as stocks, bonds, and cash, and across international boundaries.

The asset allocation strategy seems to balance risk and reward by apportioning portfolio assets according to individual goals, risk tolerance, and investment horizon. The three main asset classes, equities, fixed-income, and cash and equivalents, all have different levels of risk and return, so each will behave differently over time.

There are no simple methods for indicating the correct allocation for every individual. However, most financial experts agree that asset allocation is a key and crucial decision for investing. The selection of an individual security is secondary to how each investor allocates their investment in stocks, bonds, and cash and cash equivalents.

Some asset allocation mutual funds, typically called life cycle or target date funds, attempt to provide investors with portfolio structures that address the investor's age, risk profile, and investment objective, via an appropriate apportionment of assets among asset classes.

VANGUARD WELLINGTON FUND (VWELX)

Vanguard Wellington funds (VWELX) are one of the few funds that survived the stock market crash of 1929. Vanguard Wellington was created just months before that collapse of the stock market.

As of June 2012, VWELX has assets totaling over $30 billion. Roughly two-third of the portfolio consists of stocks that typically pay dividends. The fund can invest up to 25% of its portfolio in non-US securities.

Typically the fund maintains a balance between relatively conservative stocks and bonds. Thus, it is designed to weather bear markets, but it may not perform as well as more aggressive funds during market rallies. Such a balanced fund is a middle-of-the-road investment that seeks to provide some combination of income, capital appreciation, and conservation of capital by investing in a mix of stocks and bonds. The fund invests in a mix of undervalued and dividend-paying stocks and mostly investment-grade bonds.

MACROECONOMIC ANNOUNCEMENTS AND MONTH END MUTUAL FUND NET ASSET VALUES

Prior research has established the existence of an interrelationship between macroeconomic news and stock market valuations and volatility. This relationship is logical given the assumptions of the Capital Asset Pricing Model, the dividend growth model, and efficient market theory. This study examines the impact of the current state of the economy on the valuation of a portfolio of assets held by a specific mutual fund. Understanding this relationship is important because, as Ewing (2002) observes, the relationship between macroeconomic variables and equity markets crucially impacts strategies formulated by participants in the financial markets. Dropsy (1996), for example, notes that "Economic agents simultaneously optimize their intertemporal allocation of consumption goods and portfolio assets. As a result, excess returns depend on the covariances between asset prices and the marginal utility of consumption." Dropsy (1996) then proceeds to conclude that "The real and financial sides of the economy are thus related."

In order to understand this relationship, we use time series models to predict the end of month net asset values of VWELX using data from January 2010 through December 2011. We then use the model resulting from this data evaluation to forecast NAV for the first three months of 2012. We begin the analytic period with the first quarter of 2010, choosing not to include data for the very volatile economic period from the beginning of what has come to be known as the Great Recession till the end of December 2009. Beginning with January of 2010, then, we follow the fund through the period of recovery. Doing this gives us the ability to view the comovements of economic indicators and the net asset values of VWELX over a more stable but still quite challenging economic environment. Using time series methods enables us to track the changing impact, if any, of changing macroeconomic news on NAV valuations.

We chose to focus on VWELX net asset valuations at month end in order to capture the impact of macroeconomic news on a managed portfolio. Vanguard describes VWELX as "… Vanguard's oldest mutual fund and the nation's oldest balanced fund. It offers exposure to stocks (about two-third of the portfolio) and bonds (one-third). Another key attribute is broad diversification – the fund invests in about 100 stocks and 500 bonds across all economic sectors. This is important because one or two holdings should not have a sizeable impact on the fund. Investors with a long-term time horizon who want growth and are willing to accept stock market volatility may wish to consider this as a core holding in their portfolio." Use of VWELX, therefore, enables us to investigate the impact of key macro-economic variables on a broad portfolio of managed holdings. Vanguard funds are self-billed as low management fee funds, thus the returns on the portfolio will be minimally impacted by management exactions from the assets managed on the investors' behalf.

LITERATURE REVIEW

In this chapter, we focus on statistical methods of selecting the best macroeconomic variables to use in predicting the financial market economy variables, measured through the use of the Vanguard Wellington Index Fund. Results of a study like this, therefore, will impact perceptions of practitioners in the field. Do practitioners, for example, fund managers and institutional investors use this type of information? Conrad and McCafferty (2012) used a survey methodology to examine factors that affected the atti-tudes of UK fund managers and institutional investors toward investment in Japanese equities. Conrad and McCafferty (2012) found that such macro-economic factors, such as economic growth, GDP, deflation, demographics, and the institutional factor of corporate governance were important explanatory factors in explaining the UK fund managers' low enthusiasm for Japanese equities. Loss of enthusiasm for an equities market, as is evident in the Conrad and McCafferty study, necessarily impacts the liquidity of markets. This is especially pertinent for our study given that our initial period begins just over a year after the onset of the financial crisis of 2008, with the severe threats to the banking and financial systems leading to a seize up in the LIBOR and other interbank funding markets. We proceed with our study, therefore, with the expectation that its results will be useful to practitioners in the field, as well as researchers seeking additional tools to evaluate the impact of the so-called real economy on the financial markets.

There is a long record of research that has examined the impact of macroeconomic news on stock returns and volatility. This research has taken place across a wide variety of national settings. Ibrahim and Aziz (2003), for example, applied co-integration and vector auto-regression methodologies (vector autoregression methodology is a very popular methodology in these studies) to monthly data in order to investigate the relationship between stock prices and four macroeconomic variables in Malaysia. The four macroeconomic variables used are – the Consumer Price Index (CPI), a Production Index, the Money supply (M2, as defined in Malaysia at the time of the study), and a measure of the bilateral exchange rate between the Malaysian currency, the Ringgit, and the US dollar. Their exploration used rolling windows to test the sensitivity of the stock market values to macro-economic variables of different ages. They found that different macro-economic variables had differential long-term impacts on stock market prices. The authors note (p. 23), importantly, that "The presence of co-integration between stock prices and macroeconomic variables indicate long-run predictability of the Malaysian equity prices." While this finding seems to contradict the once iconic efficient market theory, it is consistent with results reported elsewhere in this chapter, that macroeconomic variables are predictive of stock prices and returns. Accordingly, understanding the best use of these variables is important in understanding, as Dropsy (1996) put it, the relationship between the real economy and the financial markets.

Madsen (2009) develops a model of stock prices using Tobin's q model of investment. This model is used to shed light on movements of stock prices and dividends in the medium and long run. Madsen argues that, over the long run, "equilibrium in the markets for fixed investment and labour provides a rationale for mean reversion in real share prices and earnings per unit of capital." Madsen's study uses 130 years of macroeconomic data for 22 OECD countries to test his model of mean reversion. Madsen finds, using pooled cross-section and time-series data, that factor shares (i.e., labor and capital income shares) are important determinants of stock prices and ex post stock returns. Further, Madsen finds that the estimated expected income growth coefficient is both statistically and economically significant. He argues that stock prices react strongly to business cycle fluctuations, and by definition, to events in the so-called real economy.

An illustration of the codependence of the financial markets on the status of the real economy, and feedback effects from the status of the financial markets on the real economy (a point not addressed in this study), can be seen in the recent history of the United States. Specifically, we refer to the real economy and financial market events surrounding the financial collapse of 2008. The potential for the seizing up of the financial markets in late 2008 led to a broad retreat from market risk, reflected in the sharp drop in the key US stock market indicators (e.g., the Dow Jones Industrial Index and the S&P 500 Index). Macroeconomic indicators fell as well. Investors fleeing the stock markets in order to avoid risk presaged reduced market liquidity, resulting in falling stock prices as sellers nervously repriced their holdings in search of buyers. Nervous individuals are also likely to reduce discretionary purchases and boost savings, impacting the macroeconomic situation as well. Thus the wealth effect of the sharp stock market plunge may have caused further contraction in the real economy's macroeconomic variable indicators.

Naes, Skjeltorp, and Odegaard (2011), for example, showed that there is a historical relationship between stock market liquidity and the business cycle. They found that investors changed the composition of their portfolios as the business cycle progressed, typically engaging in a flight to quality during economic downturns. Given the changing mixture of bonds and stocks in the VWELX portfolio, as well as the broad stock market representation held by the fund, its use is justified here. Ceteris paribus, bonds are typically seen as safer investments than stock in that they have a terminal (i.e., maturity) date as well as a stream of interest payments until the date of maturity. Stocks, on the other hand, fluctuate according to economic changes that alter the systematic risk of the market and the unique risk attendant upon a particular firm's business activities. The Capital Asset Pricing Model (Sharpe, 1964) argues that greater return is necessarily attendant upon greater risk, assuming relevant information is known to the market. This assumes that investors seek compensation for additional risk. So-called "style investors" may, therefore, self-select themselves into different risk-return categories based on their risk preferences (for a study examining relevant issues, see Kumar, 2010). Mutual fund managers may also have distinct "styles." In a portfolio of significant size and a certain design, however, with substantial diversification, the riskiness of a portfolio may approximate that of all financial assets combined. This argument, and Naes et al.'s (2011) findings, support our use of a managed, balanced fund, VWELX, as the indicator of financial market level.[1]

We chose as our independent variables macroeconomic news announcements in order to capture the market's knowledge of the currently known state of the economy. This information can be used by fund managers, such as the managers of the Wellington Fund, to adjust their portfolio holdings. Others, in addition to Ibrahim and Azis (2003) have also investigated the impact of macroeconomic announcements on equity returns. Arshanapalli, Nelson, and Switzer (2010), for example, investigated the relationship between macro economic announcements, Fama-French factors,[2,3] and equity returns. In their study, Arshanapalli et al. (2010) asked whether Fama-French factors substituted effectively for the news contained in the macroeconomic announcements or whether these announcements added information to that already contained in the Fama-French factors. The authors reported finding that macroeconomic announcements added information not already captured by the Fama-French three factor model, even when supplemented with the momentum factor. In the Arshanapalli et al. (2010) study, daily returns were used, with the information evaluated around the announcement date.

Macroeconomic information releases act to educate investors and fund managers about the risks in the economic environment. Leading economic indicators, for example, may impact the decisions of managers with respect to how much of a non-staple commodity to produce. A substantial, expected to be long-term, rise in the unemployment rate (UR) may lead to a reduction in car production plans. Increase in the Producer Price Index (PPI), on the other hand, may lead to a speed-up in purchases of materials in order to "beat the price rise." Changes in interest rates may have contradictory effects, in part depending on where in the yield curve the change hits. For example, an increase in longer term interest rates may lead to an expectation of further increase in rates, leading to a speed up in home purchase plans in order to avoid mortgage rate increases. Also, in portfolio terms, increase in interest rates, of course, may impact the perceived relative valuation of holding stocks versus bonds as well. On the contrary, while an increase in interest rates may spur quicker acquisition of long-term assets, increase in short-term interest rates, or an expectation thereof, may trigger avoidance of credit card financed purchases, resulting in a slowdown of production of items financed in this way and a consequent release of resources from employment in these sectors. In portfolio terms, changes in interest rates may impact the relative proportion of bonds and stocks held by an investor, or, in this case, VWELX. Success in interpreting the right mix of bonds and stocks to hold may be captured by changes in the NAV of the fund. By exploring the impact of macroeconomic variable announcements on net asset values of a broad index fund, we can gain insight into the relationship of the real economy to the financial markets. To the extent, of course, these relationships change between our initial training sample and the hold out sample, we can gain some indication of whether fund manager learning takes place, that is, the extent to which returns on the out-of-sample period exceed those predictable based on first the in-sample period, and that which would have occurred had the out-of-sample results mirrored substantially the in-sample results.[4]

This discussion points importantly to the riskiness of both bond and stock market investments. Mutual fund managers, for example, must incorporate current information about the future riskiness of the macroeconomic environment in deciding how best to allocate available investment funds. Risk exists in the short run and in the long run. As the perceived riskiness of the economic environment increases, perhaps due to the increased uncertainty that always attends anticipated events at a distance, especially at a far distance, the risk premium built into the interest rate or desired return increases. This riskiness may have both short- and long-term components, a question addressed by Adrian and Rosenberg (2008.). Adrian and Rosenberg (2008) explored cross-sectional pricing of volatility risk. They found that market skewness risk showed up with respect to short-run volatility, while business cycle risk was related to long-run volatility. Du, Denning, and Zhao (2011) examined the impact of market-wide information on stocks. They argued that prior studies which found that stocks "under react" to common information suffered methodological weaknesses, weaknesses which Du et al. (2011) addressed. Their study found that there was a statistically and economically significant stock level reaction to common information. Macroeconomic announcements are an example of such common information, and are relied on here as part of our description of the environment within which investment managers make portfolio decisions, decisions that may result in an enhanced value of the fund or not.

Obviously, investment decisions are made within environments that incorporate both macroeconomic news and political events. Macroeconomic news describes what has happened and acts to shape investor expectations of what *may* happen going forward. Based on discounted cash flow models of stock prices, economic events that suggest future cash flows will be higher than previously thought, and should lead to greater stock prices than before, assuming a constant discount rate. Macroeconomic news, based on the past in most instances, represents one influence on investor expectations. An increase in economic uncertainty may trigger an increase in the market's required discount rate, reducing the stock price at a minimum if we hold the dividend constant (see, for instance, Gordon, 1959) or the earnings constant (for early work on this, see Modigliani & Miller, 1958). The political environment represents another source of uncertainty. The interaction between the political and economic environments is obvious, given the differing interests and purported policy preferences of the two main political parties in the United States. The interplay between the major US political parties raises both the uncertainties and hopes of the investing class. Bohl, Dopke, and Pierdzioch (2008), using a real-time modeling approach and monthly data, demonstrated the usefulness of political stock market anomalies for forecasting excess stock returns. The researchers specifically argue that the investors, in making forecasts, have the problem of "combin[ing], in every month, the then available information on macro-economic, financial and political variables [in order to] forecast ... excess stock returns" (2008, p. 324). Since their study did not show a systematic impact of these variables beyond what was possible with simple trading rules, the authors argued that the usefulness of these variables does not impeach the credibility of the efficient market hypothesis. Based on the limited usefulness of these variables, and our choice of a time period for our study, a study which covers a time period entirely within the presidency of Barack Obama, we do not include political variables here.

As we have seen, risk is a vital component in predicting market valuations. Cover (2011), for example, uses a time series model to examine the association of risk, as measured by Moody's assignment of credit ratings, specifically here a BAA versus a triple A (AAA) spread, with macroeconomic outcomes. Cover (2011) specifically argues that increased risk leads to an increased likelihood of recession and decreased output.[5] Another consequence of increased risk, Cover argues, is that there will be a so-called flight-to-safety, that is, an increase in the holdings of government securities or staying in cash. Other things equal, a consequence of an increase in mutual fund holdings of government securities, or cash, would be a diminishment of yield on the fund. On the other hand, the NAV of the mutual fund faces less risk of decline, but also of increasing relative to where it would have been had it held more risky assets, due to the acquisition and holding of relatively safer, and therefore lower-return, assets. Cover (2011) finds that increases in risk result in an increase in the holdings of real money balances, relative to output. Real money balances generate minimal or no return over time, especially in the minimally inflationary economic environment we base our study within.

He et al. (2010) seek to determine which ex ante factors impact asset pricing and forecasting, and, in doing so, compare the predictions of their econometric model with the Fama and French (1993) three-factor model as well as alternative models. He et al. (2010) note that the CAPM came under research challenge by alternative models, such as Fama and French's three-factor model and the four-factor model of Carhart (1997). These models, He et al. (2010) note, have become the favorite benchmarks used in the empirical asset pricing literature. He et al. (2010) employ the Kalman filter. The latter (p. 708) "repeats a sequence of forecasting and updating as the information set develops" This approach, referred to by HHL as the dynamic factor pricing model, is compared with other asset pricing models, with the result that the dynamic factor pricing model is supported. HHL's tests incorporate both cross-sectional and time series elements. Their examination of the data across time is accomplished by generating dynamic factors as "linear combinations of both contemporaneous and past returns so that they can capture the entire history of the information set" (p. 708). In terms of teasing out the relative effectiveness of the technique that HHL uses, versus the results obtained using FF's three-factor model, HHL note that the dynamic factors they develop are highly serially correlated across successive time periods, although only weakly correlated with each other within a given time frame. This is the reverse of the situation obtaining with the FF three-factor model. He et al. (2010), drawing on Stock and Watson (1989, 1991, both cited in He et al. (2010, p. 709)), note that the latter found that "comovements in observed macroeconomic time series have a common component that can be captured by a single time-varying latent variable." Based on this finding, He et al. (2010) create a multifactor model of stock returns, with the factors based upon a prespecified factor structure. Simin (2008, cited in He et al., 2010) notes that prediction of asset pricing returns can be done simply, in that the historical average return (6% annually or 0.5% monthly) is superior in so-called one-step ahead forecasts to even much more sophisticated models. He et al. (2010) demonstrate that ex ante factors, specifically the book to market value and size factors, are very important in asset pricing and predictions.

Graham, Nikkinen, and Sahlstrom (2003) study the impact of 11 macro-economic announcements on stock valuation. Based on prior literature, they chose announcements of the results for the NAPM: Manufacturing; NAPM: Nonmanufacturing, Employment; Producer Price Index; Retail Sales; Import and Export Price indices; the Consumer Price Index; Real Earnings; Gross Domestic Product; Productivity and Costs; and the Employment Cost Index. In addition, Graham et al. (2003) measured uncertainty using the implied standard deviation, as calculated from options prices. With this data in hand, they used regression analysis to test the impact of the macro-economic variable announcements on implied volatility. The resulting adjusted r^2, with outliers removed, was 0.058, with NAPM: Manufacturing, Employment, PPI, Import and Export Price Indices, Productivity and Costs, and the Employment Cost Index significant at least the 10% significance level. Graham et al. tested the impact of the distance between the timing of the announcement and the volatility index. Specifically, as the timing of the announcement neared, volatility increased. The increase in volatility suggests the increasing relevance to the market of the forthcoming infor-mation release as well as the likely existence of heterogeneous expectations for the numbers to be released.

Brenner, Pasquariello, and Subrahmanyam (2009) also investigated the relationship between the real economy and US financial markets. Brenner et al. specifically looked at the impact of the unexpected information con-tent resident in macroeconomic information releases on both the level and volatility of the US stock, corporate bond, and Treasury instrument markets. They note that investigating the combination of these is certainly not typical of the literature. The specific macroeconomic variables employed in this study include the consumer price index (CPI), the unemployment rate, nonfarm payroll employment, and the target federal funds rate. To test the impact of unexpected macroeconomic information on the US Treasury, corporate bond and US stock volatility and levels, they employed Engle's (2002) multivariate GARCH-DCC model on seven portfolios constructed from these asset classes, covering a period beginning in January 1986 and continuing through February 14, 2002. The GARCH specification is described by Brenner et al. as "among the most widely adopted models that describe time-varying volatility and covariances" (p. 1273). In contrast to our study, however, Brenner et al. examine the differences between expectations for the announcements and the actual announcement. To the extent, of course, that the actual information was unanticipated, that information "surprised" the market. Interestingly, Brenner et al. (2009) found that the stock and bond markets reacted differently to the macro-economic information's arrival. This is of interest here because our study involves the impact of macroeconomic news on a comingled asset, the NAV of a fund which invests in a combination of stocks, bonds, and cash holdings. Brenner et al. (2009) found that conditional stock return volatility was lower before the macroeconomic news release and higher, significantly so, the day of the news' arrival. This was not true of the US bond market, whose prices were unperturbed by surprise information contained in the economic news. These findings are important, as Brenner et al. state (p. 1286), because

> The analysis of the extent to which prices in financial markets incorporate fundamental information is central to the theoretical and empirical finance literature. The traditional notion of market efficiency requires that new information about asset payoffs should be quickly and fully reflected in asset prices and drive their dynamics.

Given the demonstrated relevance of macroeconomic announcements to stock market volatility, the question arises: Which of the many available indicators should be chosen in studies studying this question? Armah and Swanson (2011) address this question. Specifically, they explore which of the many economic indicators used by policy-setters and economic forecasters should be used in research. The Armah and Swanson study does not, in contrast to ours, deal with stock market volatility and stock market levels. Instead, it addresses the question of which of many possible indicators of an economic concept should be used as representative of all the possible indicators of that concept. Accordingly, Armah and Swanson compared the predictive content of various indicators with factor proxies that they chose from various financial and macroeconomic time series. As part of their effort, they used Stock and Watson's (2002, cited in Armah & Swanson, 2011) diffusion index as well as Bai and Ng's (2006) factor proxy methodology. Armah and Swanson chose output growth and inflation as their dependent variables. The researchers reported that a subset of the many financial and macroeconomic variables can usefully serve to proxy for many others. Specifically, Armah and Swanson note that central banks, and their research, rely on real GDP, the CPI, nonfarm payroll employment, housing starts, industrial production/capacity utilization, retail sales, business sales and inventories, advanced durable goods shipments, new orders and unfilled (backlog) orders, lightweight vehicle sales, the yield on 10-year bonds, the S&P 500 stock price index, and the M2 measure of the money supply as tools to use in monitoring economic policy.

We use many of these variables in this study, a study which examines the impact of the real economy on a representative financial market portfolio, as captured in VWELX's end of month net asset values. The Armah and Swanson showing that a subset of all available economic indicators can successfully proxy for the much wider range of indicators available supports our methodological choices of using management science and statistical techniques to winnow out a subset of commonly used predictive variables to a select few, ones shown to have superior predictive power. The authors note, for example, that at the time of their research, there were nine CPI variables, etc., in the available inflation measuring data sets available. Further, the Armah and Swanson finding that macroeconomic variables do best when the inflation forecasts occur in nonvolatile time periods supports our restriction of the time series data used here to the period chosen. Spread variables, by contrast, served well in more volatile economic environments.

It has often been noted that this is the age of globalization, an age when markets are interlinked with the result that macroeconomic events in one major economic power may impact the stock market levels and volatility of other major powers' stock markets. Harju and Hussain (2011), for example, demonstrate the impact of US macroeconomic announcements on the volatility of major European stock index indices. They found that the level of indices volatility on European exchanges increases upon the opening of the US stock market. In addition, surprises in the macroeconomic news released in the United States was also found to have a powerful impact on the intraday returns and volatilities of the European stock markets, with the volatilities and returns measured in 5-minute intraday time segments. While we do not calculate intraday returns surrounding a US macroeconomic announcement, our research demonstrates the longer term impact of the release of US macroeconomic news on the month end net asset valuation of VWELX. As such, given the possibility that one US macroeconomic announcement may fully or partially contradict the momentum information given by another, our test is both more conservative and in that respect more meaningful in helping researchers understand the intersection between the real and the financial economies.

COMPUTATION ANALYSIS OF PREDICTIVE REGRESSION MODELS

The basis of this research was to develop a series of predictive regression models to forecast the NAV of the asset allocation fund VWELX. The regression models were developed from 24 months of data beginning in January 2010 and going through December 2011. The forecasting period of the model is the first three months of 2012.

After analyzing the various sets of regression models based on the set of nine economic and financial variables, the four best models (in terms of R^2

and *s*), developed using different variable selection regression techniques, are the following:

Linear Models:

Model #1 (stepwise)

$$\hat{y} = 65.8 + .14773 \text{ oil} + 36.99 \text{ beta of VWELX}$$
$$s = .770940 \quad R^2_{\text{adj}} = 78.9$$

Model #2 (forward selection)

$$\hat{y} = -5.15 + .0045 \text{ S\&P} + .105 \text{ oil} + 1.88 \text{ beta of VWELX}$$
$$s = .761 \quad R^2_{\text{adj}} = 79.37$$

Quadratic Models:

Model #3 (stepwise/forward selection) same results

$$\hat{y} = 12.42 + .00052 \text{ oil squared} + 25 \text{ beta of VWELX squared}$$
$$s = .768 \quad R^2_{\text{adj}} = 81.45$$

Square Root Model:

Model #4 (stepwise/forward selection)

$$\hat{y} = -42.39 + 2.80 \text{ oil square root} + 58 \text{ beta of VWELX square root}$$
$$s = .765 \quad R^2_{\text{adj}} = 79.18$$

Month	Forecast Errors			
	Model #1	Model #2	Model #3	Model #4
25	−.61242	−.80114	3.451868	.698800
26	.42780	−.14847	4.278704	.062680
27	.39910	−.91390	4.690244	.360880
Sum of errors	.21448	1.86351	12.420800	−.275240

Clearly models #2 and #3 are inferior in terms of sums of error to models #1 and #4. While model #1 has a sum of errors less than model #4 in absolute value terms, it is hard to judge whether model #1 or #4 produces the best forecasts of NAV. Only further study and refitting the models with more recent data will make obvious which model produces better results.

CONCLUSION

We have demonstrated in this study that it is possible to develop a powerful forecast model of financial market asset values, as captured by the asset allocation choices of VWELX, based on widely available macroeconomic variables. The result underlines the findings in other literature of the tie-in between macroeconomic variables and asset valuation levels. The results obtained here, however, did not require use of the complex methods often employed in other financial forecasting studies.

NOTES

1. Use of a fund of the Vanguard Wellington Fund's design, the design of a broad market index fund, permits us to avoid the issues raised by Elton, Gruber, and Blake (2011), issues of how best to select superior mutual funds based on holdings data and security returns. We do note, however, that the responsiveness of NAV values to the macroeconomic environment may be a tool that is useful in isolating mutual fund manager performance from performance occasioned by the macroeconomic environment itself.
2. The three Fama-French risk factors are denoted as MKT, defined as the excess return on the market portfolio; SMB, which is defined as the return on a 0 net investment portfolio that is short in large firms, but long in smaller firms; and HML. The latter is defined as the return on a 0 net investment portfolio that is short in low BTM (Book to Market) firms, but long in high BTM firms.
3. Note that He, Huh, and Lee (2010) describe the Fama-French 3 factor model as one of the most cited in the finance literature.
4. See, for example, Bossert, Füss, Rindler, and Schneider's (2010) article on the information ratio's usefulness in evaluating mutual fund managers. The information ratio is defined by Bossert et al. (2010, p. 67) as "the ratio of excess portfolio return over a specified benchmark, as well as excess return volatility."
5. Note that other research uses stock market volatility as an estimate of risk (e.g., Bloom (2009), as cited in Cover (2011)).

REFERENCES

Adrian, T., & Rosenberg, J. (2008). Stock returns and volatility: Pricing the short-run and long-run components of market risk. *Journal of Finance*, *63*(6), 2997–3030.

Armah, N. A., & Swanson, N. R. (2011). Some variables are more worthy than others: New diffusion index evidence on the monitoring of key economic indicators. *Applied Financial Economics*, *21*, 43–60.

Arshanapalli, B., Nelson, W., & Switzer, L. (2010, August). The effects of macroeconomic announcements on equity returns and their connections to Fama-French factors. *Applied Financial Economics*, *20*(16), 1257–1267.

Bai, J., & Ng, S. (2006). Evaluating latent and observedfactors in macroeconomics and finance. *Journal of Econometrics, 113*, 507–537.

Bloom, N. (2009). The impact of uncertainty shocks. *Econometrica, 77*, 623–685.

Bohl, M. T., Döpke, J., & Pierdzioch, C. (2008, August). Real-time forecasting and political stock market anomalies: Evidence for the United States. *Financial Review, 43*(3), 323–335.

Bossert, T., Füss, R., Rindler, P., & Schneider, C. (2010). How "informative" is the information ratio for evaluating mutual fund managers? *The Journal of Investing, 19*(1), 67–81.

Brenner, M., Pasquariello, P., & Subrahmanyam, M. (2009). On the volatility and comovement of U.S. financial markets around macroeconomic news announcements. *Journal of Financial and Quantitative Analysis, 44*(6), 1265–1289.

Carhart, M. (1997). On persistence in mutual fund performance. *Journal of Finance, 52*, 57–82.

Conrad, H., & McCafferty, J. (2012). United Kingdom fund managers and institutional investors' attitudes toward Japanese equities. *Japanese Economy, 39*(1), 105–130.

Cover, J. P. (2011). Risk and macroeconomic activity. *Southern Economic Journal, 78*(1), 149–166.

Dropsy, V. (1996). Do macroeconomic factors help in predicting international equity risk premia? Testing the out-of-sample accuracy of linear and nonlinear forecasts. *Journal of Applied Business Research, 12*(3), 120–132.

Du, D., Denning, K., & Zhao, X. (2011). Evidence on stock reaction to market-wide information. *Review of Pacific Basin Financial Markets & Policies, 14*(2), 297–325.

Elton, E. J., Gruber, M. J., & Blake, C. R. (2011). Holdings data, security returns, and the selection of superior mutual funds. *Journal of Financial and Quantitative Analysis, 46*(2), 341–367.

Engle, R. (2002). Dynamic conditional correlation: A simple class of multivariate generalized autoregressive conditional heteroskedasticity models. *Journal of Business and Economic Statistics, 20*, 339–350.

Ewing, B. T. (2002). Macroeconomic news and the returns of financial companies. *Managerial and Decision Economics, 23*, 439–446.

Fama, E., & French, K. (1993). Common risk factors on the returns of stocks and bonds. *Journal of Financial Economics, 33*, 3–56.

Federal Reserve Bank of St. Louis (FRED). (2012). Retrieved from http://www.stlouisfed.org/. Accessed on November 2, 2012.

Gordon, M. J. (1959). Dividends, earnings and stock prices. *Review of Economics and Statistics, 41*(2), 99–105. (The MIT Press).

Graham, M., Nikkinen, J., & Sahlstrom, P. (2003). Relative importance of scheduled macroeconomic news for stock market investors. *Journal of Economics and Finance, 27*(2), 153–165.

Harju, K., & Hussain, S. M. (2011). Intraday seasonalities and macroeconomic news announcements. *European Financial Management, 17*(2), 367–390.

He, Z., Huh, S.-W., & Lee, B.-S. (2010). Dynamic factors and asset pricing. *Journal of Financial and Quantitative Analysis, 45*(3), 707–737.

Ibrahim, M. H., & Aziz, H. (2003). Macroeconomic variables and the Malaysian equity market: A view through rolling subsamples. *Journal of Economic Studies, 30*(1), 6–27.

Kumar, A. (2010). Dynamic style preferences of individual investors and stock returns. *Journal of Financial and Quantitative Analysis, 44*(3), 607–640.

Madsen, J. B. (2009). The macroeconomics of stock prices in the medium term and in the long run. *The Manchester School, 77*, 127–152.

Modigliani, F., & Miller, M. (1958). The cost of capital, corporation finance and the theory of investment. *American Economic Review, 48*(3), 261–297.

Næs, R., Skjeltorp, J. A., & Ødegaard, B. A. (2011, February). Stock market liquidity and the business cycle. *Journal of Finance, 66*(1), 139–176.

Sharpe, W. F. (1964). Capital asset prices: A theory of market equilibrium under conditions of risk. *Journal of Finance, 19*(3), 425–442.

Simin, T. (2008). The poor predictive performance of asset pricing models. *Journal of Financial and Quantitative Analysis, 43*, 355–380.

Stock, J., & Watson, M. (2002). Macroeconomic forecasting using diffusion indexes. *Journal of Business and Economic Statistics, 20*, 147–161.

Stock, J. H., & Watson, M. W. (1989). New indexes of coincident and leading economic indicators. In O. J. Blanchard & S. Fischer (Eds.), *NBER Macroeconomics Annual* (pp. 351–394). Cambridge, MA: MIT Press.

Stock, J. H., & Watson, M. W. (1991). A probability model of the coincident economic indicators. In K. Lahiri & G. H. Moore (Eds.), *Leading economic indicators: New approaches and forecasting records* (pp. 63–89). Cambridge, UK: Cambridge University Press.

APPENDIX

Description of Macroeconomic Variables for 2010–2012.

FRED'S Variable Name	Description	Source	Unit of Measure	Reporting Frequency	Seasonal Adjustment
GDP	Gross Domestic Product, 1 decimal	US Dept. of Commerce: Bureau of Economic Analysis	Billions of dollars	Quarterly	Seasonally adjusted
UNEMP	Unemployment rate – Full-time workers	US Bureau of Labor Statistics	Percent	Monthly	Seasonally adjusted
OILPRICE	Spot oil price: West Texas intermediate	Dow Jones & Co.	Dollars per barrel	Monthly	Not adjusted
UNRATE	Civilian unemployment rate	US Bureau of Labor Statistics	Percent	Monthly	Seasonally adjusted

PART III
METHODS

APPLYING TECHNOLOGY FORECASTING TO NEW PRODUCT DEVELOPMENT TARGET SETTING OF LCD PANELS

Dong-Joon Lim, Neil Runde and
Timothy R. Anderson

ABSTRACT

This chapter illustrates the Technology Forecasting using Data Envelopment Analysis (TFDEA) process on Liquid Crystal Display (LCD) performance characteristics from 1997 to 2012. The objective of this study is to forecast future state-of-the-arts (SOAs) specifications as well as to diagnose past technological advancement of the LCD industry. Appropriate characteristics were determined from a group of LCD technologists. Data was gathered from public databases and outlying data points were cross-referenced as a validity check. The TFDEA process is defined and its application to the dataset is described in detail. The results not only provide information on how LCD industry has evolved but also provide an insight on future NPD targets.

Keywords: Technology forecasting (TF); data envelopment analysis (DEA); new product development (NPD); state-of-the-art (SOA); liquid crystal display (LCD)

Advances in Business and Management Forecasting, Volume 9, 137–152
ISSN: 1477-4070/doi:10.1108/S1477-4070(2013)0000009012

INTRODUCTION

Since the 1970s, Liquid Crystal Display (LCD) technology moved from small displays such as watches to large scale televisions/public displays. As performance demands increased, demands on manufacturing managers to plan and deliver competitive products have also increased (Craig, 2004). As demand for mobile computing and high-definition video standards took hold, worldwide sales of LCD and plasma displays increased dramatically along with decreases in unit cost. At the same time, businesses began replacing Cathode Ray Tube technology-based computer monitors with LCD displays (Take, 2003). The range of display technology is vast and the technologies are ever changing (see Fig.1) (Takiguchi, 1999).

The increasing demands pressed flat panel manufacturers to invest in larger sizes, greater resolution, and color/contrast improvements. LCD manufacturers have planning teams to forecast future LCD performance characteristics to remain competitive. Marketing companies track LCD technology trends using internal analysis. Often, advancements are constrained by external issues (i.e., broadcast standard adoption rates) that inhibit throughput or manufacturing limitations. An example of this is how LCDs are cut from "mother glass" with well-defined size constraints and do not improve in size in a continuous fashion, but increase in a step-wise mode. Weight or power usage can be improved continuously (HP, 2008).

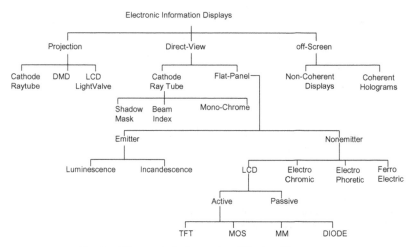

Fig. 1.   Electronic Information Display Taxonomy.

RESEARCH GOALS AND DESIGN CONSTRAINTS

Overall Research Aims

The objective of this research is to determine changing patterns in the LCD image quality and physical device characteristics to forecast future values of similar products.

Projection Horizon Goals

A "panel" of industry experts at a major flat panel manufacturer was interviewed to determine benchmark characteristics used for performance measurements. Modeling data to produce projections from 2012 to 2017 was determined by the best match to actual industry planning timeframes.

Historical Data Boundary

The history of LCD technologies goes back to the 1960s, however, 1997 was used as the starting point for this study because of the critical mass of larger (> 15″) LCD products were available in the market. This represented a point where LCD products moved beyond mobile computing and was of the most interest to our panel of experts.

Type of Displays Considered

As shown in Fig. 1, there is a range of technology options for electronic information displays. This chapter focuses on Direct-View, Flat Panel, Non-emitter, Active, and Thin-Film technologies which represent the bulk of high-definition televisions and computer monitors.

Units Measured

Working with industry experts, a list of fundamental attributes representing the core tradeoffs between products was developed. Data collected included the following:

- Release Date: (year)
- Screen Size: (inches) measured diagonally

- Bezel Size: (millimeters) derived by subtracting the beginning of the active area from the outside shell measurement
- Weight: (kilograms)
- Resolution: (pixels) horizontal times vertical resolution
- Viewing Angle (degrees)
- Contrast Ratio: (lumens) difference between 0 and 100% energized pixel(s) (Learn About LCD TV and TFT LCD Displays, 2012).

ANALYSIS

Data Gathering

Panelook.com provided two-thirds of the research data and the rest of it were collected from online scanned manuals and various other sources including review sites. Statistical outliers were verified from secondary sources and removed if unconfirmed. In order to sample the full range of data, the authors searched criteria filtered on upper, middle, or low bounds on target characteristics. Derivative products of base-models that did not add to usable differences were removed from the dataset. There were 389 models, with diagonal screen sizes ranging from 14 to 108″, in the final data set from 20 manufacturers from 1997 to 2012 (see sample data in Table 1).

Method

Modern benchmarking analyses frequently use frontier analysis (or best practice) methods. The idea is to model the frontier of the technology rather than to model the average use of the technological possibilities (Bogetoft & Otto, 2010). This approach has a strong advantage in learning from the best

Table 1. Sample Data.

Manufacturer	Product	Release Date	Screen Size	Bezel Size	Weight	Resolution	Viewing Angle	Contrast Ratio
NEC	EA192M	1997	19	43.18	3.52	1,310,720	170	1,000
AUO	T370HW01 V0	2004	37	75.44	10.00	2,073,600	178	800
Samsung	LTI700HD01-006	2012	70	80.56	45.00	2,073,600	178	2,400

rather than being influenced by the inclusion of mediocre performers. Since its founding in 1978 (Charnes, Cooper, & Rhodes, 1978), Data Envelopment Analysis (DEA), has been widely used as a frontier model for organizational benchmarking (Seiford, 1996). In 2001 it was extended to examine product-oriented performance by extending Moore's Law to a wider set of performance indicators and termed TFDEA (Technology Forecasting using DEA) (Anderson, Fare, Grosskopf, Inman, & Song, 2002). It has since been applied to a wide range of industries including battle tanks (Kim, Kim, & Kim, 2007), fighter jets (Inman, Anderson, & Harmon, 2006), disk drives (Inman, 2004), telecommunications protocols (Anderson, Daim, & Kim, 2008; Kim, Daim, & Anderson, 2010; Lim, Anderson, & Kim, 2012), and commercial airplanes (Lamb, Anderson, & Daim, 2012).

TFDEA is able to leverage DEA's natural ability to handle rich models and applications in terms of flexibly handling both multiple inputs and multiple outputs. This is particularly important in the case of technology forecasting and new product development because the tradeoffs between product characteristics can vary by manufacturer, by market segment, and over time.

Fig. 2 summarizes this model procedure. Briefly, x_{ik} represents the ith input and y_{rk} represents the rth output of technology k. The variables for the linear program underlying DEA are λ_{jk} and $\phi_k^{t_f}$ The variable $\phi_k^{t_f}$ also serves as the objective function and represents the amount of output which should be generated by technology k at time period t_f if it were state-of-the-art at that time. The variable λ_{jk} describes how much of technology j is used in setting a target of performance for technology k. Details of TFDEA procedures can be found in original research (Inman, 2004).

TFDEA can be conducted in two stages – model validation and actual extrapolation. Specifically, parameters to be used for the TFDEA model are determined in the first stage and future state-of-the-arts specifications of LCD products are estimated in the second stage.

Model Validation

Fig. 3 illustrates the model validation process to determine an appropriate model for the LCD industry. Since TFDEA measures technological superiority using an efficiency framework, suitable characteristics of LCD products need to be determined as input(s) and output(s) values. As in other recent forecasting techniques' applications, "Backtesting," was used to validate the effectiveness of forecasting model by running the current model up to a

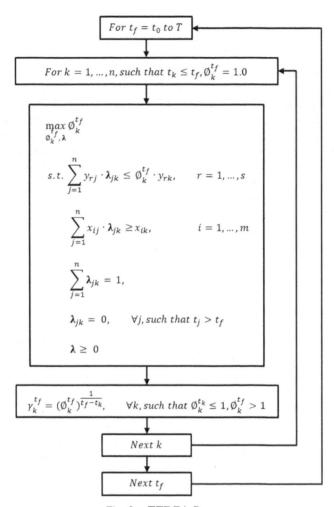

Fig. 2.   TFDEA Process.

certain point in time and calculating how it would have performed had it actually been applied in the past. It was adopted to compare the accuracy of different models (Rösch, 2005). This backtesting procedure is analogous to using a holdout sample to validate a more traditional statistical model. Therefore, it is necessary to determine a proper point of time to divide the dataset. Finally, TFDEA parameters including orientation (input/output), returns to scale (RTS) (constant returns to scale/variable return to scale/

nonincreasing return to scale/nondecreasing return to scale), and frontier (static/dynamic) are selected using this process.

Fig. 4 shows characteristics identified from the model validation process. As bezel size and weight tend to be proportional to screen size, normalized specifications, namely per-inch data, are used as inputs. For the output variables, screen size, pixel number, and contrast ratio were used to define the fundamental characteristics of display performance in terms of forecasting purpose.

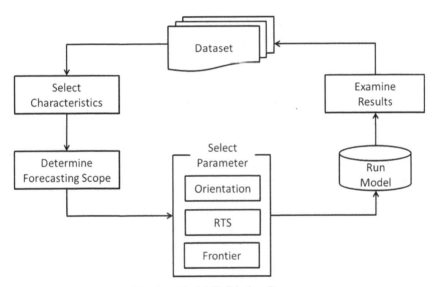

Fig. 3. Model Validation Process.

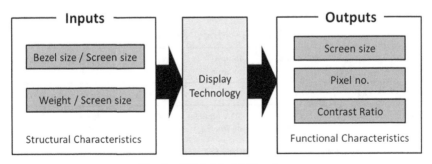

Fig. 4. DEA Model Structure.

Ideally, manufacturing cost should be included as an input but this is typically very difficult to include for many reasons:

- Each company has different ways of calculating cost and cost allocation methods.
- Cost is typically a rapidly decreasing value based on yield and learning, so a particular value in time would be needed.
- Different factories may be used for the same product with different cost functions.
- International currency fluctuations make it difficult to compare.
- Actual costs are confidential and therefore not available in industry publications.

In place of costs, a product price such as list price, manufacturer suggested retail price, or average selling price is sometimes used as a proxy for cost. Unfortunately, neither cost nor price was consistently available for the range of products.

Table 2 summarizes details of the analyzed model and results. A range of options was tested and the model was selected on the basis of characteristics of the application and accuracy in the validation stage.

TFDEA allows either static frontier or dynamic frontier to be used. The frontier year is a measure of the products that are being used to be compared against. For example, assume a 2005 LCD panel is being compared against panels from 2007 and earlier. The best comparisons for this product might be a combination of panels from 2006 and 2007. The static frontier year would use a fixed date of 2007 while a dynamic frontier year uses a combination of the dates of the products (2006 and 2007) such as 2006.5. In this application, a static frontier was used.

Table 2. Model Results.

Frontier Type	Orientation	2nd Goal	Return to Scale	Avg. RoC	Frontier Year	MAD
Static	OO	N/A	VRS	1.169682	2007	1.891382
Input(s)	Output(s)	SOA products at release	SOA products on frontier	RoC contributors	Release before forecast	Release after forecast
2	3	88	7	30	9	76

Orientation can be either input-oriented or output-oriented and can be best thought of as whether the primary goal is "input-reducing" or "output-augmenting." While both screen performance and reducing bulkiness are important, in this time period, the LCD industry is better characterized as being driven by improving screen performance taking priority over making designs lighter and more compact. Therefore, an output orientation was selected for this application but a future study might find an input orientation a better fit if improving screen performance takes a back seat to bulkiness reduction. Hence, the model evaluates technologies based on how much advancement of outputs was produced using the same level of inputs.

DEA allows for various returns to scale assumptions. The most common are variable returns to scale (VRS) and constant returns to scale (CRS). Using CRS implies that for an actual product, a doubling of each of the inputs should result in a feasible product with double each of the outputs. In our application, doubling the inputs of the LCD panel does not correspond to a realistic design with double the outputs. Therefore, a VRS model was selected.

Average Rate of Change (Avg RoC) was found to be 1.169682, which means the overall performance of LCD products has improved by an average of 17% a year. Fig. 5 displays the annualized pattern of RoC over time. Gamma values indicate the progress in a product's performance in the current year as compared to the previous year. The rate fluctuates from year to year, and in each year we can see which products had the largest advance. From 1997 to 2012, LCD products from Samsung and LG dominated the rate-of-change list (2004 and 2005 technologies were annualized by other

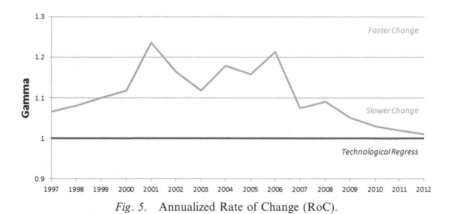

Fig. 5. Annualized Rate of Change (RoC).

Table 3.   Top 5 Rate-of-Change Products.

Rank	Release Year	Model	Producer	Rate of Change
1	2006	LM240WU2-SLB2	LG	1.555610
2	2006	LTM270M1-L01	Samsung	1.322629
3	2005	LTM240M1-L01	Samsung	1.303089
4	2004	LM300W01-A3	LG	1.245964
5	2001	SyncMaster 180T	Samsung	1.236020

mediocre technologies). The years of 2001 and 2006 had the fastest rates of change. This can be explained by breakthrough technologies introduced during those times (see Table 3).

The frontier year was defined as 2007 which means the dataset was divided into two groups. The first had LCD panels included from 1997 up to and including 2007. The second set was used for backtesting to see how well the results from 1997–2007 forecasted the 2008–2012 data for validation purposes. This was a challenge due to the slowing rate of change shown in Fig. 5.

The mean absolute deviation, MAD, was 1.89 years. Hence, it is expected that there could be a 22-month error when this forecasting model is applied to LCD industry from 2007.

Lower row of Table 2 shows the number of display technologies captured from the model; 2 inputs and 3 outputs characteristics were chosen for the model.

This model found that 88 out of 389 products were state-of-the-art when they were introduced. The non-state-of-the-art products are ones that were surpassed by a product or a combination of products.

Seven products were identified as state-of-the-art in 2007. Thirty products (out of 88 state-of-the-arts) were taken into account when the model calculated the average rate of change because they used to be state-of-the-art when they were released in the market but have been superseded by products released afterwards. In other words, TFDEA tries to capture this obsolescence process to measure the technology advancement.

The forecast result of backtesting shows that 9 products were released before the forecast, and 76 products were released after the forecast. This is consistent with the industry perception that the technology advancement has been slowing down (Tsai, 2012). Fig. 6 shows detailed results of this forecasting. Since the dataset was divided into two parts for backtesting, the model forecasted post-2007 products based on the RoC identified from

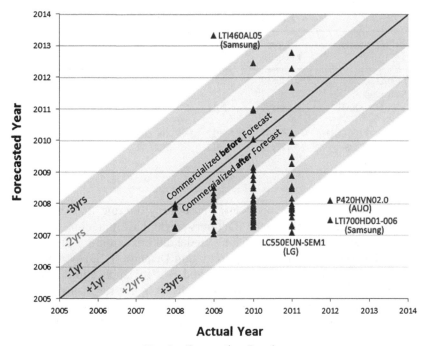

Fig. 6.   Forecasting Results.

up-through-2007 technologies. As seen in the figure, some technologies are on the diagonal line which denotes perfect forecasting. Furthermore, most of forecasts are within ±3 years range (note that mean absolute deviation is 1.891382, namely, 22 months).

Fig. 6 has four products with large forecast deviations from actual release dates; Table 4 provides more information on these products. The first model, "LTI460AL05," came out much earlier than expected and warranted attention. It had a 7.65 mm Bezel, which was much thinner than peers in 2009 (50.90 mm). The model forecasted that this level of technology (particularly a bezel this thin while maintaining the performance) would take more than 6 years from 2007 considering the average rate of change. However, it actually took only 2 years to introduce this product in the market.

On the other hand, three models came out later than were expected given their specifications. All three, "LC550EUN-SEM1," "P420HVN02.0," and "LTI700HD01-006," had relatively low contrast ratios (1400) and heavy screens (0.64 and 0.23). Therefore, they were introduced later than forecasted

Table 4. Examining Outliers.

Model (Producer)	Super Efficiency	Release Year	Forecasted Year	Error	Distinctive Feature
LTI460AL05 (Samsung)	0.370872	2009	2013.33	−4.33	Ultra-thin Bezel
LC550EUN-SEM1 (LG)	0.984897	2011	2007.10	+3.90	Low contrast ratio
P420HVN02.0 (AUO)	0.842535	2012	2008.09	+3.91	Heavy screen
LTI700HD01-006 (Samsung)	0.927418	2012	2007.48	+4.52	Heavy screen

by the model. However, this doesn't necessarily indicate that those were inferior products. Rather, manufacturers might have put more emphasis on other features that the forecasting model did not capture. For example, LTI700HD01-006 was a Digital Information Displays (DID) system which was aimed at outdoor digital signage and e-board applications requiring high reliability and robustness. In hindsight, it is not surprising that this product appears "obsolete" at time of release relative to the mainstream, indoor-oriented products. This product could be deleted from the analysis with no impact other than improving MAD (Table 4).

NPD Target Setting

With the model selected from validation process, future state-of-the-art products can be readily extrapolated. Since the model is using output oriented measurement, the simplest way is to multiply current output characteristics by average rate of change (1.169682) assuming constant input characteristics. Table 5 presents projected future state-of-the-arts from 2013 (+ 1 yr) to 2017 (+ 5 yrs) with bezel size/screen size of 1.06 and weight/screen size of 0.28. Conversely, if one wants to know when a specific level of technology can be realized as a state-of-the-art, expected time can be calculated by measuring gap between current level of technology and target specifications.

In order to facilitate planning such as focusing R&D resources on certain output performance, further application that can consider trade-offs among the output characteristics is also possible. This uses the inverse-DEA process to place a virtual product on the frontier line with given efficient, namely, state-of-the-art products.

Table 5. Projected SOAs Considering Concurrent Improvement.

Year	Screen Size (Inches)	Resolution (Megapixel)	Contrast Ratio (Luminance Ratio)
2012 (current)	41.25	2.679	2,133
2013 (+1 yr)	48.25	3.134	2,495
2014 (+2 yrs)	56.44	3.666	2,919
2015 (+3 yrs)	66.01	4.288	3,414
2016 (+4 yrs)	77.21	5.016	3,993
2017 (+5 yrs)	90.32	5.867	4,671

Table 6. Alternate 2017 SOAs Projections.

Screen size (Inches)	Resolution (Megapixel)	Contrast Ratio (Luminance Ratio)
56.93	2.189	11,385
	4.379	11,320
	6.568	10,509
	8.758	8,539
	10.947	6,678
87.58	2.189	9,196
	4.378	9,130
	6.568	8,758
	8.758	8,101
	10.947	6,658
109.47	2.189	6,787
	4,379	6,678
	6.568	6,131
	8.758	5,693
	10.947	5,036
131.37	1.095	3,941
	2.189	3,613
	4.379	3,722
	6.568	3,284

Table 6 presents diverse ranges of future state-of-the-arts specifications in 2017 (+ 5 yrs) from this process. Since each column combination can represent a state-of-the-art specification, a new product a developer may be able to get benefit from this virtual design concept when he/she tries to propose new product design.

The trend toward larger screen sizes has been very visible throughout the consumer television industry over the last decade. Table 6 allows us to examine what is expected to be state-of-the-art in 2017 for these different screen sizes. The screen sizes are similar to what might be expected for high-end home theater or certain commercial applications. The resolution values can be considered to be similar to certain video standards. For example, 1080p is currently the most common native resolution for HD televisions and is $1{,}920 \times 1{,}080$ or 2.07 megapixels. WQXGA is a higher resolution format currently used in computer monitors and is $2{,}560 \times 1{,}600$ or 4.1 megapixels. A less common format is referred to as 4K and is $4{,}096 \times 3{,}072$ or 12.6 megapixels.

Table 6 indicates that for a 57″ class HD television with resolution similar to WQXGA, the expected contrast ratio should be 11,320. Product designers could then evaluate their designs based on these specifications. If their contrast ratio is much greater, they are likely to have a product that outperforms competitors. If their contrast ratio is much lower, they should make clear why this product is different from the mass market – similar to the outdoor LCD panel discussed earlier.

LIMITATIONS AND FUTURE RESEARCH

Selection of inputs and outputs for any model is always a challenge. It is important to work with industry experts in selecting a model that balances the needs of the users, the fundamental tradeoffs in the product, data accuracy, and data availability. This model emphasized functional characteristics but could be further refined in future work with the addition of some form or proxy of manufacturing cost. Similarly, longevity (particularly for the backlights), connectivity, and power consumption are important to many buyers and could also be added in future work. It was expressed to the authors by the expert panel that contrast ratio published numbers can be "unreliable" as marketing departments take undue liberties despite attempts to create a standardized measure.

As the LCD market matures, the technologies across the specifications measured in the study are slowing down. As a result, LCD manufacturers are looking at other areas for differentiation such as display translucency, display tiling, adding computing/storage capability, or physically flexing the electronics. Adding these or other features might demonstrate greater growth or frequency of change.

Another analysis to consider would be a report on the slowing rate of change in performance characteristics and a declining sales of LCD and whether there is a relationship.

Because the average living room is limited in size and most likely will not increase significantly in the next 5 years, it seems unlikely that LCD panel sizes can continue to differentiate based on size. Innovations in other areas seem likely to increase in number and magnitude. An analysis of the market looking for this phenomenon and how the manufacturers respond might be of interest.

Further analytical refinements could be applied in future work to allow for varying rates of change. In fact, the analysis used the rate of change value (gamma) from the backtesting analysis period (1997–2007) when the industry was undergoing rapid change. Including rates of change as the industry slowed down would result in less aggressive targets for Table 6. Lastly, while TFDEA is an extreme point technique that is insensitive to poor performing products, excluding special purpose products such as outdoor displays that appear obsolete by the standards of the mainstream market would improve the diagnostics such as MAD.

CONCLUSIONS

The modeling technique generated results consistent what has been observed in the LCD market in general as components become more commoditized. The innovations in the targeted attributes are slowing down and a few of these are reaching market acceptability limits (screen size) and usefulness limit (beyond the eyes ability to distinguish resolutions). Therefore, emerging features such as refresh rate, built-in interactivity, wireless connectivity, or cloud display system, will have to be adopted as a new dimension of competition.

REFERENCES

Anderson, T. R., Daim, T. U., & Kim, J. (2008). Technology forecasting for wireless communication. *Technovation, 28*(9), 602–614.

Anderson, T. R., Fare, R., Grosskopf, S., Inman, L., & Song, X. (2002). Further examination of Moore's law with data envelopment analysis. *Technological Forecasting and Social Change, 69*(5), 465–477.

Bogetoft, P., & Otto, L. (2010). *Benchmarking with DEA, SFA, and R* (1st ed.), p. 367. New York, NY: Springer.

Charnes, A., Cooper, W. W., & Rhodes, E. (1978). Measuring the efficiency of decision making units. *European Journal of Operational Research, 2*(6), 429–444.
Craig, Z. (2004). LCD TV panels: A history of their interface technology. *Electronic Design.* Retrieved from http://electronicdesign.com/article/components/lcd-tv-panels-a-history-of-their-interface-technol. Accessed on June 11, 2012.
HP. (2008). *Contrast ratio – What does it really mean?* Hewlett-Packard Development Company, L.P. (U.S).
Inman, O. L. (2004). *Technology forecasting using data envelopment analysis.* PhD dissertation. Portland State University, Portland, OR, USA.
Inman, O., Anderson, T., & Harmon, R. (2006). Predicting U.S. jet fighter aircraft introductions from 1944 to 1982: A dogfight between regression and TFDEA. *Technological Forecasting and Social Change, 73*(9), 1178–1187.
Kim, J., Daim, T., & Anderson, T. (2010). A look into the future of wireless mobile communication technologies. *Technology Analysis & Strategic Management, 22*(8), 925–943.
Kim, J.-O., Kim, J.-H., & Kim, S.-K. (2007). A comparative study of technological forecasting methods with the case of main battle tank by ranking efficient units in DEA. *Korea Defense Management Analysis Society, 33*(2), 61–73.
Lamb, A.-M., Anderson, T. R., & Daim, T. (2012). Research and development target-setting difficulties addressed through the emergent method: Technology forecasting using data envelopment analysis. *R & D Management, 42*(4), 15.
Learn About LCD TV and TFT LCD Displays. (2012). Retrieved from http://www.ercservice.com/learning/fabricating-tft-lcd.html
Lim, D.-J., Anderson, T. R., & Kim, J. (2012). Forecast of wireless communication technology: A comparative study of regression and TFDEA Model. In *Technology Management for Emerging Technologies, 2012 Proceedings of PICMET '12.* Vancouver, Canada.
Rösch, D. (2005). An empirical comparison of default risk forecasts from alternative credit rating philosophies. *International Journal of Forecasting, 21*(1), 37–51.
Seiford, L. M. (1996, July). Data envelopment analysis: The evolution of the state of the art (1978–1995). *Journal of Productivity Analysis, 7*(2–3), 99–137.
Take, H. (2003). Market and technological trends in LCD TVs. *Sharp Technical Journal, 85,* 42–44.
Takiguchi, H. (1999). Technology-development trend of liquid crystal display. *Sharp Technical Journal, 74,* 5–11.
Tsai, B.-H. (2012). Predicting the diffusion of LCD TVs by incorporating price in the extended Gompertz Model. *Technological Forecasting and Social Change, 80*(1), 106–131.

HYBRID NEURAL NETWORK MODEL IN FORECASTING AGGREGATE U.S. RETAIL SALES

Youqin Pan, Terrance Pohlen and Saverio Manago

ABSTRACT

Retail sales usually exhibit strong trend and seasonal patterns. Practitioners have typically used seasonal autoregressive integrated moving average (ARIMA) models to predict retail sales exhibiting these patterns. Due to economic instability, recent retail sales time-series data show a higher degree of variability and nonlinearity, which makes the ARIMA model less accurate. This chapter demonstrates the feasibility and potential of applying empirical mode decomposition (EMD) in forecasting aggregate retail sales. The hybrid forecasting method of integrating EMD and neural network (EMD-NN) models was applied to two real data sets from two different time periods. The one-period ahead forecasts for both time periods show that EMD-NN outperforms the classical NN model and seasonal ARIMA. In addition, the findings also indicate that EMD-NN can significantly improve forecasting performance during the periods in which macroeconomic conditions are more volatile.

Keywords: Empirical mode decomposition; ARIMA; artificial neural network; retail sales forecasting; time-series analysis

Advances in Business and Management Forecasting, Volume 9, 153–170
Copyright © 2013 by Emerald Group Publishing Limited
All rights of reproduction in any form reserved
ISSN: 1477-4070/doi:10.1108/S1477-4070(2013)0000009013

INTRODUCTION

Forecasting plays an important role in effective operations and other business decisions (Hansen & Nelson, 2003). Accurate forecasts of future retail sales are critical to strategic planning and operational decisions (Chu & Zhang, 2003). A poor forecast usually leads to either too-much or too-little stock, which results in revenue loss and further jeopardizes a firm's competitive position (Agrawal & Schorling, 1996). For retail business and retail supply chains, accurate forecasting has been attributed to successful supply chain operations and coordination (Chopra & Meindl, 2007; Lee, Padmanabhan, & Whang, 1997). However, retail sales forecasting is a challenging task especially during periods of economic instability. The fall of 2008 showed a significant drop in customer demand, which forced firms to guess about the demand for their products. In fact, according to a report by the US Census Bureau and National Retail Federation, US retailers are losing more than 200 billion dollars a year due to large forecasting errors (Kumar & Patel, 2010). Thus, retail sales forecasting during periods of economic instability is more critical and more important for profitable retail operations.

In literature, various traditional methods are available for forecast-ing aggregate retail sales. For instance, Winter's exponential smoothing, Box–Jenkin's auto regressive integrated moving averages (ARIMA) model, and multiple linear regression have been used in forecasting retail sales. Alon (1997) found that the Winters models' forecasts for aggregate retail sales were more accurate than simple exponential and Holt's models. Alon, Qi, and Sadowski (2001) concluded that linear models such as Winter's exponential smoothing and ARIMA perform well during stable economic conditions. However, these traditional models assume that a linear correlation structure exists among time series values and work well under the assumption that the time series is stationary. Unfortunately, retail sales exhibit strong trend and seasonal patterns, which are nonstationary. Additionally, a lot of nonlinearity or irregularity is expected in retail time series due to the current volatile economic environment. Research indicates that economic forecasters made their largest prediction errors during reces-sion periods (Zarnowitz & Braun, 1993). The recessions in the US economy challenge the assumptions used in most forecasting methods including ARIMA (Hansen & Nelson, 2003), which fail to capture the nonlinear and irregular economic activities in the economy. If traditional forecasting methods are applied to the nonlinear time series, greater forecasting errors incur when the forecasting horizon increases (Wu & Lau, 2011). Therefore, these traditional models are not expected to effectively capture the nonlinear relationships in retail sales.

To overcome this limitation, neural networks (NN) have predominantly been utilized to improve retail sales prediction. The NN model is a data-driven nonparametric method which offers an alternative for better capturing dynamic nonlinear activities in a time series. Unlike the traditional forecasting methods, no prior assumptions about the underlying patterns in the data are required in the model building process. The significant advantages of NN models over other classes of nonlinear models are based on the NN model's ability to approximate a large class of functions with a high degree of accuracy (Khashei & Bijari, 2012). There have been many successful applications of NN models in time series forecasting (Kuan & Liu, 1995; Schoneburg, 1990). Hill, O'Connor, and Remus (1996) showed that ANNs significantly outperform traditional forecasting models when forecasting quarterly and monthly data. In the area of aggregate retail sales forecasting, Chu and Zhang (2003) demonstrated that the NN models with deseasonalized time series data are superior to the other models examined in their study. They also reported that nonlinear models outperformed their linear counterparts in out-of-sample forecasting. However, direct NN model's performance is worse than the performance of corresponding ARIMA models as almost all predicated values are relatively far below the actual values. Prior studies found that NN are not able to directly model seasonality and that data pre-processing (such as pre-desesonalization) is necessary to achieve improvement of forecasting accuracy (Nelson, Hill, Remus, & O'Connor, 1999). Zhang and Qi (2002) explained that the interaction of the trend movement and seasonal fluctuations in the retail sales data may cause NN models to fail in generating accurate forecasts. Thus, it was suggested that a combined approach of detrending and deseasonalization would be the efficient way for getting the best forecasting result.

Modeling seasonal and trend time series has been a main research endeavor for decades. The seasonal ARIMA model is one of the most powerful forecasting methods among the linear forecasting methods. However, seasonal ARIMA is not aiming at capturing nonlinearity in the retail sales time series. On the other hand, NN models are good at identifying nonlinear relationships in a time series, but the accuracy of NN models is adversely affected by seasonality (Kuvulmaz, Usanmaz, & Engin, 2005; Zhang & Qi, 2005) and noise (Hsieh, Hsiao, & Yeh, 2011) in the time series. There is no universal best forecasting model under all conditions, yet, recent research demonstrated that hybrid models are both interesting and promising in the area of forecasting (Hsieh et al., 2011; Khashei & Bijari, 2012). Thus, in order to improve the forecasting accuracy of retail sales, researchers could consider the use of a certain decomposition scheme to further enhance their original methods and use hybrid models to forecast aggregate retail sales.

This chapter intends to propose hybrid NN models which maintain the advantages of the NN models while reducing their drawbacks so that the accuracy of the retail sales forecasting can be improved. In recent years, the empirical mode decomposition (EMD), introduced by Huang, Shen, and Long (1998), has yielded encouraging results in the area of engineering such as image processing and fault diagnosis. EMD is an empirical and adaptive data-driven approach. It is better in dealing with nonlinear and nonstationary data. Using EMD, any complex raw data can be decomposed into a small number of independent and almost periodic intrinsic modes based on a local characteristic time scale of the data series. These derived intrinsic modes not only reveal the characteristics of the data but also uncover the underlying rules of reality (Zhang, Lai, & Wang, 2008). The EMD analysis is useful in isolating meaningful seasonal components (Huang et al., 1998), revealing structure breaks and volatility clusters (Zhang, Yu, Wang, & Lai, 2009), and identifying local and global dynamic properties of a process at specific time scales (Huang et al., 1998; Zhang et al., 2009). In particular, EMD analysis is useful in analyzing and modeling the behavior of nonlinear and nonstationary financial time series. Huang, Wu, Qu, Long, and Shen (2003) first applied EMD to examine the changeability of the markets using financial data. More recent studies (Yu, Wang, & Lai, 2008; Yu, Wang, Lai, & Wen, 2010) demonstrate the superior performance of EMD-based hybrid models over traditional forecasting models in forecasting oil prices and financial crises. EMD and NN models have been used to predict short-term metro passenger flow (Wei & Chen, 2012) and to forecast tourism demand (Chen, Lai, & Yeh, 2012). However, our literature search did not turn up a case where the EMD approach has been applied to monthly data with a strong seasonal pattern. Clearly, there are no applications of EMD in retail sales forecasting. Improving accuracy in retail sales forecasting is an important yet often difficult task. EMD-based hybrid models may be an effective way to provide accurate forecasts.

In this chapter, we apply the EMD-based hybrid models to retail sales time series data over periods in which recessions occurred. The organization of the remainder of the chapteris as follows: the second section provides background on the experimental plan and forecasting models; the third section presents the results and findings; and the fourth section concludes the chapter.

EXPERIMENTAL PLAN

Empirical Mode Decomposition

Empirical mode decomposition proposed by Huang et al. (1998) is a signal analysis method which has been widely applied in the area of engineering such as image processing and fault diagnosis. Recently, EMD has attracted much attention in forecasting because it is applicable to nonlinear and nonstationary data. EMD assumes that different coexisting modes of oscillations in a time series may occur at the same time, thus, a complicated time series can be decomposed into a finite and often small number of intrinsic mode functions (IMFs). Each IMF must meet the following two conditions (Huang et al., 1998):

(1) In the whole data series, the number of extrema (either maxima or minima) and the number of zero crossings is the same, or differ at most by one.
(2) The mean value of the envelopes defined by local maxima and the envelopes defined by the local minima must be zero at all points.

With these two conditions, some meaningful IMFs can be well defined. Using the definition, any data series $x(t)$ ($t = 1, 2, \ldots, n$) can be decomposed according to the following sifting procedure:

(1) Identify all the local extrema of the time series $x(t)$.
(2) Form an upper envelope (e.g., $e_{max}(t)$) by interpolating the local maxima and a lower envelope (e.g., $e_{min}(t)$) by interpolating the local minima.
(3) Compute the mean of the upper and lower envelopes for each data point. That is, $m(t) = (e_{min}(t) + e_{max}(t))/2$.
(4) Subtract the mean $m(t)$ from the time series $x(t)$, $h(t) = x(t) - m(t)$.
(5) Check whether $h(t)$ meets the criteria for an IMF as given above:

  – If $h(t)$ satisfies the IMF conditions, $h(t)$ becomes a new IMF, then replace $x(t)$ with the residue $r(t) = x(t) - h(t)$.
  – If $h(t)$ is not an IMF, then replace $x(t)$ with $h(t)$.

The sifting process (step 1 through step 5) continues until no more IMF can be extracted. During this process, the highest frequency IMF is derived first. Then the next highest frequency IMF is extracted from the remainder between the data and the extracted IMF. The iterations continue until no IMF is contained in the residual. Eventually, the data series $x(t)$ can be decomposed into a finite number of IMFs and one residue. In other words, the time series can be expressed by the sum of the empirical mode functions and the residue as the following equation:

$$x(t) = \sum_{j=1}^{n} h_j(t) + r_n(t) \tag{1}$$

where n is the number of IMF extracted from $x(t)$, $h_j(t)$ $(j=1,2,..n)$ represent the IMFs, and $r_n(t)$ is the final residue which captures the main trend of $x(t)$.

ARIMA

ARIMA represents an autoregressive integrated moving average and was developed by Box and Jenkins (1976). For a given time series of $x(t)$, an ARIMA(p,q) process can be expressed as follows:

$$X(t) = c + \varphi_1 x_{t-1} + \varphi_2 x_{t-2} + \cdots + \varphi_p x_{t-p} + \varepsilon_t - \theta_1 \varepsilon_{t-1} - \theta_2 \varepsilon_{t-2} - \cdots - \theta_q \varepsilon_{t-q} \tag{2}$$

Where c is a constant, $\varphi_1, \varphi_2, \ldots \varphi_p$ are parameters of autoregressive (AR), $\theta_1, \theta_2 \ldots, \theta_q$ are parameters of moving average (MA), t is an integer index, and $x(t)$ are real numbers. ARIMA models have been one of the most popular and powerful methods for stationary time series forecasting since their introduction. Nonstationary time series need to be differenced in order to use ARIMA model. The parameter d in the ARIMA (p,d,q) model represents the number of difference needed to make the series stationary. In order to identify the appropriate ARIMA model, we followed the three steps: model identification, parameter estimation, and diagnostic checking. The model that gives the minimum Akaike Information Critierion (AIC) is selected as the best model. We use the ARIMA models as benchmarks for evaluating the performance of the forecasting models since ARIMA models achieve extensive use and acceptance among the statistical techniques (Hansen & Nelson, 2003).

Artificial Neural Networks (ANNs)

ANNs are biologically inspired semi-parametric models used to capture complex nonlinear relationships which violate the assumptions of traditional forecasting methods. These models are more flexible in modeling dynamic time series since they don't require specific assumptions about the underlying model. A large number of successful applications have established the role of NN in time series modeling and forecasting (Zhang & Beradi, 2001). One of the most popular NN is the single multilayer feedforward model (MLP). A single output multilayer feedforward model actually performs the following mapping from the inputs to the output based on Eq. (3) (Zhang & Qi, 2005).

$$y_t = \alpha_0 + \sum_{\substack{j=1 \\ q}} \alpha_j f \left(\sum_{\substack{i=1 \\ p}} \beta_{ij} x_{it} + \beta_{0j} \right) + \varepsilon_t \tag{3}$$

where x_{it} ($i = 0,1,2, \ldots, p$) is the input, y_t is the output at time t, p is the number of the input nodes, q is the number of hidden nodes, and f is a nonlinear activation function (such as logistic transfer function) determined by the MLP structure and the data. α_j ($j = 0,1,2, \ldots, n$) are the weights from the hidden to the output nodes. Since we use univariate retail sales to predict the future, the inputs of NN model is the past observations, and the output is the forecast. Although NN models are the most versatile non-linear models, the desirable benefits of ANNs can only be realized through constructing the proper network for a particular application. In fact, one of the most difficult tasks is to choose the "best" network that generates the "optimal" prediction for a particular time series (Alon et al., 2001; Bodyanskiy & Popov, 2006). The most common NN architecture is the MLP and it seems to perform well in time series financial forecasting (Makridakis et al., 1982). Cybenko (1989) demonstrated that one hidden layer with the sigmoid function is sufficient for most NN learning problems. Therefore, one hidden layer MLP NN models are used in this study. In addition, the selection for the other parameters of the network is based on trial-and-error methods since there are no general rules for the choice of the network structure.

EMD-Based Neural Network Model (EMD-NN)

In order to overcome the problems with direct NN models, we first applied the EMD algorithm to the original time series to extract the intrinsic mode functions (IMFs) with different time scales. In fact, after the EMD decomposition, each IMF becomes more regular and less nonstationary compared to the original data series. Then, the lagged time series of each IMF is treated as inputs of a two layer MLP NN to generate forecasts for the corresponding IMF. It is expected that the tendencies of these IMF components can be predicted accurately since the interactions of different patterns are significantly reduced due to the EMD decomposition. Finally, the predicted IMFs are used as inputs to feed a two layer MLP NN in order to predict the future value of the aggregate retail sales. Fig. 1 illustrates a complete procedure of the hybrid EMD-NN model.

Data

The data used in this study are monthly retail sales compiled by the US Bureau of the Census. Data from two sampling periods were examined in this study. The first period is from January 1977 to December 1987. Fig. 2 indicates that a trend pattern still dominates the time series for the data

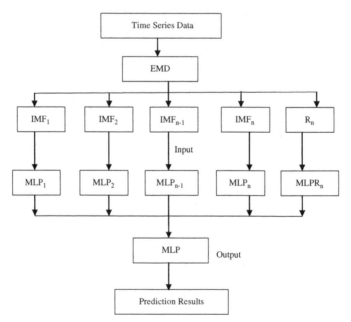

Fig. 1. The Procedure of the EMD-Based Neural Network Model.

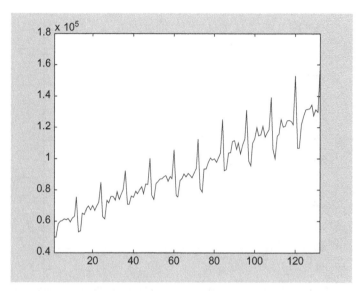

Fig. 2. Plot of US Aggregate Retail Sales (January 1977–December 1987).

from January 1977 to December 1986 even though several recessions occurred during this time period. The second period is from January 2000 to December 2008. Fig. 3 clearly shows that US retail sales contain both strong trend and seasonal patterns in which the last quarter of 2008 showed a dramatic drop in sales due to the financial crisis. Because aggregate retail sales are influenced by macroeconomic instability, we expect the forecasts for the second time period to be more accurate because EMD can capture the nonlinear activities well if there are large fluctuations in the time series.

Performance Measures

In this study, we use the mean absolute percentage error (MAPE) to compare and evaluate the forecasting accuracy of the forecasting models. The choice of MAPE is due to its popularity in the forecasting literature and the fact that it is not prone to changes in the magnitude of the time series to be predicted (Alon et al., 2001). This study focuses on out-of-sample performance since the purpose is to accurately predict future retail sales. In addition, the variance of absolute percentage error (VAPE) is used to evaluate the prediction stability of the forecasting models. These

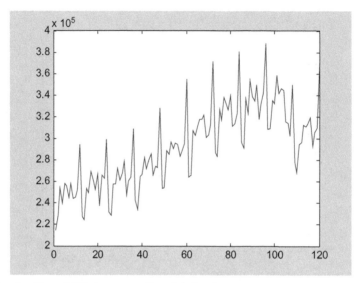

Fig. 3. Plot of US Aggregate Retail Sales (January 2000–December 2009).

performance measures are commonly used in prior studies (Wei & Chen, 2012; Zhang & Ye, 2008). MAPE and VAPE are defined in Eqs. (4) and (5) respectively:

$$\text{MAPE}(\%) = \frac{100}{n} \sum_{i=1}^{n} \frac{|Y_i - \hat{Y}_i|}{Y_i} \tag{4}$$

$$\text{VAPE}(\%) = Var\left(\frac{|Y_i - \hat{Y}_i|}{Y_i}\right) \times 100 \tag{5}$$

RESULTS

In this study, the EMD procedure was implemented in Matlab (version 7.5). The original data series was decomposed into several intrinsic modes and one residue. Figs. 4 and 5 show the decomposition results. Then Neuro-Solution 6.0 was used to generate the forecasts for each component using direct NN model with lag one and lag two data as inputs. SAS (version 9.2) ARIMA procedure was used to generate the forecasts for the original retail sales.

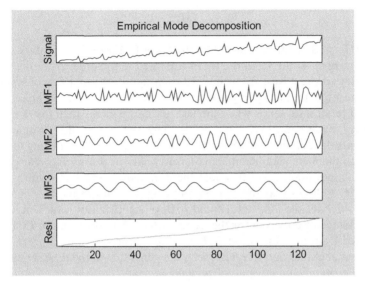

Fig. 4. EMD Decomposition of Retail Sales (1977–1987).

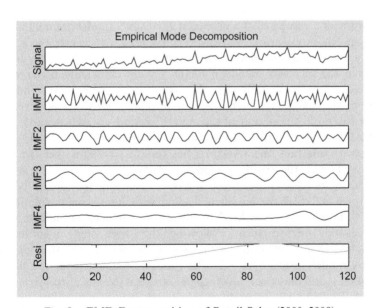

Fig. 5. EMD Decomposition of Retail Sales (2000–2009).

IMFs

The IMFs and residue extracted by applying EMD to the two data sets are shown in Figs. 4 and 5. All the IMFs are listed in the order from the highest frequency to the lowest frequency. In each figure, the first few components with the high frequency represent the high time variant or noise in the original retail sales series while the last few components with low frequency represent underlying cycles or trends. The last one is the residue which represents the dominant trend pattern in the time series. According to Fig. 4, although there are significant short-term variations during the year of 1986, these changes don't seem to affect the dominant trend significantly. However, Fig. 5 shows that the sudden and deep changes in the last quarter of 2008 do impact the long-term trend pattern significantly, which may result in the change of direction for the trend pattern. Moreover, more IMFs were extracted from data in period 2. This is not surprising since a great deal of nonlinear activities and irregularities were generated in the time series due to volatile economic conditions since 2000.

General Forecasting Results

The forecasting results of the proposed EMD-NN model are compared to the direct NN model using non-EMD forecasting, which uses the previous month's retail sales to predict future month's retail sales. The findings show that the forecasts based on EMD-NN are expectedly better when a highly volatile pattern exhibits in the decomposed component. Under this situation, the EMD-NN model is better than SARIMA and direct NN models for both one-period ahead and 12-period ahead forecasts, which indicates that the EMD decomposition benefits the forecasting in this situation. In addition, the SARIMA has some advantages over the EMD-NN model since the strong seasonal component in retail sales is better captured in its forecasting, thus, it is not surprising that EMD-NN will outperform ARIMA model when dealing with nonseasonal volatile time series. As benchmarks, the ARIMA models are included in the comparison of forecasting performance. Following the three steps mentioned in section "ARIMA" and utilizing the AIC value, we identify the "optimal" ARIMA models using SAS 9.2. The models obtained from the data set (1977–1986) and data set (2000–2008) are ARIMA $(2,1,0)(0,1,1)_{12}$ and ARIMA$(2,1,2)(0,1,1)_{12}$ respectively.

In NN forecasting, the inputs of the NN model are the past and lagged observations, and the output is the forecast. Depending on the time series, either one-period lagged or two-period lagged observations were used as inputs to feed the MLP model to predict future values. The Levenberg (1944) method was selected as the learning algorithm, and the MLP network was trained through 1,000 epochs. The available data were divided into a training set for constructing the NN, a validation data set for cross-validation and a test data set for testing the forecasting performance of the networks. In particular, for the second period data set, data from January 2000 to December 2007 with 96 observations were used for model building, and the 12 observations in 2008 were used for validation purpose, the test data set consisted of 12 observations in 2009. Moreover, the network model was trained three times with different random initial conditions and the best network weights were saved. Once the "best" network model was identified, it was applied to the test data to generate forecasts.

Figs. 6 and 7 show the out-of-sample forecasts for the three models for both time periods, clearly, the one-period ahead forecasts of EMD-NN are closer to the actual values than forecasts based on SARIMA and direct NN model. These results demonstrate that EMD-NN models are able to

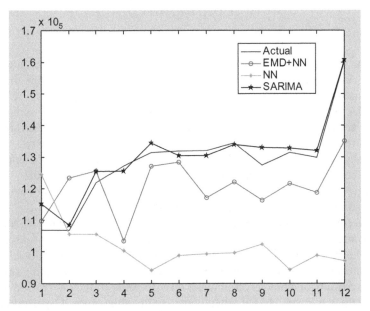

Fig. 6. Comparison of Forecasting Performance among Forecasting Models Based on Data for Period 1.

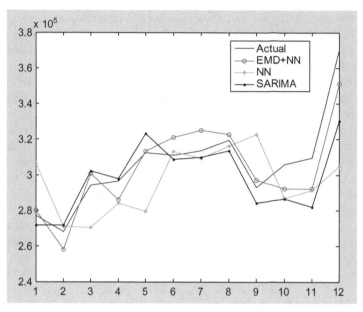

Fig. 7. Comparison of Forecasting Performance among Forecasting Models Based on Data for Period 2.

capture the significant nonlinearity, irregularity, and seasonality in a time series. As to the 12 period forecasts, the EMD-NN model outperforms the other models during periods of economic instability. However, the seasonal ARIMA outperforms EMD-NN during periods with relatively stable economic activities. In addition, direct NN models generate the worst forecasts due to the interaction effect of trend, seasonality, and nonlinearity.

As shown in Tables 1 and 2, the MAPE value increases from one-period ahead to 12 periods ahead in direct NN and EMD-NN models, which indicates that forecasting more periods ahead could result in lower forecasting accuracy. However, the SARIMA model generates the lowest MAPE for 12-period ahead forecast among these three models. This result can be explained by the characteristics of the time series. Since seasonality rather than irregularity is very strong in the retail sales for period 1, which dominates the time series, the SARIMA is still a viable forecasting method during periods of stable economic activity. In general, the one-period ahead forecast has a lower MAPE when compared to that of the 12-period ahead forecast since it incorporates recently updated information.

Table 1. Forecasting Error Measures of Different Models Based on Period 1 Data (January 1977 through December 1986).

	One-Period Ahead Forecast	12-Period Ahead Forecasts	12-Period Ahead Forecasts
Model	MAPE (%)	MAPE (%)	VAPE (%)
SARIMA	7.8	2.1	0.04
Direct NN	16.6	22.3	0.88
EMD-NN	2.6	8.9	0.31

Table 2. Forecasting Error Measures of Different Models Based on Period 2 Data (January 2000 through December 2008).

	One-Period Ahead Forecast	12-Period Ahead Forecasts	12-Period Ahead Forecasts
Model	MAPE (%)	MAPE (%)	VAPE (%)
SARIMA	1.96	3.56	0.11
Direct NN	10.6	6.46	0.27
EMD-NN	0.93	2.92	0.03

In terms of VAPE, a forecasting model with a smaller VAPE is more stable than the one with a larger VAPE. Table 2 indicates that the performance of the hybrid NN model is more stable compared to direct NN model and SARIMA during volatile economy in period 2. However, during relatively stable economic activity, SARIMA performs consistently well despite the fact that the hybrid model NN model significantly reduces the VAPE compared to that of direct NN model.

One-Period versus Multiple-Period Forecasts

Overall, the results of our analysis show that one-period forecasts are better than multiple-period forecasts for both time periods except for the out-of-sample forecasts of SARIMA model for period 1. This make senses because one-period forecasts incorporate recently updated information, thus, one-period forecasts are more accurate than multiple-period forecasts. The only exception for period 1 can be explained by the fact that the trend and seasonal patterns still dominate the series, thus, multiple-period forecasts are more accurate than the one-period forecasts generated by the SARIMA model. Moreover, one-step forecasts may be preferred by practitioners and managers under different macroeconomic conditions since multiple-period forecasts may not provide better results because they do not incorporate recently updated information.

CONCLUSIONS AND IMPLICATIONS

Forecasting aggregate retail sales is often difficult and complex because of the presence of dynamic nonlinear trend and seasonal patterns in the time series. The findings of this study have important managerial and practical implications. The proposed method preprocesses the retail sales data into less nonstationary components (IMFs) based on the EMD algorithm. Then the corresponding NN models for each component are built and trained. Through trial and error, the "optimal" NN models are identified and used to make forecasts. The forecasts thus obtained from these components are combined to obtain the final forecast. The findings of this study demonstrate that the hybrid NN model generates more accurate one-step forecasts for both periods investigated. The results also show that both one-step ahead and 12-step forecasts of the proposed method are better than those forecasts of SARIMA and direct NN models when highly volatile patterns exhibit in the decomposed components. The results indicate that the EMD decomposition benefits the forecasting in this situation. Thus, the EMD-based NN successfully overcomes the limitations of direct NN models and significantly improves the forecasting performance. Overall, in forecasting retail sales, EMD-NN model proves to be more efficient and robust.

As shown in period 1, although EMD decomposition has proven to be successful in improving the performance of NN models during periods of economic instability, the seasonal ARIMA model remains viable in delivering multi-step forecasts during periods where economic activity is more stable. Thus, practitioners and managers should evaluate the costs and benefits of each model before choosing an appropriate forecasting model. Managers and practitioners should have a better understanding of the characteristics of the time series and the economic conditions when selecting forecasting models. EMD-based NN is a promising tool which may be used to improve the accuracy of forecasts, especially when the economic system experiences great fluctuations as is common during recessions. Since traditional forecasting methods are not good at capturing nonlinear activities in a time series, EMD-based NN model should be promoted in forecasting aggregated retails sales so that firms can use it to reduce costs during volatile economy.

Our study has some limitations that need further research. One of the limitations of EMD decomposition is its mode mixing phenomenon (Huang et al., 1998). When it occurs, one IMF component may include both high frequency and low frequency, or a similar frequency may exist in different IMFs. To fix this issue, the ensemble empirical model decomposition method (Wu & Huang, 2008) can be used to extract IMFs. Thus, future studies should combine ensemble EMD and other nonlinear forecasting models such as time-lag recurrent networks and support vector machines to evaluate the proposed forecasting scheme.

REFERENCES

Agrawal, D., & Schorling, C. (1996). Market share forecasting: An empirical comparison of artificial neural networks and multinomial logit model. *Journal of Retailing, 72*(4), 383–407.

Alon, I. (1997). Forecasting aggregate retail sales: The winters' model revisited. In J. C. Goodale (Ed.), *The 1997 Annual Proceedings* (pp. 234–236). Midwest Decision Science Institute.

Alon, I., Qi, M., & Sadowski, R. J. (2001). Forecasting aggregate retail sales: A comparison of artificial neural networks and traditional methods. *Journal of Retailing and Consumer Services, 8*(3), 147–156.

Bodyanskiy, Y., & Popov, S. (2006). Neural network approach to forecasting of quasiperiodic financial time series. *European Journal of Operational Research, 175,* 1357–1366.

Box, G. E. P., & Jenkins, G. M. (1976). *Time series analysis: Forecasting and control.* San Francisco, CA: Holdan-Day.

Chen, C., Lai, M., & Yeh, C. (2012). Forecasting tourism demand based on empirical mode decomposition and neural network. *Knowledge-Based Systems, 26,* 281–287.

Chopra, S., & Meindl, P. (2007). *Supply chain management: Strategy, planning, and operation* (3rd ed.). Upper Saddle River, NJ: Prentice Hall.

Chu, C., & Zhang, G. (2003). A comparative study of linear and nonlinear models for aggregate retail sales forecasting. *International Journal of Production Economics, 86,* 217–231.

Cybenko, G. (1989). Approximation by superpositions of a sigmoidal function. *Mathematics of Control, Signals and Systems, 2,* 303–314.

Hansen, J. V., & Nelson, R. D. (2003). Forecasting and recombining time-series components by using neural networks. *The Journal of the Operational Research Society, 54*(3), 307–317.

Hill, T., O'Connor, M., & Remus, W. (1996). Neural network models for time series forecasts. *Management Science, 42*(7), 1082–1092.

Hsieh, T., Hsiao, H., & Yeh, W. (2011). Forecasting stock markets using wavelet transforms and recurrent neural networks: An integrated system based on artificial bee colony algorithm. *Applied Soft Computing, 11,* 2510–2525.

Huang, N. E., Shen, Z., Long, S. R. (1998). The empirical mode decomposition and the Hilbert spectrum for nonlinear and non-stationary time series analysis. *Proceedings of the Royal Society of London* A, *459,* 2317–2345.

Huang, N. E., Wu, M. L., Qu, W. D., Long, S. R., & Shen, S. S. P. (2003). Applications of Hilbert–Huang transform to nonstationary financial time series analysis. *Applied Stochastic Models in Business and Industry, 19*, 245–268.

Khashei, M., & Bijari, M. (2012). A new class of hybrid models for time series forecasting. *Expert Systems with Applications, 39*, 4344–4357.

Kuan, C.-M., & Liu, T. (1995). Forecasting exchange rates using feed forward and recurrent neural networks. *Journal of Applied Econometrics, 10*, 347–364.

Kumar, M., & Patel, N. (2010). Using clustering to improve sales forecasts in retail merchandising. *Annals of Operations Research, 174*, 33–46.

Kuvulmaz, J., Usanmaz, S., & Engin, S. N. (2005). *Time-series forecasting by means of linear and nonlinear models. Advances in artificial intelligence.* Springer Berlin: Heidelberg.

Lee, H., Padmanabhan, V., & Whang, S. (1997). The bullwhip effect in supply chains. *Sloan Management Review, 38*, 93–102.

Levenberg, K. (1944). A method for the solution of certain problems in least squares. *Quarterly of Applied Mathematics, 2*, 164–168.

Makridakis, S., Anderson, A., Carbone, R., Fildes, R., Hibon, M., Lewandowski, R., ... Winkler, R. (1982). The accuracy of extrapolation (time series) methods: Results of a forecasting competition. *Journal of Forecasting, 1*, 111–153.

Nelson, M., Hill, T., Remus, W., & O'Connor, M. (1999). Time series forecasting using neural networks: Should the data be deseasonalized first? *Journal of Forecasting, 18*, 359–367.

Schoneburg, E. (1990). Stock price prediction using neural net-works: A project report. *Neurocomputing, 2*, 17–27.

Wei, Y., & Chen, M. (2012). Forecasting the short-term metro passenger flow with empirical model decomposition and neural networks. *Transportation Research Part C, 21*, 148–162.

Wu, Z., & Huang, N. E. (2008). Ensemble empirical mode decomposition: A noise-assisted data analysis method. *Advance in Adaptive Data Analysis, 1*, 1–41.

Yu, L., Wang, S., & Lai, K. (2008). Forecasting crude oil price with an EMD-based neural network ensemble learning paradigm. *Energy Economics, 30*, 2623–2635.

Yu, L., Wang, S., Lai, K. K., & Wen, F. (2010). A multiscale neural network learning paradigm for financial crisis forecasting. *Neurocomputing, 73*, 716–725.

Zarnowitz, V., & Braun, P. A. (1993). Twenty-two years of the NBER-ASA quarterly economic outlook surveys: Aspects and comparisons of forecasting performance. In J. H. Stock & M. W. Watson (Eds.), *Business cycles, indicators, and forecasting.* Chicago, IL: University of Chicago Press.

Zhang, G. P., & Qi, M. (2002). Predicting consumer retail sales using neural networks. In K. Smith & J. Gupta (Eds.), *Neural networks in business: Techniques and applications* (pp. 26–40). Hershey, PA: Idea Group Publishing.

Zhang, G. P., & Qi, M. (2005). Neural network forecasting for seasonal and trend time series. *European Journal of Operational Research, 160*, 501–514.

Zhang, X., Lai, K. K., & Wang, S. (2008). A new approach for crude oil price analysis based on empirical mode decomposition. *Energy Economics, 30*, 905–918.

Zhang, X., Yu, L., Wang, S., & Lai, K. (2009). Estimating the impact of extreme events on crude oil price: An EMD-based event analysis method. *Energy Economics, 31*, 768–778.

Zhang, Y., & Ye, Z. (2008). Short-term traffic flow forecasting using fuzzy logic system methods. *Journal of Intelligent Transportation Systems, 12*(3), 102–112.

A METHODOLOGY FOR COMBINING BIASED DEMAND FORECASTS

Joanne Utley

ABSTRACT

Past research has shown that forecast combination typically improves demand forecast accuracy even when only two component forecasts are used; however, systematic bias in the component forecasts can reduce the effectiveness of combination. This study proposes a methodology for combining demand forecasts that are biased. Data from an actual manufacturing shop are used to develop the methodology and compare its accuracy with the accuracy of the standard approach of correcting for bias prior to combination. Results indicate that the proposed methodology outperforms the standard approach.

Keywords: Bias correction; demand forecasts; forecast combination; linear programming; systematic bias

INTRODUCTION

In their classic paper on the combination of forecasts, Bates and Granger (1969) argued that if two demand forecasts for the same product are based

Advances in Business and Management Forecasting, Volume 9, 171–183
ISSN: 1477-4070/doi:10.1108/S1477-4070(2013)0000009014

on different information, then combining the forecasts will improve accuracy. Forty years of research on forecast combination has supported this claim (Clemen, 1989; De Menzes, Bunn, & Taylor, 2000; Hendry & Clements, 2002). Much of this research was based on the assumption that the component forecasts used in the combination are unbiased (Goodwin, 2000). When component forecasts exhibit systematic bias, forecasters typically correct for bias first and then combine the de-biased forecasts. However, this approach does not guarantee greater accuracy for out of sample forecasts. In particular, when error patterns change over time the correct-then-combine method may actually reduce the accuracy of the combination (Goodwin, 2000).

This chapter proposes an alternative approach for combining component demand forecasts that exhibit systematic bias. The proposed method replaces the standard correct-then-combine approach with a linear model that simultaneously selects optimal weights for linear combination and addresses the problem of systematic bias in the component forecasts. Data from an actual manufacturing shop are used to illustrate the proposed model and compare its accuracy to that of the standard approach. Prior to model formulation, a brief review of the literature on de-biasing techniques and forecast combination will be presented in the following section.

BIAS CORRECTION AND FORECAST COMBINATION

The standard approach for combining forecasts with systemic bias consists of two steps: (1) de-biasing the component forecasts and (2) combining the bias corrected forecasts with a well-established combination procedure. In completing these two steps the manager has a range of de-biasing and combination techniques to choose from.

One of the most widely used approaches to bias correction was devised by Theil (1971), who demonstrated that the mean square error (MSE) of a forecast series can be decomposed into three terms as follows:

$$\text{MSE} = (A - F)^2 + (S_F - rS_A)^2 + (1 - r^2)S_A^2$$

where

$A =$ the mean of the actual demand values

$F =$ the mean of the demand forecasts

$S_A =$ the standard deviation of the actual demand values

$S_F =$ the standard deviation of the demand forecasts

$r =$ the correlation coefficient between the actual demand and the forecast demand values.

The first term in this decomposition represents the mean bias or tendency of the forecast model to underestimate or overestimate demand. The second term reflects the regression bias or inability of the forecast to track the pattern in the actual demand values (Sanders & Ritzman, 2004). Taken together, these two terms correspond to the systematic forecast bias (Ahlburg, 1984). The third term, or random error term, represents the unexplained variation in actual demand.

Theil (1971) argued that when the decomposition of the MSE revealed systematic forecast bias, a linear correction based on ordinary least squares (OLS) regression could be used to remove this bias. Theil's (1971) linear correction takes the form:

$$\hat{A}(t) = b_0 + b_1 F(t)$$

where
t = a particular time period
$A(t)$ = actual demand for time period t
$F(t)$ = forecast demand for time period t.

As long as the systematic bias remains constant, the linear correction can also be used to correct for bias in out of sample forecasts. However, if a change occurs in the relationship between the demand and the forecast, use of the correction may be counterproductive (Goodwin & Lawton, 2003; Sanders & Ritzman, 2004).

Given the possibility of such a change over time, several researchers have studied the use of weighted linear correction models in which older observations and forecasts receive smaller weights than more recent values. For instance, Ameen and Harrison (1984) devised a discounted weighted regression (DWR) model that recursively generated model parameters for Theil's linear correction. Goodwin (1997) used a laboratory experiment to compare the accuracy of Ameen and Harrison's (1984) model and Theil's (1971) linear correction and found that the DWR model was more robust to sudden change. Jex (1994) also found that the use of a weighed correction model improved forecast accuracy. Despite these findings, a manager may be less inclined to use weighted correction models in practice given their mathematical complexity.

Once systematic bias has been removed from component forecasts, the manager can combine the corrected forecasts with one of the several established mathematical techniques. De Menzes et al. (2000) provide an excellent review of these combination techniques which include the simple average, the outperformance method, the optimal technique, and the ordinary least squares (OLS) regression model; De Menzes et al. (2000) also offer guidance on the choice of combining methods.

The simplest of the combination methods is based on the arithmetic mean of the component forecasts and takes the form:

$$F_t = \frac{\sum f_j}{n}$$

where
f_j = component forecast j
n = the number of component forecasts to be combined.

The arithmetic mean (or simple average) has been widely used by researchers and practitioners alike (Clemen, 1989; De Menzes et al., 2000). It is especially useful when demand data are limited as is the case in industrial contexts where products undergo rapid development and change (Bunn, 1987; Goodwin, 2000; Watson, 1996). Armstrong and Collopy (1998) advocate the use of the simple mean when demand series are unstable and it is difficult to determine which combination technique will provide the most accurate forecast. De Menzes et al. (2000, p. 191) note that the strengths of the simple average include its robustness, impartiality and strong "track record" in business forecasting.

The outperformance technique devised by Bunn (1975) also performs well when data are limited (Bunn, 1985). The outperformance technique utilizes a weighted average in which each weight corresponds to the proportion of time that a specific component forecast outperformed the other component forecasts in the combination. The optimal method proposed by Bates and Granger (1969) also utilizes linear weights. Granger and Ramanathan (1984) demonstrated that the optimal method is equivalent to an OLS regression model in which the weights are constrained to one and the constant term is suppressed.

In the OLS approach, the actual demand is the dependent variable while component forecasts are the independent variables. Assuming that f_1 and f_2 represent two component forecasts that are used in the combination, the OLS model has the form:

$$D_t = b_0 + b_1 f_{1t} + b_2 f_{2t} + e_t$$

where
D_t = the actual value of the forecasted variable for period t
f_{jt} = the forecast for period t generated by component forecast model j
b_0 = the constant term
b_j = the regression coefficient for component forecast j
e_t = the error term for period t.

A number of researchers have compared the relative performance of the OLS model shown above with that of alternative combination approaches. Mills and Stephenson (1985), Clemen (1986), Holden and Peel (1986), and Lobo (1991) found that the optimal approach outperformed the OLS model, while Guerard (1987), Holmen (1987), and Holden, Peel, and Thomson (1990) advocated the use of the OLS method. Gunter (1992) and Asku and Gunter (1992) studied a number of variations of the OLS model and found that the model in which weights are subject to a nonnegativity constraint was comparable to the simple average in accuracy and robustness. They further determined that the simple average and this specific OLS model outperformed unconstrained OLS models and OLS models which constrain weights to sum to one but do not force the weights to be nonnegative.

The OLS model shown above minimizes the mean square error (MSE) of the combination forecast; however, in applications where one wishes to minimize the mean absolute deviation (MAD) of the combined forecast, a Least Absolute Value (LAV) regression model is preferable. Multiple LAV regression can constitute an attractive alternative combination technique because the LAV approach tends to be less sensitive to outliers than the OLS model (Dielman & Pfaffenberger, 1988).

The preceding discussion suggests that a forecaster has a number of alternatives in devising a correct-then-combine strategy for biased component forecasts. No matter which models are chosen for de-biasing and combination, the strategy used to implement these models remains a sequential one in which the component forecasts are first corrected for bias. In practice, this initial de-biasing can potentially reduce the effectiveness of the combination (Goodwin, 2000). For instance, Sanders and Ritzman (2004) observe that forecast correction can prove problematic when rapid or sporadic change occurs in systematic bias and the correction no longer suits the data. In addition, the initial correction may produce such an accurate forecast for one of the component models that combination does not appear useful. If this occurs, the forecaster may decide to rely only on the more accurate component forecast, thereby losing valuable information contained in the discarded component forecast (Goodwin, 2000). It is also possible that initial correction of the components will eliminate cancellation of errors of opposite signs during the combining process. This would reduce the effectiveness of the combination.

Given the possible shortcomings of a correct-then-combine strategy, this study will propose a linear model that reflects a correct-and-combine approach. The correct-and-combine approach models actual demand values as a function of component forecast values while simultaneously minimizing the weighted absolute error of the combined forecast. As shown below, the correct-and-combine model is a variation of the standard multiple LAV regression model formulated as a linear program. Unlike the standard LAV regression approach, the proposed model contains separate constraints for each set of component forecasts and additional constraints that force the weights of the component forecasts to be non-negative and to sum to one. In addition, the terms in the objective function are weighed by time period to compensate for change in the forecast bias.

$$\text{Minimize} \sum w_i(P_i + N_i) + \sum w_i(R_i + S_i)$$

Subject to:

$$b_0 + b_1 f_{1i} + P_i - N_i = D_i \quad \text{for } i = 1, 2, \ldots n$$

$$b_0 + b_2 f_{2i} + R_i - S_i = D_i \quad \text{for } i = 1, 2, \ldots n$$

$$b_1 + b_2 = 1$$

$$\text{All } P_i, \ N_i, \ R_i, \ S_i \geq 0, \quad b_0 = 0 \text{ and } b_1 \geq 0, \ b_2 \geq 0$$

where
b_0 = the regression constant
b_j = the regression coefficient for component forecast model j ($j = 1, 2$)
f_{1i} = the component forecast 1 for period i
f_{2i} = the component forecast 2 for period i
D_i = the actual value of total demand in period i
$P_i = D_i - (b_0 + b_1 f_{1i})$ (the positive deviational variable for period i and component model (1)
$N_i = (b_0 + b_1 f_{1i}) - D_i$ (the negative deviational variable for period i and component model (1)
$R_i = D_i - (b_0 + b_2 f_{2i})$ (the positive deviational variable for period i and component model (2)
$S_i = (b_0 + b_2 f_{2i}) - D_i$ (the negative deviational variable for period i and component model (2)
$w_i = k^{(n+1)-i}$ = the time-based weight for a deviation for period i where k is constant and $0 < k < 1$
n = the number of observations in the data set.

The following section illustrates how the linear programming model shown above can be used to implement a correct-and-combine strategy to produce a forecast for product demand. The performance of the correct-and-combine strategy will then be compared to the performance of a standard correct-then-combine approach that applies Theil's (1971) linear correction to component forecasts and then combines them with the simple average.

CASE STUDY

To evaluate the performance of the weighed LAV model discussed in the preceding section, the model was applied to data from an actual manufacturing shop. For simplicity, this section will address the problem of forecasting demand for just one of the electronic components produced by this shop. Two distinct types of data were available for this component: (1) historical demand data and (2) advance order data. Analysis of these data showed that both the order quantity and customer designated lead times varied with each customer order. Typically, customer designated lead times ranged from 1 month to 4 months.

The initial data set consisted of 9 months of historical and advance order data for this product. The historical data for demand that was actually realized were used to generate an exponentially smoothed forecast (with $\alpha = .2$) for months 2–9. These forecasts are listed in Table 1 as the f_1 time series. In contrast, the advance order data for months 1–9 were used to generate simple additive forecasts (for months 2–9) in which total demand

Table 1. Component Forecasts and Corrected Component Forecasts For Months 2–9.

Month	Actual Demand	f_1 (Exponentially Smoothed Forecast)	f_2 Additive Model for Partial Data	Corrected f_1	Corrected f_2
2	266	321	268	240	266
3	260	310	264	236	262
4	193	300	200	234	208
5	253	279	246	227	247
6	193	273	195	225	204
7	182	257	177	220	189
8	210	242	172	215	185
9	262	235	253	213	253
MSE		3940.75	211.375	1057	142.63

was modeled as the sum of the partially accumulated demand (known via the advance orders) and an estimate of the unknown (or as yet unrevealed) segment of total demand. A forecast $F(t,h)$ for month t generated by the simple additive model, h or more periods in advance of month t is given by

$$F(t,h) = D(t,h) + S(t,h)$$

where

$D(t,h) =$ the partially accumulated demand for month t occurring h or more months in advance of month t

$S(t,h) =$ the smoothed value of the unknown segment of total demand

$h =$ the customer designated lead time.

These forecasts are listed in Table 1 as the f_2 time series. A detailed discussion of the simple additive model for advance order data can be found in Kekre, Morton, and Smunt (1990).

Theil's (1971) decomposition of the MSE for f_1 time series and MSE for the f_2 time series revealed the presence of systematic bias. The exponentially smoothed forecast (f_1) series had a systematic bias $= 82.3\%$ (mean bias of 63.3% and a regression bias $= 19\%$); in addition, a simple t-test for systematic bias (DeLurgio, 1998), with t-calculated $= 2.81 > t$-table $= 2.365$ ($n = 7$ and prob $= .05$), indicated statistically significant bias. The simple additive forecasts (f_2 time series) had a systematic bias $= 32.6\%$ (mean bias $= 15.0\%$ and regression bias $= 17.6\%$).

The forecast problem was to use the f_1 time series and the f_2 time series to develop combined forecasts for months 10–13. The forecast process consisted of a series of stages which are summarized below.

Stage 1: Correction of the Component Forecasts

Theil's (1971) correction was used to de-bias the f_1 time series and the f_2 time series. The estimated OLS regression model for the f_1 time series was $\hat{A}(t) = 137.68 + .32F(t)$. The estimated OLS regression model for the f_2 time series was $\hat{A}(t) = 39.56 + .845F(t)$. The bias-corrected time series for these two models are shown in Table 1. The correction process improved the forecast accuracy for both component models. As shown in Table 1, the MSE for the exponentially smoothed forecasts decreased from 3940.75 to 1057 while the MSE for the additive forecasts declined from 211.375 to 142.625.

Stage 2: Combination of the Corrected Component Forecasts with the Simple Average

The corrected forecasts found in stage 1 were combined using the simple average. These combined forecasts for months 2–9 are shown in Table 2. Results indicate that the de-biased additive model actually outperformed the combined model for months 2–9. The MSE for de-biased additive model was 142.63 while the MSE for the simple average model was 403.594. The corrected component forecasts and the combined forecasts for months 10–13 are given in Table 3. For months 10–13, the MSE for the combination

Table 2. Simple Average Combined Forecasts and Weighted LAV Forecasts For Months 2–9.

Month	Actual Demand	Simple Average Combination	Error Simple Average	Weighted LAV Combination	Error LAV Combination
2	266	253	13	305.47	−39.47
3	260	249.5	10.5	269.522	−36.52
4	193	221	−28	270.7	−77.7
5	253	237	16	267.917	−14.917
6	193	214.5	−21.5	250.146	−57.146
7	182	204.5	22.5	233.56	−51.56
8	210	200	10	221.49	−11.49
9	262	233	29	239.274	22.726
MAD			18.81		38.94
MAPE			8.63%		18.4%
MSE			403.594		1965.53

Table 3. Corrected Component Forecasts and Simple Average Combination Forecasts For Months 10–13.

Month	Actual Demand	Corrected f_1	Corrected f_2	Simple Average Combination
10	235	214.82	214.7	214.7
11	405	214.44	306.42	260.43
12	264	225.0	127.15	176.08
13	206	224.4	108.62	166.52
MAD		67.04	88.27	73.05
MAPE		19.8%	33.0%	24.2%
MSE		9645.56	9584.78	7649.43

forecast based on the simple average (MSE = 7649.43) outperformed the MSE for the corrected f_1 time series (MSE = 9645.56) and MSE for the corrected f_2 time series (MSE = 9584.78) The combination did not outperform both corrected component forecasts in terms of the MAD and the MAPE for out of sample data.

Stage 3: Establishing the LAV Combination Forecasts

The uncorrected f_1 and f_2 time series for months 2–9 were used to generate a weighted LAV forecast model for months 2–9. The LAV model took the form $F(t) = .707f_{1t} + .293f_{2t}$. The LAV forecasts for months 2–9 are shown in Table 2. This table shows that the simple average combination outperformed the LAV model in months 2–9.

Stage 4: Model Comparison for Months 10–13

The uncorrected f_1 and f_2 time series for months 10–13 were used in conjunction with the weighted LAV model to generate a series of combined forecasts for months 10–13. These forecasts are given in Table 4. The weighted LAV model outperformed both of the uncorrected forecasts – as well as both of the corrected forecasts – for months 10–13 in terms of the MAD, MAPE, and MSE. Table 5 reveals that the weighted LAV approach outperformed the simple average of the corrected component forecasts for months10–13.The MAD for the simple average was 73.05 while the MAD for the weighted LAV model was 49.25. The MAPE for the simple average combination was 24.2% while the MAPE for the weighed LAV model was 14.25%. The MSE for the simple average combination was 7650.29 while the MSE for the weighted LAV model was 5544.69.

Table 4. Uncorrected Component Forecasts and Weighted LAV Combination For Months 10–13.

Month	Actual Demand	Uncorrected f_1	Uncorrected f_2	LAV Combination
10	235	241.07	207.27	231.17
11	405	239.86	315.82	262.11
12	264	272.89	103.67	223.31
13	206	271.11	81.72	215.62
MAD		61.3	100.38	44.45
MAPE		19.58%	38.72%	11.9%
MSE		7906.6	12468.31	5544.69

Table 5.   Comparison of Simple Average Forecasts and Weighted LAV
Forecasts For Months 10–13.

Month	Actual Demand	Simple Average Combination	Error Simple Average	Weighted LAV Combination	Error LAV Combination
10	235	214.7	20.3	231.17	3.83
11	405	260.43	144.57	262.11	142.88
12	264	176.08	87.92	223.31	40.69
13	206	166.52	39.48	215.62	-9.6
MAD			73.05		49.25
MAPE			24.2%		14.25%
MSE			7650.29		5544.69

DISCUSSION

The case application results illustrated that the proposed weighted LAV model could support an effective correct-and-combine approach for combining component forecasts that exhibit systematic bias. In months 10–13, the LAV approach outperformed the standard correct-then-combine approach which was based on Theil's (1971) correction and subsequent averaging of the de-biased component forecasts. The case application demonstrated that the standard correct-then-combine approach does not guarantee improved accuracy, particularly when the amount of demand data is limited and the error pattern changes over time, as was the case at this manufacturing shop. In contrast with the standard approach, in which the monthly forecasts receive equal weights, the proposed LAV model utilized time-based weights to compensate for changes in forecast bias.

The case application results also demonstrate that initial de-biasing of component forecasts may appear so effective that there does not seem to be any point in developing combined forecasts. The corrected f_2 time series for months 2–9 had a lower MSE (142.63) than either the simple average combination (MSE = 403.594) or the corrected f_1 time series (MSE = 1057). Given this disparity in initial forecast performance, the manager might decide to discard the exponentially smoothed model altogether and simply use the additive model for advance order data. As the results from the out of sample forecasts show, this would be misguided because it means that the manager would be throwing away information about past total demand – which was contained in the exponential forecasts – and would be using only the information contained in the partial order forecasts.

The weighted LAV model proposed in this study should not be harder to implement in practice than the standard correct-then-combine approach. Instead of requiring an OLS regression to reduce bias, the weighed LAV model uses linear programming to simultaneously address bias problems and solve for optimal combination weights. User friendly software tools like Excel and LINGO can be used to implement the LAV approach. In addition, the sensitivity analysis reports available with these packages can provide further insight on the effect of outliers or mis-specified points on model parameters.

Additional research on the proposed correct-and-combine approach is needed to test its effectiveness in other demand contexts, such as service contexts. Other weighting schemes besides the time-based weighting method used in this study should be investigated. There are also many variations on the constraints in the linear programming model that could be examined. Although a number of alternative weighted LAV models could be developed, the linear programming model presented in this study does illustrate the potential of the combine-and-correct approach in improving forecast accuracy.

REFERENCES

Ahlburg, D. (1984). Forecast evaluation and improvement using Theils' decomposition. *Journal of Forecasting*, *3*(3), 345–361.

Ameen, J., & Harrison, P. (1984). Discounted weighted estimation. *Journal of Forecasting*, *9*, 285–296.

Armstrong, J., & Collopy, F. (1998). Integration of statistical methods and judgment for time series forecasting: Principles from empirical research. In G. Wright & P. Goodwin (Eds.), *Forecasting with judgment* (pp. 269–293). Chichester: Wiley.

Asku, C., & Gunter, S. (1992). An empirical analysis of the accuracy of the SA, OLS, ERLS and NRLS combination forecasts. *International Journal of Forecasting*, *8*(1), 27–43.

Bates, J. M., & Granger, C. W. J. (1969). The combination of forecasts. *Operational Research Quarterly*, *20*(4), 451–468.

Bunn, D. (1975). A Bayesian approach to linear combination of forecasts. *Operational Research Quarterly*, *26*(2), 325–329.

Bunn, D. (1985). Statistical efficiency on the linear combination of forecasts. *International Journal of Forecasting*, *1*, 151–163.

Bunn, D. (1987). Expert use of forecasts: Bootstrapping and linear models. In G. Wright & P. Ayton (Eds.), *Judgmental forecasting* (pp. 229–241). Chichester: Wiley.

Clemen, R. (1986). Linear constraints and the efficiency of combined forecasts. *Journal of Forecasting*, *5*(1), 31–38.

Clemen, R. (1989). Combining forecasts: A review and annotated bibliography. *International Journal of Forecasting*, *5*(4), 559–583.

DeLurgio, S. (1998). *Forecasting principles and applications*. Boston, MA: Irwin McGraw-Hill.
De Menzes, L., Bunn, D., & Taylor, J. (2000). Review of guidelines for the use of combined forecasts. *European Journal of Operational Research, 120*, 190–204.
Dielman, T., & Pfaffenberger, R. (1988). Least absolute value regression: Necessary sample sizes to use normal theory inference procedures. *Decision Sciences, 19*(4), 734–743.
Goodwin, P. (1997). Adjusting judgmental extrapolations using Theil's method and discounted weighted regression. *Journal of Forecasting, 16*(1), 37–46.
Goodwin, P. (2000). Correct or combine? Mechanically integrating judgmental forecasts with statistical methods. *International Journal of Forecasting, 16*(2), 261–275.
Goodwin, P., & Lawton, R. (2003). Debiasing forecasts: How useful is the unbiasedness test? *International Journal of Forecasting, 19*, 467–475.
Granger, C., & Ramanathan, R. (1984). Improved methods of forecasting. *Journal of Forecasting, 3*(2), 197–204.
Guerard, J. (1987). Linear constraints, robust-weighting and efficient composite modeling. *Journal of Forecasting, 6*(3), 193–199.
Gunter, S. (1992). Nonnegativity restricted least squares combinations. *International Journal of Forecasting, 8*(1), 45–59.
Hendry, D., & Clements, M. (2002). Pooling of forecasts. *Econometrics Journal, 5*, 1–26.
Holden, K., & Peel, D. (1986). An empirical investigation of combinations of economic forecasts. *Journal of Forecasting, 5*(4), 229–242.
Holden, K., Peel, D., & Thomson, J. (1990). Economic forecasting: An introduction. *International Journal of Forecasting, 3*, 239–243. Cambridge: Cambridge University Press.
Holmen, J. (1987). A note on the value of combining short-term earnings forecasts. *International Journal of Forecasting, 3*, 239–243.
Jex, C. (1994). Recursive estimation as an aid to exploratory data analysis: An application to market share models. *International Journal of Forecasting, 10*, 445–453.
Kekre, S., Morton, T., & Smunt, T. (1990). Forecasting using partially known demands. *International Journal of Forecasting, 6*(1), 115–125.
Lobo, G. (1991). Alternative methods of combining security analysts' and statistical forecasts of annual corporate earnings. *International Journal of Forecasting, 19*, 57–63.
Mills, T., & Stephenson, M. (1985). Forecasting contemporaneous aggregates and the combination of forecasts: The case of the UK monetary aggregates. *Journal of Forecasting, 4*, 273–281.
Sanders, N., & Ritzman, L. (2004). Integrating judgmental forecasts and quantitative forecasts; Methodologies for pooling marketing and operations information. *International Journal of Operations and Production Management, 24*(5), 514–529.
Theil, H. (1971). *Applied economic forecasting*. Amsterdam, NY: North Holland.
Watson, M. (1996). Forecasting in the Scottish electronics industry. *International Journal of Forecasting, 12*(3), 361–371.

ASSESSING A MODIFICATION TO CROSTON'S METHOD TO INCORPORATE A SEASONAL COMPONENT

Matthew Lindsey and Robert Pavur

ABSTRACT

One aspect of forecasting intermittent demand for slow-moving inventory that has not been investigated to any depth in the literature is seasonality. This is due in part to the reliability of computed seasonal indexes when many of the periods have zero demand. This chapter proposes an innovative approach which adapts Croston's (1970) method to data with a multiplicative seasonal component. Adaptations of Croston's (1970) method are popular in the literature. This method is one of the most popular techniques to forecast items with intermittent demand. A simulation is conducted to examine the effectiveness of the proposed technique extending Croston's (1970) method to incorporate seasonality.

Keywords: Seasonality; Croston's method; intermittent demand; forecasting

Advances in Business and Management Forecasting, Volume 9, 185–195
ISSN: 1477-4070/doi:10.1108/S1477-4070(2013)0000009015

INTRODUCTION

Forecasting techniques for slow-moving inventory have been explored extensively in the last 10 years. Examples of this research are numerous. New and improved forecasting methodologies (Altay, Rudisill, & Litteral, 2008; Boylan & Syntetos, 2007; Levén & Segerstedt, 2004; Lindsey & Pavur, 2009; Shale, Boylan, & Johnston, 2006; Shenstone & Hyndman, 2005; Snyder, 2002; Syntetos & Boylan, 2001, 2005, 2006; Willemain, Smart, & Schwarz, 2004), inventory systems (Chang, Chung, & Yang, 2001; Chung & Hou, 2003), method comparisons (Dolgui & Pashkevich, 2008; Ghobbar, 2004), and case studies (Hua, Zhang, Yang, & Tan, 2007) are many of the areas that have been studied related to slow-moving inventory. However, many of the characteristics of forecasting times series with regular demand have not been thoroughly investigated for items with intermittent or slow-moving demand. Altay et al. (2008) demonstrated that a modification of Holt's method can be used to satisfactorily forecast demand for spare parts when trends are present. Lindsey and Pavur (2008) studied the effect of trends when forecasting slow-moving inventory. Recently Altay, Litteral, and Rudisill (2012) examined the effects of correlation when demand is intermittent. However, the aspect of seasonality has been largely ignored in practice and in the literature. Furthermore, the usual assumption when forecasting slow-moving demand is that seasonality is absent (Tuenter, 2009).

The presence of seasonality is generally ignored due to difficulty in computing reliable estimates when there are so few positive demand observations over long stretches of time. It is reasonable to think that seasonality might even make demand intermittent. Spare parts could easily be influenced by seasonality. Many industries have "shut downs" in a slow season to retool or change model years. These shut downs could influence demand at similar times each year. Car assembly lines generally retool each summer at the end of model years and many heavy industries shut down at the end of the year for maintenance and upgrades. Accessories for seasonal products could have low demand and occur on a seasonal basis.

This chapter examines the effect of seasonality on one method of forecasting intermittent demand. Croston's method (1972) is arguably one of the leading techniques for forecasting slow-moving demand. This chapter proposes an adaptation of Croston's method to account for the effects of seasonality. A simulation is conducted to examine the proposed model. First Croston's method and seasonality are reviewed, and then the special considerations of slow-moving inventory when seasonality is expected are explored. The proposed model and the simulation used to validate the model are then described.

CROSTON'S METHOD

Croston's (1972) method is summarized below and is similar to the notation for single exponential smoothing. The method utilizes a smoothing constant α, like exponential smoothing, and assumes a constant mean demand of size of μ occurring every p periods, so the demand per period is not just μ/p under the assumptions of Croston (1972), but rather

$$y^* = \left(\frac{\alpha}{p}\right)\left\{\frac{p\mu}{[1-(1-\alpha)^p]}\right\} \tag{1}$$

Boylan and Syntetos (2007) demonstrated that Croston's method was not unbiased and provided the correction of multiplying the demand per period by $1 - \alpha/2$. This research utilizes Willemain, Smart, Shockor, and DeSautels (1994) methodology in implementing Croston's (1972) method. The following notation is utilized:

$X_t =$ binary indicator of demand at time t
$Z_t =$ size of demand
$Y_t = X_t Z_t =$ demand for an item at time t
$\mu =$ mean value of demand when nonzero
$\sigma^2 =$ variance of demand when nonzero
$p =$ average number of time periods between demands
$\alpha =$ smoothing parameter
$q =$ time interval since last demand
$P_t'' =$ Croston's estimate of mean interval between demands
$Z_t'' =$ Croston's estimate of mean demand size
$v_t'' =$ Croston's estimate of mean demand per period

Separate exponential smoothing estimates are made for the average demand and the interval between the demands for Croston's method with updates only occurring if a demand occurs (Willemain et al., 1994).

$$\text{If } X_t = 0, \quad Z''_t = Z''_{t-1}$$
$$P''_t = P''_{t-1} \tag{2}$$
$$q = q + 1$$

$$\text{Else } X_t = 1, \quad Z''_t = Z''_{t-1} + \alpha(y_t - Z''_{t-1}) \tag{3}$$

$$P''_t = P''_{t-1} + \alpha(q - P''_{t-1}) \tag{4}$$

$$q = 1 \tag{5}$$

The mean demand per period is then $y''_t = Z''_t / P''_t$.

Furthermore, immediately following demand, the expected value is $E\{y''_t\} = \frac{\mu}{p}$, with the approximate variance

$$V(y''_t) = \left[\frac{\alpha}{2-\alpha}\right]\left[\frac{(p-1)^2\mu^2}{p^4} + \frac{\sigma^2}{p^2}\right] \tag{6}$$

When demand is not slow-moving, Croston's method can be used, but it is basically the same as single exponential smoothing (SES). Since this is the case, Croston's method can be used for either slow-moving (intermittent demand) or regular demand.

SEASONALITY

Seasonality is a data pattern that repeats itself after a certain period. The repeating period can be days, weeks, months, or quarters. Seasonal variations appear in data sets due to recurring events like hot weather during the summer or holidays. Seasonality is basically the amount that actual values differ from the average value or from some trend in a time series due to the influence of a recurring event. That is, due to the season, the particular time period is either greater or less than the overall average.

The effect of seasonality can be multiplicative or additive. When seasonality is multiplicative, the magnitude of the seasonal variation changes in relation to the present trend. That is, if the trend increases, the seasonal variation increases proportionally. When seasonality is additive, the magnitude of the seasonal variation is constant each season, even if an increasing or decreasing trend is present. Additive seasonality is less common than multiplicative seasonality (Derksen, 1969).

For multiplicative seasonality, a seasonal index, which is the ratio of the average period demand to the overall demand, is used to adjust seasonal demand for each period. For example, if the average monthly demand for an item for the past three years is 100 units per month but the average demand in January over the last three years is 80 units per month, January would have a seasonal index of 0.8 indicating that demand in January is 80% of the normal demand due to the seasonal influence. When preparing a forecast, seasonality is first removed from the data (divide actual data by seasonal index), then a trend or mean estimate is computed using the deseasonalized data, and finally a forecast is made by multiplying this estimate by the seasonal index for the respective period.

SEASONALITY AND SLOW-MOVING INVENTORY

Hyndman (2006) suggests that seasonality can be a factor in forecasting demand for slow-moving items. The difficulty of computing seasonal index values is that many periods have no demand (Eaves & Kingsman, 2004). Thus, seasonality is generally assumed to be absent when forecasting slow-moving demand (Tuenter & Duncan, 2009). While comparing methods for forecasting slow-moving demand by Sani and Kingsman (1997) neither Croston's method, single exponential smoothing, nor did moving averages explicitly account for seasonality in data.

The problem with accounting for seasonality in intermittent data is that it is likely that a particular seasonal period (i.e., January's demand when demand is monthly) might never experience demand. Several possible options were considered for dealing with this situation. One option might be to find a similar product with regular demand and use the same seasonal index for the slow-moving item. Another possible solution is to combine smaller periods (combine weekly data into monthly data or monthly data into quarterly data). Another option might be to use a seasonal index of 1 until actual demand is experienced and an index can be computed.

The model investigated in this chapter assumes multiplicative seasonality. Multiplicative seasonality with no trend can be described as follows: $y_t = (\beta_0)SN(t) + \varepsilon_t$, where β_0 is a constant and $SN(t)$ is a seasonal component that is assumed to be mostly constant over certain time periods within a year. These parameters may change slowly from year to year. The β_0 parameter can be thought of as the average deseasonalized value of the time series. The error term ε_t is assumed to have a mean of zero and a constant variance. If the $SN(t)$ component was equal to one over all time periods, then the time series could be forecasted used single exponential smoothing. The "No Trend Winter's Method" can be used to smooth values in this time series. This method is described as follows and assumes one observation per season. This procedure allows for any number of seasonal periods.

$$a_0(t) = a(y_t/SN(t - L)) + (1 - a)a_0(t - 1) \tag{7}$$

$$SN(t) = a(y_T/a_0(t)) + (1 - a)SN(t - L) \tag{8}$$

$$\hat{Y}_{t+1}(t) = a_0(t)^*SN(t + 1 - L) \tag{9}$$

where L represents the seasonal length, t represents the current time, $a_0(t)$ is the smoothed value of the deseasonalized value β_0, $SN(t - L)$ is the most recent smoothed seasonal value made L periods ago, and $\hat{y}_{t+1}(T)$ is the forecasted value of y_t made at time t for time period $t + 1$.

A Croston method modified for seasonality is presented below. One adaptation to this procedure is that multiple observations are allowed per seasonal period. The "No Trend Winter's Method" exponential smoothing can also be modified to have multiple observations per season. To accommodate this change $SN(t - L)$ is changed to $SN_t(T - L)$ where T is a counting variable for the seasons and t is the count for each time period for a each possible demand. Note that there may be several time periods within a season. As an example to clarify the use of T and t, one may think of t as a counting variable for observations made once a month and T as a counting variable for each quarter. The $SN(t - L)$ term previously used is changed to $SN_t(T - L)$ to reflect that the seasonal index $SN(T - L)$ is updated in time period t. The notation t^* represents the most recent time period in which $SN(T - L)$ was updated. That is, $SN_{t^*}(T - L)$ means that the seasonal index at $T - L$ was last updated at time period t^*. Note that t^* may be $t - 1$ or it may be a t value from four quarters ago.

$$\begin{aligned}
&\text{If } X_t = 0, \ a_0(t) = a_0(t - 1) \\
&\qquad P_t'' = P_{t-1}'' \\
&\qquad SN_t(T) = SN_{t^*}(T - L) \\
&\qquad q = q + 1
\end{aligned} \tag{10}$$

$$\begin{aligned}
&\text{Else } X_t = 1, \ a_0(t) = a_0(t - 1) + \alpha((y_t/SN_{t^*}(T - L)) - a_0(t - 1)) \\
&\qquad P_t'' = P_{t-1}'' + \alpha(q - P_{t-1}'') \\
&\qquad SN_t(T) = \alpha(y_t/a_0(t)) + (1 - \alpha)SN_{t^*}(T - L) \\
&\qquad q = 1.
\end{aligned} \tag{11}$$

The forecasted demand for time period t that is made in time period $t - 1$ is $y_t'' = a_0(t - 1)^*SN_{t^*}(T - L)/P_{t-1}''$. Note that the same smoothing constant is being used for both P_t and $SN_t(T)$. In practice, separate smoothing constants can be used particularly if one component varies more than the other.

SIMULATION DESCRIPTION

To investigate the effect of seasonality when using Croston's method to forecast intermittent data, a simulation was performed. For this investigation, 36 test situations were reported. Three smoothing constants were compared, three seasonality scenarios, and two standard deviations were compared for regular and slow demand levels. Each test consisted of 100 simulation repetitions. For each simulation, 12 years of quarterly data (or 48 time periods) were used. The actual data was recorded on a monthly basis. So a total of $12 \times 4 \times 3 = 144$ data points were used. The forecast for the first two years were not included in the computation of the Root Mean Square Error (RMSE). While this would be a long period to collect data in most real life situations, the same technique could be used with shorter periods, for example, observed weekly data within monthly seasons could be used instead of observed monthly data within quarters. The error component of the multiplicative seasonality model is normally distributed with a mean of zero and a two different value for the standard deviation.

Three seasonality scenarios were examined. First with no seasonality – all seasonal indexes are equal to 1, then with seasonal indexes of 1, 1.8, 0.5, and 0.7 in quarters 1, 2, 3, and 4, respectively, and finally with a seasonal index of 1.2 in quarters 1 and 2 and 0.8 in quarters 3 and 4. Each scenario is shown in the following graphs. The first scenario of "no seasonality" provides a baseline of comparison (Fig. 1).

Two demand situations were used. Regular demand had a probability of demand of 50% and slow demand had a probability of demand of 25%. That is the probability of demand occurring in a given period is 25% or the probability of no demand is 75%. This rate was selected to be in the range of rates used commonly in the literature on slow-moving inventory (Johnston, Boylan, & Shale, 2003; Razi & Tarn, 2003; Segerstedt, 1994).

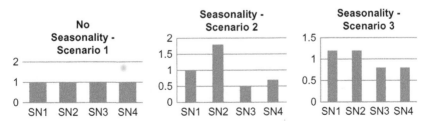

Fig. 1. Seasonality Scenarios Used in Simulation Study.

Table 1. Comparison of Croston's Seasonality Model with the Exponential Smoothing Model Adjusted for Seasonality.

Smoothing Constant (α)	Seasonality Scenario	SE	Regular Demand (Probability of Demand is 0.5)			Slow Demand (Probability of Demand is 0.25)		
			Average RMSE		Percent	Average RMSE		Percent
			Exponential Smoothing	Seasonal Croston	Reduction in RMSE	Exponential Smoothing	Seasonal Croston	Reduction in Error
0.1	1.0	10	52.5	50.4	3.9	47.7	45.9	3.9
0.2	1.0	10	64.1	50.6	21.0	58.2	47.2	18.9
0.3	1.0	10	95.2	51.4	46.0	84.1	48.4	42.4
0.1	1.0	20	53.6	51.5	3.8	48.3	46.4	3.9
0.2	1.0	20	65.2	51.8	20.6	58.7	47.8	18.5
0.3	1.0	20	96.2	52.7	45.3	83.8	49.2	41.4
0.1	2.0	10	57.1	57.4	-0.5	44.0	40.1	9.0
0.2	2.0	10	63.2	57.1	9.6	64.3	41.2	35.9
0.3	2.0	10	78.9	57.3	27.3	114.1	42.5	62.8
0.1	2.0	20	58.2	58.4	-0.3	43.4	39.4	9.1
0.2	2.0	20	64.3	58.3	9.4	63.7	40.6	36.3
0.3	2.0	20	80.4	58.9	26.7	113.6	41.8	63.2
0.1	3.0	10	52.7	52.0	1.4	43.2	40.8	5.5
0.2	3.0	10	61.0	52.1	14.5	57.5	42.1	26.8
0.3	3.0	10	84.1	52.9	37.1	95.0	43.3	54.4
0.1	3.0	20	53.8	53.1	1.4	43.9	41.5	5.5
0.2	3.0	20	62.0	53.3	14.0	58.0	42.7	26.3
0.3	3.0	20	84.7	54.3	35.9	94.9	44.0	53.6

The simulations also compare two levels of dispersion. A "high" standard deviation of 20 and a "low" standard deviation of 10 are used. The simulations also compare the forecasts using three smoothing constants. Lower smoothing constants take a smaller percentage of the forecast error into account when adjusting the forecast for the next period, resulting in a smoother forecast. Three results values are provided. The RMSE for the forecast using exponential smoothing, the RMSE for the forecast using Croston's method adjusted for seasonality, and the percent improvement (possibly negative) of Croston's method adjusted for seasonality over exponential smoothing.

RESULTS

The results of the 36 exploratory simulations are provided in Table 1. The simulations were conducted using three alpha levels, for three seasonality scenarios and two standard error levels identified on the left section of the table. The center section of the table provides the error and percent improvement for the seasonal Croston method for regular demand. The right section provides the error and percent improvement for slow demand.

The seasonal Croston method percent improvement always increased for regular demand and slow demand as the alpha levels increased as confirmed by the column in Table 1 showing the reduction in the RMSE by the Croston's method. The only time that the seasonal Croston's method did not show an improvement over exponential smoothing was for regular demand with the seasonality scenario 2 at both standard error levels when a smoothing constant of 0.1 was used. The greatest improvement came for seasonality scenario 2 with an alpha level of 0.3 for the slow demand level for the high standard error and next for the low standard error. Overall very little difference was realized between the low standard error levels and the high standard error levels. Seasonality scenario 1 reflects that Croston's method with the seasonality adjustment is still superior to the exponential smoothing method with seasonality even when no actual seasonality is present.

CONCLUSIONS

In this chapter, we have proposed a modification of Croston's method that utilizes the seasonality to improve the ability to forecast the demand rates for items with intermittent demand. As in most forecasting methods, utilizing additional information should give a method an advantage over a method that uses less information. The proposed Croston with seasonality procedure attempts to gain an advantage by utilizing seasonal demand information.

In general seasonality has been ignored in the research for intermittent and slow-moving demand. This research suggests that considering seasonality can improve the forecast in some situations.

REFERENCES

Altay, N., Litteral, L. A., & Rudisill, F. (2012). Effects of correlation on intermittent demand forecasting and stock control. *International Journal of Production Economics, 135*(1), 275–283.

Altay, N., Rudisill, F., & Litteral, L. A. (2008). Adapting Wright's modification of Holt's method to forecasting intermittent demand. *International Journal of Production Economics, 111*(2), 389–408.

Boylan, J. E., & Syntetos, A. A. (2007). The accuracy of a modified Croston procedure. *International Journal of Production Economics, 107*(2), 511–517.

Chang, S.-L., Chung, K.-J., & Yang, W.-D. (2001). The (s, Q) inventory system for slow-moving items. *Journal of Information & Optimization Sciences, 22*(2), 383–395.

Chung, K.-J., & Hou, K.-L. (2003). The determination of the optimal safety stock of the (s, Q) inventory system for slow moving items. *Journal of Statistics & Management Systems, 6*(2), 229–240.

Croston, J. D. (1972). Forecasting and stock control for intermittent demands. *Operational Research Quarterly, 23*(3), 289–303.

Derksen, J. B. D. (1969). Adjustments for seasonal movements with the census method II: Recent experiences. *Statistica Neerlandica, 23*(2), 151–159.

Dolgui, A., & Pashkevich, M. (2008). On the performance of binomial and beta-binomial models of demand forecasting for multiple slow-moving inventory items. *Computers and Operations Research, 35*(3), 893–905.

Eaves, A. H. C., & Kingsman, B. G. (2004). Forecasting for the ordering and stock-holding of spare parts. *Journal of the Operational Research Society, 55*(4), 431–437.

Ghobbar, A. A. (2004). Forecasting intermittent demand for aircraft spare parts: A comparative evaluation of methods. *Journal of Aircraft, 41*(3), 665–673.

Hua, Z. S., Zhang, B., Yang, J., & Tan, D. S. (2007). A new approach of forecasting intermittent demand for spare parts inventories in the process industries. *Journal of the Operational Research Society, 58*, 52–61.

Hyndman, R. J. (2006). Another look at forecast accuracy metrics for intermittent demand. *Foresight: The International Journal of Applied Forecasting, 4*, 43–46.

Johnston, F. R., Boylan, J. E., & Shale, E. A. (2003). An examination of the size of orders from customers, their characterization, and the implications for inventory control of slow moving items. *Journal of the Operational Research Society, 54*(8), 833–837.

Levén, E., & Segerstedt, A. (2004). Inventory control with a modified croston procedure and Erlang distribution. *International Journal of Production Economics, 90*(3), 361–367.

Lindsey, M. D., & Pavur, R. (2008). A comparison of methods for forecasting intermittent demand with increasing or decreasing probability of demand occurrences. *Advances in Business and Management Forecasting, 5*, 115–132.

Lindsey, M. D., & Pavur, R. (2009). Prediction intervals for future demand of existing products with an observed demand of zero. *International Journal of Production Economics, 119*(1), 75–89.

Razi, M. A., & Tarn, J. M. (2003). An applied model for improving inventory management in ERP systems. *Logistics Information Management, 16*(2), 114–124.

Sani, B., & Kingsman, B. G. (1997). Selecting the best periodic inventory control and demand forecasting methods for low demand items. *Journal of the Operational Research Society, 48*(7), 700–713.

Segerstedt, A. (1994). Inventory control with variation in lead times, especially when demand is intermittent. *International Journal of Production Economics, 35*(1/3), 365–372.

Shale, E. A., Boylan, J. E., & Johnston, F. R. (2006). Forecasting for intermittent demand: The estimation of an unbiased average. *Journal of the Operational Research Society, 57*(5), 588–592.

Shenstone, L., & Hyndman, R. J. (2005). Stochastic models underlying Croston's method for intermittent demand forecasting. *Journal of Forecasting, 24*(6), 389–402.

Snyder, R. D. (2002). Forecasting sales of slow and fast moving inventories. *European Journal of Operational Research, 140*(3), 684–699.

Syntetos, A. A., & Boylan, J. E. (2001). On the bias of intermittent demand estimates. *International Journal of Production Economics, 71*(1/3), 457–466.

Syntetos, A. A., & Boylan, J. E. (2005). The accuracy of intermittent demand estimates. *International Journal of Forecasting, 21*(2), 303–314.

Syntetos, A. A., & Boylan, J. E. (2006). On the stock-control performance of intermittent demand estimators. *International Journal of Production Economics, 103*(1), 36–47.

Teunter, R. H., & Duncan, L. (2009). Forecasting intermittent demand: A comparative study. *The Journal of the Operational Research Society, 60*(3), 321–329.

Willemain, T. R., Smart, C. N., & Schwarz, H. F. (2004). A new approach to forecasting intermittent demand for service parts inventories. *International Journal of Forecasting, 20*(3), 375–387.

Willemain, T. R., Smart, C. N., Shockor, J. H., & DeSautels, P. A. (1994). Forecasting intermittent demand in manufacturing: A comparative evaluation of Croston's method. *International Journal of Forecasting, 10*(4), 529–538.

PREDICTING THE PERFORMANCE OF A TWO-STAGE FLOWSHOP: LOWER BOUNDS AND HEURISTICS FOR SINGLE AND BICRITERIA MEASURES

Mark T. Leung

ABSTRACT

This study examines the scheduling problem for a two-stage flowshop. All jobs are immediately available for processing and job characteristics including the processing times and due dates are known and certain. The goals of the scheduling problem are (1) to minimize the total flowtime for all jobs, (2) to minimize the total number of tardy jobs, and (3) to minimize both the total flowtime and the total number of tardy jobs simultaneously. Lower bound performances with respect to the total flowtime and the total number of tardy jobs are presented. Subsequently, this study identifies the special structure of schedules with minimum flowtime and minimum number of tardy jobs and develops three sets of heuristics which generate a Pareto set of bicriteria schedules. For each heuristic procedure, there are four options available for schedule generation. In addition, we provide enhancements to a variety of lower

Advances in Business and Management Forecasting, Volume 9, 197–225
Copyright © 2013 by Emerald Group Publishing Limited
All rights of reproduction in any form reserved
ISSN: 1477-4070/doi:10.1108/S1477-4070(2013)0000009016

bounds with respect to flowtime and number of tardy jobs in a flowshop environment. Proofs and discussions to lower bound results are also included.

Keywords: Production scheduling; flowshop; multi-objective decision making; operations research

INTRODUCTION

Effectively scheduling jobs on machines has long been a crucial problem widely studied in the field of operations management. The quality of the generated machine schedules often has direct influence on the performance outcomes (costs, delay, throughput, etc.) of the production line. Hence, in this chapter, we examine how to effectively generate machine schedules and predict the "bottom line" performance with respect to a variety of single and bicriteria measures. Traditional research on machine scheduling usually focuses on problems with a single objective measure. However, in the past decades, there has been an increasing need for addressing multiple managerial concerns. To cope with the reality, researchers have expanded their scheduling studies to the multi-objective dimension. Based on the machine layout, the multi-objective scheduling research can be broken into four major categories:

- single machine
- multiple-machine jobshop
- multiple-machine flowshop
- special configuration (e.g., flexible manufacturing system (FMS) and cellular manufacturing system (CMS))

While most multi-objective studies in the literature focus on single-machine problems, there has been a trend of studying and developing scheduling algorithms for systems with multiple machines. Because of the complexity of the problem structure, many multiple-machine scheduling issues remain unsolved, even when there is a single objective. Thus, most multi-objective scheduling problems involve only two performance measures or they fall into the class of bicriteria scheduling.

In this chapter, we focus on a two-stage flowshop with a single machine in each stage. The goals of the scheduling problem are (1) to minimize the total flowtime for all jobs, (2) to minimize the total number of tardy jobs, and (3) to minimize both the total flowtime and the total number of tardy jobs simultaneously. Goals 1 and 2 are based on single-performance measure whereas goal 3 involves bicriteria scheduling which strategically combines goals 1 and 2. Using the conventional notation, the bicriteria problem (goal 3) can be denoted as $n/2/F/(F,n_T)$. Such a situation can be found in an assembly environment where a delay in completion causes a shutdown of the station located downstream in the production flow line. Minimizing flowtime improves customer response time and tends to reduce inventory. On the other hand, less tardy jobs can lead to smoother material flows and higher customer satisfaction. This bicriteria scheduling problem can also be found in a linked-cellular manufacturing system where fabrication cells with flow-line structure are supporting a major assembly line. Any tardy job from a cell will cause disruption of the final assembly process and thus disrupt the entire cellular manufacturing system. However, in this scenario, the adverse impact of not reducing the flowtime is not as significant as not meeting the due date. For both of these production systems, it is obvious that a manager needs to take into account the tradeoffs between the two measures (i.e., total flowtime and total number of tardy jobs) during machine scheduling. It is because, in most situations, a performance measure of the schedule cannot be improved without a sacrifice in the other one.

An examination of the literature provides many ways to handle these tradeoffs. Despite the variety of their model assumptions, system configuration, or choice of performance measures, the algorithms follow one of the two approaches. If Z_1 and Z_2 represent the two performance measures, then the first approach optimizes Z_1 and Z_2 at the same time while the second approach attempts to find the best value of Z_1 while keeping Z_2 at no more than a certain level. In the following, these two approaches and their conceptual foundation are discussed in more detail.

For the first approach, most studies combine/aggregate Z_1 and Z_2 into a single performance measure using weighted linear combinations. In a number of more recent articles, nonlinear functions are used to describe the tradeoffs between the two measures. These methods usually require the designation of a tradeoff ratio between the two measures, that is, how one measure is expressed as a function of another. Nevertheless, the tradeoff ratio may not be obvious in the real world and a manager's preference may change from time to time. Taking this into account, some researchers also propose to eliminate inferior schedules based on dominance. This elimination method calls for comparison of the tuple (Z_1, Z_2) from different schedules, instead of a combined objective function value. No matter how the approaches eliminate the inferior schedules, their logic shares the common conceptual background:

$$\text{Minimize } F(Z_1(s), \ Z_2(s))$$
$$\text{subject to } s \in \{S\}$$

where $\{S\}$ is the set containing all possible schedules s and $F(\bullet)$ is a function of Z_1 and Z_2. It is the form of $F(\bullet)$ that distinguishes the two types of elimination methods stated above. When a tradeoff ratio between Z_1 and Z_2 is specified and used by the scheduler, $F(\bullet)$ represents a linear or a nonlinear combination of the two performance measures and yields a single value. On the other hand, a tuple (Z_1 and Z_2) is maintained for each schedule when dominance elimination is used.

The second approach attempts to find the best value of Z_1 while keeping Z_2 at a certain level. Some former studies refer this approach as hierarchical optimization. An example of such a study can be seen in Chand and Schneeberger (1988). Their scheduling model is formulated such that the total weighted earliness for the job set is minimized subject to zero tardy jobs. The generic formulation for the second approach is:

$$\text{Minimize } Z_1(s)$$
$$\text{subject to } s \in \{S'\}$$

where s is a schedule, $\{S'\}$ is the set of all schedules satisfying the condition $Z_2(s) \leq Z^*$, and Z^* is a value given by the decision maker. The second approach seems to be more attractive than the first one when a scheduler would like to generate an efficient set of schedules or the preference relationship between Z_1 and Z_2 is not clear. In addition, this approach becomes especially appealing when there is only a finite set of values for $Z_2(s)$, like the number of tardy jobs in our problem. For these reasons, the heuristics proposed in our study follow the second approach. In other words, we attempt to find a schedule with good flowtime given a designated number of tardy jobs.

The remainder of this chapter is organized as follows: the related literature is briefly summarized in the next section. In the third section, we provide a description of the two-stage flowshop problem. Basic notations and assumptions pertinent to this study are also established. The fourth section presents a variety of lower bounds with respect to total flowtime and number of tardy jobs. A detailed discussion of and possible improvements to some of the existing bounds are also provided. Then, three sets of heuristic algorithms for bicriteria scheduling are described in the fifth section. To facilitate better understanding of the heuristic logic, numerical examples are included. Finally, the chapter is concluded in the sixth section.

LITERATURE REVIEW

Since the pioneer work by Johnson (1954) for minimizing the makespan of jobs in a two-stage flowshop, there has been an immense growth of research related to flowshop scheduling. A significant number of these studies are related to solving the sequencing problem with the objective of minimizing the makespan although other criteria such as average (or total) flow-time, tardiness, and proportion of tardy jobs have also been attempted. Because of the vast amount of studies in machine scheduling, the following discussion focuses on the relevant articles in multi-objective flowshop scheduling.

Gupta and Dudek (1971) suggest a number of cost criteria for flowshop scheduling. Their empirical findings indicate that none of their tested scheduling rules consistently outperforms the others with respect to these cost criteria. Further, Dudek, Panwalkar, and Smith (1992) point out that some research studies may find a lack of application in industry because "the problem may exist but with multiple criteria" (p. 9). With these notions, many studies within the last decade extend the single objective flowshop problem to the multi-objective arena where multiple shop performance measures are used to determine the optimal production schedules.

The multi-objective flowshop problems usually pose a challenge to schedulers. Morton and Pentico (1993) state that optimizing even a single objective such as flowtime, tardiness, number of tardy, or any regular measure other than makespan is NP hard. Hence, trying to solve a flowshop problem with multiple measures is also an NP hard task. Thus, researchers have proposed a wide range of procedures to attack this difficult problem. For a systematic overview of the scheduling algorithms for flowshop, interested readers can refer to Morton and Pentico (1993) and Rajendran (1995).

Because of their complexity, most of the multi-objective flowshop problems deal with two criteria with a few exceptions which examine three criteria at the same time. Daniels and Chambers (1990) develop a bicriteria deterministic scheduling algorithm for the flowshop. The shop performance is evaluated by a minimization of both makespan and maximum job tardiness. The paper provides an exact algorithm that identifies an efficient set of schedules for the two-machine case. For those systems with more machines, the paper proposes a heuristic to approximate the efficient set.

In a separate study, Nagar, Heragu, and Haddock (1995) give a branch and bound algorithm for two-machine flowshops where the objectives minimize flowtime and makespan. Effective heuristic algorithms to compute upper and lower bounds are also given. The bicriteria flowshop scheduling study by Liao, Yu, and Joe (1997) examines two problems, one dealing with the objectives of minimizing makespan and number of tardy jobs and the other one with makespan and total tardiness. Like most other precursory studies with two objectives, this paper also uses a branch and bound algorithm to develop efficient schedules.

In Rajendran (1992), the author presents a branch and bound procedure to minimize the total flowtime subject to an optimal makespan. The procedure makes use of the previous work by Ignall and Schrage (1965) and develops heuristics for bounding conditions. A later study by Rajendran (1995) extended the previous work to consider the scheduling problem of minimizing makespan, total flowtime, and machine idle time simultaneously. They report better results relative to a former tri-criteria study by Ho and Chang (1991). In their paper, they develop a heuristic for optimizing the same three performance measures – makespan, total flowtime, and machine utilization (which is equivalent to minimizing idle time). Experimental results show that the proposed heuristic performs better in all criteria than those heuristics which aim at optimizing a single measure.

Apart from the traditional procedures which are based on a branch and bound framework, there are several studies that explore the use of non-conventional search paradigms to solve the bicriteria scheduling problem. Gangadharan and Rajendran (1994) propose a simulated annealing (SA) framework to handle the flowshop problem with the objectives of minimizing makespan and total flowtime. Together with the proposed framework are two heuristics to provide the seed sequences for the SA improvement algorithm. The reported results suggest that the solutions found by the SA framework have better performance than those generated by Ho and Chang's heuristic. Murata, Ishibuchi, and Tanaka (1996) develop a multi-objective genetic algorithm to tackle the flowshop problem. Their study applied the proposed algorithm to two scheduling problems with different objectives. The first one is a bicriteria problem with the objectives of minimizing the makespan and total tardiness whereas the second one is a tri-criteria problem with the objectives of minimizing makespan, total tardiness, and total flowtime.

PROBLEM FORMULATION AND NOTATION

In this study, we consider a deterministic two-machine flowshop problem without preemption. There is a single machine in each of the two stages. A machine is available for processing immediately after the previous job is completed (i.e., no explicit setup is considered). There are exactly n jobs available for processing at time zero and all information pertinent to the jobs is known and certain. Each of the n jobs requires processing once and only once on each of the two machines and a job's processing on Machine A must precede its processing on Machine B. For job j, let a_j be the processing time on Machine A, b_j be the processing time on Machine B, and F_j be the completion time of the job on Machine B. Also let J be a sequence (permutation) of n jobs. In addition, there is a due date d_j assigned to job j.

There are two performance measures in our scheduling problem, that is, minimizing the total flowtime F and minimizing the total number of tardy jobs n_T. First, we examine how to generate effective job schedules with respect to each individual performance measure. Then, we develop heuristics to generate bicriteria schedules which encompass the two measures simultaneously. As mentioned in section "Introduction", our heuristic procedures follows the second approach of bicriteria optimization, that is, improving performance measure Z_1 after a schedule with a good value of Z_2 has been found. Therefore, there are two major formats in our proposed bicriteria heuristics, representing the two possibilities of optimizing F or n_T in the first stage and the other measure in the second stage. The first format tries to obtain a schedule with the minimum n_T in the first stage. Then, the algorithm improves F without increasing the value of n_T. Likewise, the second format focuses on the F measure in the first stage and attempts to improve n_T in the second stage. This kind of hierarchical optimization of two criteria parallels the frameworks used by Liao et al. (1997) and Chand and Schneeberger (1988).

Rather than looking at the two performance measure at the same time, we can focus on a single measure by isolating the other. As a result, we can compute lower bounds and generate feasible schedules (upper bounds) based on flowtime F and on the number of tardy jobs n_T separately. It means that a specific schedule J can be evaluated by F and n_T simultaneously. To be consistent throughout the paper, for a sequence J, we use $F(J)$ and $n_T(J)$ to indicate the flowtime and the number of tardy jobs. The lower bound and the final value of heuristic solution on the flowtime for J are denoted as $LB[F(J)]$ and $F'(J)$, respectively. Similarly, their n_T counterparts are written as LB[$n_T(J)$] and $n_{T'}(J)$. Additional notations will be defined when they are used.

Before we move to the next section, it is important to point out a special characteristic of the optimal schedules for two-stage flowshops. According to Morton and Pentico (1993), since both F and n_T are regular measures, only permutation schedules, in which the processing sequence in the first stage is identical to the processing sequence in the second stage, will lead to the optimal solution(s). This notion allows us to substantially reduce the size of state space for searching and paves the road to problem relaxation described below.

LOWER BOUNDS

In this section, we present a number of lower bounds for two-stage flowshop schedules. These lower bounds focus on a single measure, that is, they are the bounds on the performance of F or on the performance of n_T. Having conducted a significant amount of preliminary work, it is obvious to us that more developments on these single-criterion bounds are needed before proceeding to the multi-criteria level. It is because good and efficient bounds on F and n_T are not available and multi-criteria bounds, which simultaneously consider any two measures, are non-existent. Therefore, we perceive any development or improvement to the few existing methods for obtaining the bound for single performance measure as a crucial step to create multi-criteria lower bound.

Formulation for Two-Stage Flowshop Scheduling Problem

Before we describe the lower bounds, let us provide a general formulation of the two-stage flowshop scheduling problem with the objective of minimizing the total flowtime. This model is useful in helping us to explain the foundation and logic of the lower bounds presented later. Let $F_{[j]}$ indicate the flowtime of the job in the j-th position of sequence J. Also let $a_{[j]}$ and $b_{[j]}$ denote the processing times a and b, respectively, of the job in the j-th position of sequence J. The model can be written as:

$$\text{Min } F(J) = \sum_i F_{[i]} \qquad (1)$$

subject to

$$F_{[i]} = \max(A_{[i]},\ B_{[i]}) \qquad (2)$$

$$A_{[1]} = a_{[1]} + b_{[1]} \tag{3}$$

$$A_{[1]} \geq \min(a_{[i]}) + b_{[1]} \tag{4}$$

$$A_{[i]} = \sum_{j=1,i} a_{[j]} + b_{[i]}, \quad \text{for } i = 2, \ldots, n \tag{5}$$

$$B_{[1]} = 0 \tag{6}$$

Objective function (1) indicates that this is a flowtime scheduling problem. Constraint (2) means that the flowtime of the i-th job in the sequence is the maximum of two quantities, $A_{[i]}$ and $B_{[i]}$, which represents two possible scenarios. In scenario A, job i receives immediately processing on Machine B after its completion on Machine A. In scenario B, job i does not receive immediate processing on Machine B because the second-stage machine is still occupied with the previous job when job i is completed on Machine A and preemption is not allowed.

Constraints (3), (4), and (5) belong to a set which describes the calculation of $A_{[i]}$. Constraint (3) simply says that the completion time of the first job in sequence J is the sum of its processing times on both stages. Constraint (4) implies that the flowtime of the first job must be at least as great as the sum of its second stage processing time $b_{[1]}$ and the smallest first stage processing time among all jobs in the sequence. Constraint (5) shows how to compute the $A_{[i]}$ for jobs after the first one in the sequence.

Constraints (6) and (5) are for the calculation of $B_{[i]}$. Constraint (6) complements constraints (2) and (3) in that there is only one way to compute the flowtime for the first job in sequence. Constraint (7) shows the flowtime of job i when scenario B arises. Now, we describe the lower bounds on F.

Lower Bounds on F

$LB_1[F(J)]$
While it is well-known that the Johnson's algorithm minimizes the makespan of a group of jobs in a two-machine flowshop, there does not exist any algorithm which guarantees an optimal flowtime schedule. As mentioned earlier, the total flowtime problem in a two-machine flowshop environment is NP-hard. Thus, many researchers have developed specialized branch and bound procedures and heuristics to solve this problem. The first lower bound presented here focuses on the F measure and follows the conceptual background of a bound used by Ignall and Schrage (1965) in their branch and bound procedure.

Theorem 1. A lower bound on the flowtime can be obtained by, first, arranging the jobs in SPT sequence such that $a_{[1]} \leq a_{[2]} \leq \ldots \leq a_{[n]}$ and then computing the sum of flowtimes for all jobs in J:

$$LB_1[F(J)] = \sum_{j=1}^{n} F_j = \sum_{j=1}^{n} \left[\sum_{i=1}^{j} a_{[i]} + b_{[j]} \right]$$

Proof: The calculation of LB_1 is based on the assumption that a job always receives processing on Machine B immediately after its completion on Machine A. In other words, the scenario A described in the last section is always true. Therefore, constraints (6) and (7) are relaxed and constraint (2) is reduced to a simpler form of $F_{[i]} = A_{[i]}$. As a result, LB_1 represents a relaxation of the original problem and thereby a valid lower bound.

Theorem 2. If the dominance condition $\min_{j \in J} a_j \geq \max_{j \in J} b_j$ exists, then the SPT sequence obtained by applying the lower bound $LB_1[F(J)]$ is the optimal flowtime schedule for the two-stage flowshop problem.

Proof: The dominance condition suggests that the processing times on Machine A completely dominate the ones on Machine B. When this condition is true, the previous job in J is completed on Machine B before the current job's completion on Machine A. In other words, there is always an idle time between successive jobs on Machine B. Because the processing times b_j, for $j = 1, \ldots, n$, are irrelevant in the determination of the optimal permutation of J, only the processing times a_j and the permutation on Machine A are the factors to be considered.

Hence, we have reduced the problem to a single machine problem (Machine A) with the objective of minimizing the flowtime. Since idle time is always absent in the first stage of a flowshop schedule when we try to minimize the flowtime, an optimal schedule can be obtained by the SPT sequence with respect to the processing times a_j on Machine A, that is, the jobs should be arranged in the order of $a_{[1]} \leq a_{[2]} \leq \ldots \leq a_{[n]}$. This concept is illustrated in Fig. 1.

$LB_2[F(J)]$

$LB_1[F(J)]$ described above can be viewed as a relaxation to the scheduling problem by restricting the attention to Machine A, the first stage in the flowshop. Using the same logic, Ignall and Schrage (1965) propose another lower bound based on a restriction to Machine B, the second stage in the flowshop.

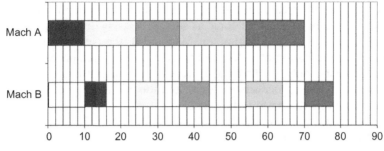

Fig. 1. Example for Theorem 2.

Theorem 3. A lower bound on the flowtime can be obtained by, first, arranging the jobs in SPT sequence such that $b_{[1]} \leq b_{[2]} \leq \ldots \leq b_{[n]}$, second, finding the minimum first-stage processing time among all jobs ($\min_{i \in IJ} a_j$), and, third, computing the sum of flowtimes for all jobs in J:

$$LB_2[F(J)] = \sum_{j=1}^{n} F_j = \sum_{j=1}^{n} \left[\min_{i \in J} a_i + \sum_{i=1}^{j} b_{[j]} \right]$$

Proof: The calculation of $LB_2[F(J)]$ implies that a job does not receive processing on Machine B immediately after its completion on Machine A because Machine B is occupied at that moment. Thus the job has to wait till Machine B is available. This situation suggests that the scenario B described earlier is always true and constraint (5) in the formulation is relaxed. Constraint (7) is then reduced to $B_{[i]} = F_{[i-1]} + b_{[i]}$, which implies $A_{[i]} = F_{[i]}$. In addition, since we use the minimum of all a_i as the first stage processing time, we have relaxed the restriction of the first job processed on Machine A being the same as the first job processed on Machine B. This also relaxes constraint (3). As a result, LB_2 represents a relaxation of the original problem and thereby a valid lower bound.

Theorem 4. If the dominance condition $\min_{j \in J} b_j \geq \max_{j \in J} a_j$ is true and both the smallest processing times on Machines A and B, $\min_{i \in J} a_i$ $\min_{i \in J} b_i$, belong to the same job i, then the SPT sequence obtained by applying the lower bound $LB_2[F(J)]$ is the optimal flowtime schedule for the two-stage flowshop problem.

Proof: The dominance condition above implies that Machine B processing times completely dominate those of Machine A. With this special structure, a job can receive immediate processing on Machine B once it is completed on Machine A. It follows that there is no delay in the schedule on Machine B. Because the processing times in the second stage b_j, for $j = 1,\ldots,n$, are at least as long as any processing time a_j in the first stage and there is no idle time on Machine B, the determination of the optimal permutation of J does not need to consider the processing times a_j. Therefore, only the first-stage processing time of the first job in the sequence $a_{[1]}$, the processing times b_j, and the permutation on Machine B are the factors that need to be considered.

The problem is now reduced to two subproblems: (1) determining the permutation of schedule on Machine B and (2) choosing the first-stage processing time for the first job ($a_{[1]}$). The optimal schedule on Machine B can be obtained by the SPT sequence with respect to the processing times b_j, that is, the jobs should be arranged in the order of $b_{[1]} \le b_{[2]} \le \ldots \le b_{[n]}$. Since the special condition that there is a job i satisfying $\min_{i \in J} a_i \min_{i \in J} b_i$ holds, the first job processed on Machine B is also the first job on Machine A, that is, $\min_{i \in J} a_i = a_{[1]}$ and $\min_{i \in J} b_i = b_{[1]}$. When $\min_{i \in J} a_i = a_{[1]}$ there is a minimum delay before the commencement of processing on Machine B, and the SPT schedule is optimal when both conditions in Theorem 4 are met. Fig. 2 depicts this concept.

Corollary. If the dominance condition $\min_{j \in J} b_j \ge \max_{j \in J} a_j$ exists and the SPT ordering of $b_{[1]} \le b_{[2]} \le \ldots \le b_{[n]}$ results in the $j_{[1]}$ such that $a_{[1]} = \min_{i \in J} a_i$, then $LB_2[F(J)]$ gives the optimal flowtime schedule for the two-stage flowshop problem.

Lower Bound on n_T

Although there is no known sequencing rule to minimize the number of tardy jobs for the two-stage flowshop, Moore (1968) presents an algorithm

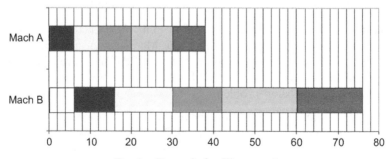

Fig. 2. Example for Theorem 4.

which solves the n_T problem for a single machine case. Moore's algorithm sequences the jobs in EDD order until the first tardy job is encountered. Then, the job with the largest processing time from the early sequence is removed and put in a late set. This procedure is then repeated until none of the jobs in the early sequence is tardy. The jobs in the late set are appended to the early sequence in the order they are identified because the order of these late jobs does not affect n_T. For our flowshop scheduling problem, it will be advantageous to sequence the set of late jobs according to the SPT order. The foundation of this Moore's algorithm is then extended to the two-stage flowshop environment and, later, to our multi-objective scheduling problem.

Liao et al. (1997) extend the single-machine Moore's algorithm to a branch and bound framework to solve the two-stage flowshop problem. Our procedure for the computation of lower bound on n_T is a modified version of theirs. Given a set of n jobs, we can determine $LB[n_T(J)]$ for the complete schedule J.

$LB_5[n_T(J)]$

Described in the computation of the lower bound on F, one of the ideal scenarios is that a job receive processing on Machine B immediately after its completion on Machine A. Suppose d_j is the due date for job j. If job j is to be non-tardy, the latest completion time of the job on Machine A must be $d'_j = d_j - b_j$.

Theorem 5. A lower bound on the number of tardy jobs can be found by, first, applying Moore's algorithm to sequence J using a_j as the processing time and d'_j as the due date, for $j = 1,\ldots,n$, and subsequently, setting the lower bound $LB_5[n_T(J)]$ to be the number of tardy jobs based on the constructed Moore's sequence.

Proof: The calculation of $LB_5[n_T(J)]$ is based on ignoring the second stage (Machine B) processing, except for the due date offset. Also, the use of d'_j, $j = 1,\ldots,n$, as the due dates for sequencing implies that the processing sequence on Machine B can be in any order as long as the final due dates d_j are met. Hence, $LB_5[n_T(J)]$ represents a relaxation of the original flowshop problem such that the two stages in processing is reduced to a single stage. It follows that the n_T of a feasible schedule will be at least as large as $LB_5[n_T(J)]$ and thereby $LB_5[n_T(J)]$ is a valid lower bound.

$LB_6[n_T(J)]$

In the last section, we describe a lower bound which is built on the concept of isolating a single stage. Essentially, $LB_5[n_T(J)]$ concentrates on the first stage (Machine A) while ignoring the scheduling issues on the second stage (Machine B). In the following, we present the counterpart of $LB_5[n_T(J)]$ in which the processing sequence on the second stage is used to generate a lower bound.

Theorem 6. A lower bound on the number of tardy jobs can be found by, first, applying Moore's algorithm to sequence J using b_j as the processing time and d_j as the due date, for $j = 1,...,$ n, and subsequently, setting the lower bound $LB_6[n_T(J)]$ to be the number of tardy jobs based on the constructed Moore's sequence. All jobs share a common arrival time, $\min_{i \in J} a_i$, to Machine B.

Proof: The arguments are similar to those for $LB_5[n_T(J)]$ except that the first stage (Machine A) processing is ignored. The use of $\min_{i \in J} a_i$ as the start time of production sequence on Machine B ensures that the idle time is kept to a minimum. Any deviation from the use of $\min_{i \in J} a_i$ will push the schedule in Machine B forward and may lead to an n_T higher than or equal to $LB_6[n_T(J)]$. Hence, $LB_6[n_T(J)]$ represents a relaxation of the original flowshop problem such that the two stages in processing is reduced to a single stage. It follows that the n_T of a feasible schedule will be at least as large as $LB_6[n_T(J)]$.

Theorem 7. If the following three conditions exist:

$\min_{j \in J} b_j \geq \max_{j \in J} a_j$

$\min_{i \in J} a_i, \min_{i \in J} b_i,$ $\min_{i \in J} d_i$ belong to the same job i, and

$(\min_{i \in J} a_i + \min_{i \in J} b_i) \leq \min_{i \in J} d_i$ for job i

then the SPT sequence obtained by applying the lower bound $LB_6[F(J)]$ is the optimal schedule for the bicriteria (flowtime and number of tardy jobs) two-stage flowshop problem.

Proof: The dominance condition $\min_{j \in J} b_j \geq \max_{j \in J} a_j$ implies that there is no idle time on Machine B and, with the exception of the first position, the processing sequence on Machine A is irrelevant. This reduces the scheduling problem to be a sequencing problem on Machine B and the selection of the first job for the processing sequence on Machine A. The second condition ensures that the first job $j_{[1]}$ (with $\min_{i \in J} a_i$) to be processed on Machine A is also in the first position in the EDD sequence initiated by the Moore's algorithm. On the other hand, when both $\min_{i \in J} a_i$ and $\min_{i \in J} a_i$ belong to the same job, the first job position in the EDD sequence cannot be put in the late set by the Moore's algorithm and thus remains as the first job in the final Moore's sequence. The only exception to this case is that the first job $j_{[1]}$ is tardy, in which the job will be put into the late set according to the Moore's algorithm. However, the third condition guarantees that $j_{[1]}$ is non-tardy and rules out this possibility. Because the Moore's sequence yields the optimal n_T schedule, the schedule which yields $LB_6[F(J)]$ is optimal for the flowshop problem.

Bicriteria Lower Bound

As discussed earlier in section "Lower Bounds," models for computing a truly bicriteria lower bound which specifies the bound of one measure subject to the lower limit of another do not exist. For our study, more insights on the generation of more efficient lower bounds on F and n_T and identification of special problem characteristics need to be obtained before the goal of developing bicriteria lower bound can be attained. Nevertheless, we have made some attempts to create such lower bounds. The results and corresponding proofs for some of our works are presented in the appendix.

BICRITERIA HEURISTICS

Bicriteria Moore's Heuristics for Flowshop

As stated earlier, Moore's algorithm produces optimal schedules for the minimization of n_T in a single machine case. We extend this algorithm to the two-stage flowshop environment and, at the same time, try to capture the special characteristics of a minimum flowtime schedule.

The heuristic uses some of the ideas from the two-stage Moore's algorithm for the calculation of $LB[n_T(J)]$. In this bicriteria version, there are several options to generate schedules with the characteristics found in Moore's sequence. Since there is no definite way to tell which option outperforms the others, different schedules are created. Then, the flowtimes of these n_T-based schedules are reduced until further improvement in F cannot be obtained. The heuristic procedure is outlined as follows:

Options:

Option 1:	Use Machine A processing times.
	Set arrival time = zero,
	processing time $p_j = a_j$, and
	due date $dd_j = d_j - b_j$, for $j = 1, \ldots, n$
Option 2:	Use Machine B processing times.
	Set arrival time = $\min_{j \in J} a_j$,
	processing time $p_j = b_j$, and
	due date $dd_j = d_j$, for $j = 1, \ldots, n$.
Option 3:	Use sum of processing times.
	Set arrival time = zero,
	processing time $p_j = a_j + b_j$, and
	due date $dd_j = d_j$, for $j = 1, \ldots, n$.
Option 4:	Use difference of processing times.
	Set arrival time = $\min_{j \in J} a_j$,
	processing time $p_j = |a_j - b_j|$, where $|\bullet|$ indicate the absolute value, and
	due date $dd_j = d_j$, for $j = 1, \ldots, n$.

Heuristic Procedure:

Step 1:	Select the option for heuristic procedure. Perform Moore's algorithm: sequence all jobs in EDD order of dd_j such that $dd_{[1]} \leq dd_{[2]} \leq \ldots \leq dd_{[n]}$. This EDD sequence is initialized as J_E. The flowtimes are calculated using processing times p_j. When the first tardy job t in the sequence J_E is encountered, the job with $\max_{j=1}^{t} p_{[j]}$ is removed from J_E and put into the late set J_L. This procedure is then repeated until none of the jobs in J_E is tardy. Find $n_T(J)$. The number of jobs in J_L is the minimum n_T obtained by this heuristic. Set $n_T = n_T(J)$ and record the sequence in candidate list $S(i = n_T)$.
Step 2:	The jobs in J_E are then sequenced by the SPT order of p_j. Also perform SPT sequencing to the jobs in J_L.
Step 3:	Insert the last job in J_E to the every possible position in J_L. Recompute the number of tardy jobs $n_{T'}(J)$ for the entire sequence every time the job is placed in a new position. If $n_{T'}(J) \leq n_T + 1$, then calculate $F(J)$ and record the entire sequence

	J in candidate list $S(i=n_{T'})$. Otherwise, discard the sequence J, select the second last job in J_E, and repeat this step. Repeat step 3 until all jobs in J_E have been considered.
Step 4:	Select from list $S(i=n_T)$ the candidate sequence with the lowest $F(J)$ and set it as the new sequence J. Update J_E and J_L (i.e., remove the job from J_E and add it to J_L). Increment $n_T=n_T+1$ and repeat step 3 until there is no more job in J_E. Then select the next list $S(i=n_T+1)$ and repeat the procedure.
Step 5:	When all candidate lists have been gone through, select from each list $S(i)$ the candidate sequence with $\min_{S(i)} F(J)$. Use this schedule to find the actual flowtime $F(J|n_T*)$ with a given number of tardy jobs $n_T* = n_T, n_T+1,...$

This heuristic procedure can be repeated with different options described above. Each option will lead to a Pareto set of schedules describing the tradeoff between F and n_T. In the following, we provide an example to illustrate the operations of this heuristic.

Example:
Suppose there are $n=5$ jobs available for scheduling on a two-machine flowshop. The processing times for the jobs are as follows:

Job	a_j	b_j	d_j
1	2	9	20
2	9	6	30
3	10	12	36
4	14	16	42
5	12	15	45

All jobs are arrived at time zero and currently available for processing. If option 1 is chosen, the processing time and due date for each job is:

Job	p_j	dd_j
1	2	11
2	9	24
3	10	24
4	14	26
5	12	30

Step 1:   The initial EDD schedule is 1-2-3-4-5 and called it J_E. Job 4 (the
           4th job in J_E) is the first tardy job and therefore job 4, which has
           $\max_{j=1}^4 p_{[j]}$, is removed and put into the late set J_L. Then J_E becomes
           1-2-3-5 and job 5 (the 4th job in J_E) is the only tardy job. We
           remove job 5, which has $\max_{j=1}^4 p_{[j]}$, to the late set J_L. Then, there is
           no tardy job in J_E. So the Moore's algorithm is completed. The
           final Moore's schedule is 1-2-3-4-5 with $F(J) = 116$ and $n_T(J) = 2$.
           Set $n_T = 2$. The sequence is stored in the candidate list $S(2)$.

Step 2:   We sequence the jobs in J_E in SPT order of p_j and do the same
           to J_L. The resulting sequence is 1-2-3-5-4.

Step 3:   Insert job 5, the first job in J_L, to the first position in J_E. The
           schedule becomes 5-1-2-3-4. $n_{T'}(J) = 3$ and $F(J) = 129$. Since
           $n_{T'}(J) = 3 \leq n_T + 1 = 3$, record 5-1-2-3-4 to $S(3)$. Insert job 5 to the
           second position in J_E. The schedule becomes 1-5-2-3-4. $n_{T'}(J) = 2$
           and $F(J) = 119$. Since $n_{T'}(J) = 2 \leq n_T + 1 = 3$, 5-1-2-3-4 is stored in
           list $S(2)$. Inserting job 5 to the third position gives 1-2-5-3-4 with
           $n_{T'}(J) = 2$ and $F(J) = 116$. Since $n_{T'}(J) = 2 \leq n_T + 1 = 3$, 1-2-5-3-4 is
           stored in list $S(2)$. The last one give 1-2-3-5-4 with $n_{T'}(J) = 2$ and
           $F(J) = 114$. Then insert job 4, the second job in J_L, to the first
           position in J_E. This gives 4-1-2-3-5 with $n_{T'}(J) = 4$ and $F(J) = 137$.
           Since $n_{T'}(J) = 4 > n_T + 1 = 3$, the sequence is discarded. We
           continue this step by inserting job 4 to the remaining possible
           positions in J_E.

Step 4:   From $S(2)$, 1-2-3-5-4 gives the lowest $F(J) = 114$. So this is set as
           the new sequence. Now, $J_E = $ 1-2-3-5 and $J_L = 4$. $n_T = n_T + 1 = 3$.
           Insert job 4, the first job in J_L, to the first position in J_E. The
           schedule becomes 4-1-2-3-5 with $n_{T'}(J) = 4$ and $F(J) = 137$. Since
           $n_{T'}(J) = 4 \leq n_T + 1 = 4$, 4-1-2-3-5 is stored in list $S(4)$. This
           procedure is continued until job 4 has been inserted to every
           possible position in J_E. Then, we repeat this step with $S(3)$ and
           $S(4)$. Please note that the heuristic cannot identify any schedule
           with $n_T(J) = 5$.

Step 5:   After all evaluations have been completed, we can construct the
           Pareto set. From $S(2)$, 1-2-3-5-4 gives the lowest $F(J) = 114$. From
           $S(3)$, 1-2-4-3-5 gives the lowest $F(J) = 120$. From $S(4)$, 1-4-2-3-5
           gives the lowest $F(J) = 125$. The heuristic flowtimes for the actual
           schedules are: $F(J|n_T* = 0) = $ infeasible; $F(J|n_T* = 1) = $ infeasible;
           $F(J|n_T* = 2) = 173$ $F(J|n_T* = 3) = 190$; $F(J|n_T* = 4) = 202$; and
           $F(J|n_T* = 5) = $ unknown.

There is an interesting observation here – the Pareto does not give a tradeoff between F and n_T. These results are then verified by complete enumeration of all possible permutations of sequence. The enumeration results indicate that the minimum flowtime schedule has an $n_T = 2$ and this may be the global optimal solution for the bicriteria scheduling problem. If we try to increase the number of tardy jobs, then we are implicitly forcing the schedule to delay the flowtime in order to make more jobs tardy. This is our conjecture that this phenomenon will become less obvious and less frequent when the size of problem increases.

For comparison, the results of the optimal schedules found by enumeration are: $F(J|n_T* = 0) = $ infeasible; $F(J|n_T* = 1) = $ infeasible; $F(J|n_T* = 2) = 173$ $F(J|n_T* = 3) = 184$; $F(J|n_T* = 4) = 196$; and $F(J|n_T* = 5) = 232$.

Modified Woo and Yim Heuristic for F *and* n_T

The Woo and Yim (1998) propose a heuristic to minimize the total flowtime for flowshops. The foundation of their algorithm is based on the job insertion principle which constructs the schedule one job at a time. Essentially, the heuristic inserts each non-scheduled job into each possible slot of the constructed sequence and examines all possible sequences resulting from different insertions. The one which leads to the lowest flowtime is then selected and becomes part of the constructed sequence. The heuristic continues to build the schedule until all non-scheduled jobs have been put into the constructed sequence.

In this study, we modify the Woo and Yim heuristic to account for the number of tardy jobs in the schedule. Given an upper limit n_T^* of tardy jobs, the modified heuristic builds feasible schedules using minimum flowtime sequences. The details of the procedure are summarized as follows:

Options:

Option 1:	Use Machine A processing times.
	Set arrival time = zero,
	processing time $p_j = a_j$, and
	due date $dd_j = d_j - b_j$, for $j = 1, \ldots, n$.
Option 2:	Use Machine B processing times.
	Set arrival time = $\min_{j \in J} a_j$,
	processing time $p_j = b_j$, and
	due date $dd_j = d_j$, for $j = 1, \ldots, n$.

Option 3:   Use sum of processing times.
                Set arrival time = zero,
                processing time $p_j = a_j + b_j$, and
                due date $dd_j = d_j$, for $j = 1, \ldots, n$.

Option 4:   Use difference of processing times.
                Set arrival time = $\min_{j \in J} a_j$,
                processing time $p_j = |a_j - b_j|$, where $|\bullet|$ indicate the absolute
                value, and
                due date $dd_j = d_j$, for $j = 1, \ldots, n$.

Heuristic Procedure:

Step 1:   Initialize $n_T^* = 0$. Set the partial schedule J_r to be null and
                the non-scheduled set J_r to include all n jobs available for
                scheduling. Select job j from J_r and put it in J_r. Compute the
                flowtime $F(J_r)$ and the number of tardy jobs $n_T(J_r)$. Repeat this
                step for $j = 1, \ldots, n$. Delete all sequences with the numbers of
                tardy jobs $n_T(J_r) > n_T^*$. If there is no sequence left after the
                deletion, stop. It is impossible to generate a feasible schedule and
                go to step 6. Otherwise, select the sequence which yields the
                lowest $F(J_r)$ and set it as J_r. Remove the newly scheduled job
                from J_r.

Step 2:   Select job j from the non-scheduled set J_r and insert the job to
                every possible position in J_r. Compute the flowtime $F(J_r)$ and the
                number of tardy $n_T(J_r)$ for each of the sequences obtained from
                insertion. Delete all sequences with $n_T(J_r) > n_T*$. If there is no
                sequence left, put job j back to J_r and go to step 3. Otherwise,
                select the sequence with the lowest total flowtime $F(J_r)$ and put
                this sequence to S, the set of candidate sequences.

Step 3:   Select another job from J_r and repeat step 2 until all jobs in J_r
                have been examined.

Step 4:   If S is empty, go to step 6. Otherwise, select from S the candidate
                sequence with the lowest total flowtime $F(J_r)$. Set this sequence as
                the new J_r. Remove the newly scheduled job from J_r.

Step 5:   Repeat step 2 through step 4 until there is no remaining job in J_r.
                The flowtime of the final complete schedule is $F_2'(J|n_T = n_T*)$.

Step 6:   If $n_T* = n$, stop. Otherwise, increment $n_T* = n_T* + 1$. Go to step
                1.

Like the bicriteria Moore's heuristic, this procedure generates an efficient frontier of schedules within the whole range of possible n_T.

Example:
Again, we use the same problem outlined in the last section to illustrate the operation of this heuristic.

Step 1:	Set $n_T^* = 0$. $J_r = \{1, 2, 3, 4, 5\}$. Select job 1 and put it in J_r. Compute $F(J_r) = 11$ and $n_T(J_r) = 0$. Repeat with job 2. $F(J_r) = 15$ and $n_T(J_r) = 0$. Do the same for jobs 3, 4, and 5. Since $\{1\}$, $\{2\}$, ..., $\{5\}$ are all $\leq n_T^* = 0$, select $\{1\}$ as J_r, which gives the lowest $F(J_r) = 11$. Update $J_r = \{2, 3, 4, 5\}$.
Step 2:	Select job 2 and put it in the first position of J_r. This gives 1-2 with $F(J_r) = 17$ and $n_T(J_r) = 0$. Select job 2 and put it in the second position of J_r. This gives 2-1 with $F(J_r) = 24$ and $n_T(J_r) = 0$. Sequence 1–2 gives the lowest flowtime and put it in S.
Step 3:	Select job 3 from J_r and put it in the first position of J_r. This gives 1-3 with $F(J_r) = 24$ and $n_T(J_r) = 0$. Select job 3 and put it in the second position of J_r. This gives 3-1 with $F(J_r) = 31$ and $n_T(J_r) = 0$. Sequence 1–2 gives the lowest flowtime and put it in S. This step is repeated until all jobs in J_r have been evaluated in every position.
Step 4:	Sequence 1–2, which gives the lowest flowtime in S is selected and set as the new J_r. Update $J_r = \{3,4,5\}$.
Step 5:	Evaluate sequences 3-1-2, 1-3-2, 1-2-3, 4-1-2, and so on until all combinations have been examined. The best sequence in S is 1-3-2. The evaluation procedure continues with 4-1-3-2, 1-4-3-2, 1-3-4-2, 1-3-2-4, and so on. However, all of these schedules have $n_T(J_r) > 0$, therefore, they are discarded. Because S is empty, we go to step 6 and there is no feasible schedule with $n_T = 0$.
Step 6:	Increment $n_T^* = n_T^* + 1 = 1$. Repeat the whole schedule building procedure again.

The heuristic for this example generates about the same schedules as found by the bicriteria Moore's heuristic. If the number of jobs increases, we should be able to see deviation between the two heuristics as the state space for searching substantially expands.

Bicriteria SPT Heuristics

In this section, we present an array of bicriteria extensions to the well-known SPT algorithm which guarantees minimum flowtime schedule for a single machine. Like that of the extended Moore's heuristic described previously, the background of the bicriteria SPT heuristic is based on the isolation of one processing stage and focusing on the other. It is hoped that this will lead to a schedule with good flowtime performance.

Given this notion, we can first focus on the flowtime measure and generate a schedule. Then an improvement heuristic can be used to reduce the number of tardy jobs in the schedule. Because there are several options to generate the flowtime schedule in the first phase of sequencing, our heuristic algorithm will create a set of final schedules.

Options:

Option 1:	Use Machine A processing times. Set arrival time = zero, processing time $p_j = a_j$, and due date $dd_j = d_j - b_j$, for $j = 1,\ldots,n$.
Option 2:	Use Machine B processing times. Set arrival time $= \min_{j \in J} a_j$, processing time $p_j = b_j$, and due date $dd_j = d_j$, for $j = 1,\ldots,n$.
Option 3:	Use sum of processing times. Set arrival time = zero, processing time $p_j = a_j + b_j$, and due date $dd_j = d_j$, for $j = 1,\ldots,n$.
Option 4:	Use difference of processing times. Set arrival time $= \min_{j \in J} a_j$ min, processing time $p_j = |a_j - b_j|$, where $|\bullet|$ indicate the absolute value, and due date $dd_j = d_j$, for $j = 1,\ldots,n$.

Heuristic Procedure:

Step 1:	Sequence the jobs in the SPT order of p_j and set this sequence as J_E. Find the number of tardy jobs $n_T{}'(J_E)$. This is the maximum limit of n_T for this heuristic. Assign $n_T = n_T{}'$. Record the sequence in candidate list $S(i = n_T)$.

Step 2: When the first tardy job t in J_E is encountered, the job with $\max_{j=1}^{t} p_j$ max is removed from the sequence and put into the late set J_L. Recompute $n_{T'}(J_E)$. If $n_{T'} \leq n_T - 1$, sequence J_L in SPT order and calculate $F(J)$. Put the entire sequence J in candidate list $S(i = n_{T'})$.

Step 3: Select from list $S(i = n_T)$ the candidate sequence with the lowest $F(J)$ and set it as the new sequence J. Update J_E and J_L (i.e., remove the job from J_L and add it to J_E). Decrement $n_T = n_T - 1$ and repeat step 2 until there is no more tardy job in J_E. Then select the next list $S(i = n_T - 1)$ and repeat the procedure.

Step 4: When all candidate list have been gone through, select from each list $S(i)$ the candidate sequence with the lowest $F(J)$. The heuristic flowtime $F(J|n_T^*)$ with a given number of tardy jobs $n_T^* = n_T, n_T + 1, \ldots, n$ is $\min_{S(i)} F(J)$.

This heuristic procedure can be repeated with different options described above. Each option will lead to an efficient frontier describing the tradeoff between F and n_T.

For the sake of brevity, we do not include a full illustrative example for this heuristic. The operation and logic of the bicriteria SPT heurisitc is similar to the ideas of the modified Moore's heuristic. The major difference in their operations is that the SPT heuristic starts with an SPT schedule with high value of n_T and iteratively builds in the characteristics of Moore (EDD) schedule whereas the Moore's heuristic starts with a Moore's schedule with low value of n_T and iteratively builds in the characteristics of SPT schedule.

CONCLUSIONS

In this study, the job scheduling problem for a two-stage flowshop is considered. All jobs are immediately available for processing and job characteristics including the processing times and due dates are known and certain. The objective of the problem is to develop efficient schedules which simultaneously minimize the total flowtime and the number of tardy jobs. We present a number of bicriteria heuristics which exploit the special structure of schedules with minimum flowtime and minimum number of tardy jobs. Each of the proposed procedures generates a Pareto set of schedules in which the flowtime is heuristically minimized given a specified number of tardy jobs.

This study also provides some foundation for research on the development of bicriteria lower bounds. Based on the knowledge and experience obtained from conducting this research, we strongly suspect that the goal of developing such bicriteria lower bounds cannot be easily accomplished unless more fundamental insights are obtained from the more simplified scenarios. For example, one of such avenues is the development of bicriteria lower bounds for a single machine, a problem which has never been attempted before.

REFERENCES

Chand, S., & Schneeberger, H. (1988). Single machine scheduling to minimize weighted earliness subject to no tardy jobs. *European Journal of Operational Research, 34*, 221–230.

Daniels, R. L., & Chambers, R. J. (1990). Multiobjective flow-shop scheduling. *Naval Research Logistics, 37*, 981–995.

Dudek, R. A., Panwalkar, S. S., & Smith, M. L. (1992). The lessons of flowshop scheduling research. *Operations Research, 40*, 7–13.

Gangadharan, R., & Rajendran, C. (1994). A simulated annealing heuristic for scheduling in a flowshop with bicriteria. *Computers and Industrial Engineering, 27*, 473–476.

Gupta, J. T. D., & Dudek, R. A. (1971). Optimality criteria for flowshop schedules. *AIIE Transactions, 3*, 199–205.

Ho, J. C., & Chang, Y. L. (1991). A new heuristic for the n-job, M-machine flow-shop problem. *European Journal of Operational Research, 52*, 194–202.

Ignall, E., & Schrage, L. (1965). Application of the branch and bound technique to some flow-shop scheduling problems. *Operations Research, 13*, 400–412.

Johnson, S. M. (1954). Optimal two and three-stage production schedules with setup times included. *Naval Research Logistics Quarterly, 1*, 61–68.

Liao, C. J., Yu, W. C., & Joe, C. B. (1997). Bicriterion scheduling in the two-machine flowshop. *Journal of Operational Research Society, 48*, 929–935.

Moore, J. M. (1968). An *n* job, one machine sequencing algorithm for minimizing the number of late jobs. *Management Science, 15*, 102–109.

Morton, T. E., & Pentico, D. W. (1993). *Heuristic scheduling systems with applications to production systems and project management.* New York, NY: Wiley.

Murata, T., Ishibuchi, H., & Tanaka, H. (1996). Multi-objective genetic algorithm and its applications to flowshop scheduling. *Computers and Industrial Engineering, 30*, 957–968.

Nagar, A., Heragu, S. S., & Haddock, J. (1995). A branch-and-bound approach for a two-machine flowshop scheduling problem. *Journal of Operational Research Society, 46*, 721–734.

Rajendran, C. (1992). Two-stage flowshop scheduling problem with bicriteria. *Journal of Operational Research Society, 43*, 871–884.

Rajendran, C. (1995). Heuristics for scheduling in flowshop with multiple objectives. *European Journal of Operational Research, 82,* 540–555.
Woo, H. S., & Yim, D. S. (1998). A heuristic algorithm for mean flowtime objective in flowshop scheduling. *Computers and Operations Research, 25,* 175–182.

APPENDIX

The following hypotheses and proofs are served as references only. They have not been verified to be valid for the more general condition.

Hypothesis A1. Given a sequence J and the condition $\min_{j \in J} b_j \geq \max_{j \in J} a_j$, the SPT ordering of $b_{[1]} \leq b_{[2]} \leq \ldots \leq b_{[n]}$ does not necessarily minimize F.

Proof: If the condition $\min_{j \in J} b_j \geq \max_{j \in J} a_j$ holds, the processing sequence of J on Machine B will not contain any idle time and the sum of flowtimes for all n jobs is:

$$(a_{[1]} + b_{[1]}) + (a_{[1]} + b_{[1]} + b_{[2]}) + \ldots + (a_{[1]} + b_{[1]} + b_{[2]} + \ldots + b_{[n]})$$
$$= (n)b_{[1]} + (n-1)b_{[2]} + \ldots + b_{[n]}$$

Suppose the jobs in J are arranged in the SPT order of $b_{[1]} \leq b_{[2]} \leq \ldots \leq b_{[n]}$. Therefore, $b_{[2]} = b_{[1]} + x$ and $x \geq 0$ Now, if we inter-exchange the positions of $j_{[1]}$ and $j_{[2]}$, the jobs in J will no longer be in the SPT order with respect to $b_{[j]}$.

The difference of the sums of completion times between the two sequences is:

$$[(n)a_{[1]} + (n)b_{[1]} + (n-1)b_{[2]} + \ldots + b_{[n]}]$$
$$- [(n)a_{[2]} + (n)b_{[2]} + (n-1)b_{[1]} + \ldots + b_{[n]}]$$
$$= (n)\, a_{[1]} - (n)a_{[2]} + (n)b_{[1]} - (n)(b_{[1]} + x)$$
$$+ [(n-1)(b_{[1]} + x)] - (n-1)b_{[1]}$$
$$= (n)(a_{[1]} - a_{[2]}) - x$$

Hence, we will realize a reduction in the sum of completion times by deviating from the SPT order if the term $(n)(a_{[1]} - a_{[2]}) - x$ is positive. Since $x \geq 0$ by definition, there will be a reduction in the sum of completion times F if $(n)(a_{[1]} - a_{[2]}) > x$.

Hypothesis A2. Given a partial sequence J. If the condition $\min_{j \in J} b_j \geq \max_{j \in J} a_j$ exists, a reduction in the sum of flowtimes (F) can be achieved by exchanging the positions of the first job $j_{[1]}$ and any other job $j_{[p]}$, for $p \neq 1$, in the sequence as long as the following conditions are satisfied:

$$\frac{n}{(p-1)} > \frac{(b_{[p]} - b_{[1]})}{(a_{[1]} - a_{[p]})} > 0$$

where

$$(a_{[1]} - a_{[p]}) > 0$$
$$(b_{[p]} - b_{[1]}) > 0$$

Proof: Given any arbitrary sequence J with $j_{[1]}$ as the first job and $j_{[p]}$ as the job in the p-th position. The two jobs do not have to be adjacent to each other. Let $b_{[p]} = b_{[1]} + y$. If we inter-exchange the positions of $j_{[1]}$ and $j_{[p]}$, based on the proof for Theorem 1, the difference of the sums of completion times between the original and the exchanged sequences is:

$$[(n)a_{[1]} + (n)b_{[1]} + \ldots + (n - p + 1)\, b_{[p]} + \ldots + b_{[n]}]$$
$$- [(n)a_{[p]} + (n)b_{[p]} + \ldots + (n - p + 1)b_{[1]} + \ldots + b_{[n]}]$$
$$= (n)(a_{[1]} - a_{[2]}) + (1 - p)y$$

We can attain a reduction in the sum of completion times when the sum is positive, that is,

$$(n)(a_{[1]} - a_{[2]}) + (1 - p)y > 0$$

This inequality is equivalent to:

$$(n)(a_{[1]} - a_{[p]}) > (p - 1)(b_{[p]} - b_{[1]})$$

For $(a_{[1]} - a_{[p]}) > 0$ $(b_{[p]} - b_{[1]}) > 0$, the expression can be rewritten as:

$$\frac{n}{(p - 1)} > \frac{(b_{[p]} - b_{[1]})}{(a_{[1]} - a_{[p]})} > 0$$

Example:
Suppose there are $n = 5$ jobs available for scheduling on the two-machine flowshop. The processing times for the jobs are as follows:

Job	a_i	b_i
1	7	12
2	9	13
3	10	13
4	6	14
5	4	15

Based on the job characteristics, it is obvious that the condition $\min_{j \in J} b_j \geq \max_{j \in J} a_j$ is true. An SPT ordering with respect to b_j yields the production sequence J of 1-2-3-4-5. The total flowtime for this schedule is $F(J) = 229$.

Consider jobs $j_{[1]}$ and $j_{[5]}$. By the theorem, we see that the condition $5/(5-1) > (15-12)/(7-4) > 0$ holds and thereby we should be able to realize a reduction in the sum of flowtimes by exchanging the positions of $j_{[1]}$

and $j_{[5]}$. The resulting total flowtime for the exchanged schedule 5-2-3-4-1 is $F(J) = 226$.

Lower Bound on F Given an Upper Limit on n_T

The lower bounds described previously focus on a specific criterion. They have to be used collectively when we try to evaluate the tradeoff and the dominance in a bicriteria framework. However, the use of these bounds collectively may not be as effective as a bound which accounts for both measures. In this section, we present two "hybrid" lower bounds – the lower bounds on flowtime F given an upper limit n_T^* on the number of tardy jobs. It should be noted that the value of n_T^* can be iterated to create a Pareto set of lower bounds.

$LB_7[F(J)]$
Conjecture Lower Bound:
A lower bound on F given a maximum limit n_T^* on the number of tardy jobs can be computed using the following procedure:

Step 1:	Sequence J in SPT order of a_j for $j = 1, \ldots, n$ such that $a_{[1]} \leq a_{[2]} \leq \ldots \leq a_{[n]}$ and compute $AF_j = \sum_{i=1}^{j} a_{[i]} + b_{[j]}$ for $j = 1, \ldots, n$.
Step 2:	Find the number of tardy jobs $n_T(J)$. If $n_T(J) > n_T^*$ then select the first tardy job t and reduce $AF_t, AF_{t+1}, \ldots, AF_n$ by the difference $(AF_t - d_t)$, where d_t is the due date for job t. Repeat this step until $n_T(J) > n_T^*$.

When the procedure is completed, the lower bound on F given n_T^* is:

$$LB_7[F(J)] = \sum_{j=1}^{n} AF_j$$

Conjecture:
$LB_7[F(J)]$ can be viewed as a bicriteria extension of $LB_1[F(J)]$ in that the lower bound on F will be reduced in order to fulfill a maximum limit set on n_T, that is, to observe the tradeoff between the two measures. In step 1, the job sequence is arranged in the order of $a_{[1]} \leq a_{[2]} \leq \ldots \leq a_{[n]}$, and then the flowtime AF_j for each job is computed. This entire step follows exactly the same logic to obtain $LB_1[F(J)]$. Hence, the proof by Ignall and Schrage (1965) can be used to show that the total flowtime $F(J)$ is a lower bound.

In step 2, we count the number of tardy jobs for the schedule implied by $LB_1[F(J)]$. If its $n_T(J)$ exceeds the maximum limit n_T^*, all the individual flowtimes AF_j from the first tardy job $j_{[t]}$ up to and including the final job $j_{[n]}$ in sequence J are reduced. Thus, the sum of flowtimes $F(J)$ and thereby the lower bound $LB_1[F(J)]$ is reduced to $LB_1'[F(J)]$. Since $LB_1[F(J)]$ is a lower bound and $LB_1'[F(J)] < LB_1[F(J)]$, $LB_1'[F(J)]$ is also a lower bound. If $n_T(J)$ does not exceed the maximum limit n_T^*, the lower bound will remain to be $LB_1[F(J)]$.

This step is repeated until the condition $n_T(J) \leq n_T^*$ is met. As a result, the final lower bound $LB_7[F(J)] \leq LB_1'[F(J)] \leq LB_1[F(J)]$ and $LB_7[F(J)]$ is thus a lower bound on F.

$LB_8[F(J)]$
Conjecture Lower Bound:
A lower bound on F given a maximum limit n_T^* on the number of tardy jobs can be computed using the following procedure:

Step 1:   Sequence J in SPT order of b_j for $j = 1, \ldots, n$ such that
$b_{[1]} \leq b_{[2]} \leq \ldots \leq b_{[n]}$ and compute $BF_j = \min_{i \in J} a_i + \sum_{i=1}^{j} b_{[j]}$
for $j = 1, \ldots, n$.

Step 2:   Find the number of tardy jobs $n_T(J)$. If $n_T(J) > n_T^*$ then select the first tardy job t and reduce $BF_t, BF_{t+1}, \ldots, BF_n$ by the difference $(BF_t - d_t)$, where d_t is the due date for job t. Repeat this step until $n_T(J) \leq n_T^*$

When the procedure is completed, the lower bound on F given n_T^* is:

$$LB_8[F(J)] = \sum_{j=1}^{n} BF_j.$$

Conjecture:
$LB_8[F(J)]$ can be viewed as a bicriteria extension of $LB_2[F(J)]$ in that the lower bound on F will be reduced in order to fulfill a maximum limit set on n_T, that is, to observe the tradeoff between the two measures. In step 1, the job sequence is arranged in the order of $b_{[1]} \leq b_{[2]} \leq \ldots \leq b_{[n]}$, and then the flowtime BF_j for each job is computed. This entire step follows exactly the same logic to obtain $LB_2[F(J)]$. Hence, the proof by Ignall and Schrage (1965) can be used to show that the total flowtime $F(J)$ is a lower bound. The rest of the proof follows that of $LB_7[F(J)]$.